Memories 3

Vernon Coleman

Vernon Coleman: What the papers say

'Vernon Coleman writes brilliant books.' – The Good Book Guide
'No thinking person can ignore him.' – The Ecologist
'The calmest voice of reason.' – The Observer
'A godsend.' – Daily Telegraph
'Superstar.' – Independent on Sunday
'Brilliant!' – The People
'Compulsive reading.' – The Guardian
'His message is important.' – The Economist
'He's the Lone Ranger, Robin Hood and the Equalizer rolled into one.' – Glasgow Evening Times
'The man is a national treasure.' – What Doctors Don't Tell You
'His advice is optimistic and enthusiastic.' – British Medical Journal
'Revered guru of medicine.' – Nursing Times
'Gentle, kind and caring' – Western Daily Press
'His trademark is that he doesn't mince words. Far funnier than the usual tone of soupy piety you get from his colleagues.' – The Guardian
'Dr Coleman is one of our most enlightened, trenchant and sensitive dispensers of medical advice.' – The Observer
'I would much rather spend an evening in his company than be trapped for five minutes in a radio commentary box with Mr Geoffrey Boycott.' – Peter Tinniswood, Punch
'Hard hitting...inimitably forthright.' – Hull Daily Mail
'Refreshingly forthright.' – Liverpool Daily Post
'Outspoken and alert.' – Sunday Express
'Dr Coleman made me think again.' – BBC World Service
'Marvellously succinct, refreshingly sensible.' – The Spectator
'Probably one of the most brilliant men alive today.' – Irish Times
'King of the media docs.' – The Independent
'Britain's leading medical author.' – The Star
'Britain's leading health care campaigner.' – The Sun
'Perhaps the best known health writer for the general public in the world today.' – The Therapist
'The patient's champion.' – Birmingham Post

Books by Vernon Coleman include:

Medical
The Medicine Men
Paper Doctors
Everything You Want To Know About Ageing
The Home Pharmacy
Aspirin or Ambulance
Face Values
Stress and Your Stomach
A Guide to Child Health
Guilt
The Good Medicine Guide
An A to Z of Women's Problems
Bodypower
Bodysense
Taking Care of Your Skin
Life without Tranquillisers
High Blood Pressure
Diabetes
Arthritis
Eczema and Dermatitis
The Story of Medicine
Natural Pain Control
Mindpower
Addicts and Addictions
Dr Vernon Coleman's Guide to Alternative Medicine
Stress Management Techniques
Overcoming Stress
The Health Scandal
The 20 Minute Health Check
Sex for Everyone
Mind over Body
Eat Green Lose Weight
Why Doctors Do More Harm Than Good
The Drugs Myth

Complete Guide to Sex
How to Conquer Backache
How to Conquer Pain
Betrayal of Trust
Know Your Drugs
Food for Thought
The Traditional Home Doctor
Relief from IBS
The Parent's Handbook
Men in Bras, Panties and Dresses
Power over Cancer
How to Conquer Arthritis
How to Stop Your Doctor Killing You
Superbody
Stomach Problems – Relief at Last
How to Overcome Guilt
How to Live Longer
Coleman's Laws
Millions of Alzheimer Patients Have Been Misdiagnosed
Climbing Trees at 112
Is Your Health Written in the Stars?
The Kick-Ass A–Z for over 60s
Briefs Encounter
The Benzos Story
Dementia Myth
Waiting

Psychology/Sociology
Stress Control
How to Overcome Toxic Stress
Know Yourself (1988)
Stress and Relaxation
People Watching
Spiritpower
Toxic Stress
I Hope Your Penis Shrivels Up
Oral Sex: Bad Taste and Hard To Swallow
Other People's Problems

The 100 Sexiest, Craziest, Most Outrageous Agony Column
Questions (and Answers) Of All Time
How to Relax and Overcome Stress
Too Sexy To Print
Psychiatry
Are You Living With a Psychopath?

Politics and General
England Our England
Rogue Nation
Confronting the Global Bully
Saving England
Why Everything Is Going To Get Worse Before It Gets Better
The Truth They Won't Tell You...About The EU
Living In a Fascist Country
How to Protect & Preserve Your Freedom, Identity & Privacy
Oil Apocalypse
Gordon is a Moron
The OFPIS File
What Happens Next?
Bloodless Revolution
2020
Stuffed
The Shocking History of the EU
Coming Apocalypse
Covid-19: The Greatest Hoax in History
Old Man in a Chair
Endgame
Proof that Masks do more Harm than Good
Covid-19: The Fraud Continues
Covid-19: Exposing the Lies
Social Credit: Nightmare on Your Street
NHS: What's wrong and how to put it right
Diaries and Autobiographies
Diary of a Disgruntled Man
Just another Bloody Year
Bugger off and Leave Me Alone
Return of the Disgruntled Man

Life on the Edge
The Game's Afoot
Tickety Tonk
Memories 1
Memories 2
Memories 3
My Favourite Books
Animals
Why Animal Experiments Must Stop
Fighting For Animals
Alice and Other Friends
Animal Rights – Human Wrongs
Animal Experiments – Simple Truths

General Non Fiction

How to Publish Your Own Book
How to Make Money While Watching TV
Strange but True
Daily Inspirations
Why Is Public Hair Curly
People Push Bottles Up Peaceniks
Secrets of Paris
Moneypower
101 Things I Have Learned
100 Greatest Englishmen and Englishwomen
Cheese Rolling, Shin Kicking and Ugly Tattoos
One Thing after Another

Novels (General)

Mrs Caldicot's Cabbage War
Mrs Caldicot's Knickerbocker Glory
Mrs Caldicot's Oyster Parade
Mrs Caldicot's Turkish Delight
Deadline
Second Chance
Tunnel
Mr Henry Mulligan
The Truth Kills

Revolt
My Secret Years with Elvis
Balancing the Books
Doctor in Paris
Stories with a Twist in the Tale (short stories)
Dr Bullock's Annals

The Young Country Doctor Series
Bilbury Chronicles
Bilbury Grange
Bilbury Revels
Bilbury Country
Bilbury Village
Bilbury Pie (short stories)
Bilbury Pudding (short stories)
Bilbury Tonic
Bilbury Relish
Bilbury Mixture
Bilbury Delights
Bilbury Joys
Bilbury Tales
Bilbury Days
Bilbury Memories

Novels (Sport)
Thomas Winsden's Cricketing Almanack
Diary of a Cricket Lover
The Village Cricket Tour
The Man Who Inherited a Golf Course
Around the Wicket
Too Many Clubs and Not Enough Balls

Cat books
Alice's Diary
Alice's Adventures
We Love Cats
Cats Own Annual
The Secret Lives of Cats

Cat Basket
The Cataholics' Handbook
Cat Fables
Cat Tales
Catoons from Catland

As Edward Vernon
Practice Makes Perfect
Practise What You Preach
Getting Into Practice
Aphrodisiacs – An Owner's Manual
The Complete Guide to Life

Written with Donna Antoinette Coleman
How to Conquer Health Problems between Ages 50 & 120
Health Secrets Doctors Share With Their Families
Animal Miscellany
England's Glory
Wisdom of Animals

Dedication

To Antoinette
Thank you for the joy when there was sadness, the hope when there was despair and the memories when there were none. You are my hope, my purpose and my reason for living

'Of making many books there is no end' – Ecclesiastes, Holy Bible

Contents List

20)

Introduction

Books about people's lives fall into two main categories.

First, there are the formal biographies. These are not written by the subject and these days, unless the biography is authorised by the subject, the biographer will usually be inclined (or persuaded) to concentrate on anything scandalous in the individual's life. It is scandal, and the inside story on events which may have already been well publicised, which will put the book into the bestseller lists, ensure a paperback sale and encourage a newspaper or magazine editor to pay a large sum for the right to gut the book and use the best bits in a serialisation.

Second, there are autobiographies. These should be written by the subject but often they are written by a ghost who may or may not be credited. Usually, these volumes concentrate on the wonderful things the subject has done. (It seems that, these days, if you have ever put a £1 coin into a Salvation Army collection tin then you may describe yourself as a philanthropist.) Sometimes the alleged author may be so far removed from the process that they have no idea what is going into the book. A pop singer and celebrity often promoted by the Guardian newspaper called Pete Docherty was apparently surprised when the publisher sent him a copy of his own autobiography and he discovered that it was written in the first person. This sort of thing is by no means unusual.

Most autobiographies can be divided into one of two varieties.

Type A begins with the writer recounting their experiences at school and college and detailing their family life. The story then plods on until the writer reaches the point in their life when they are considered rich enough or famous enough to merit an autobiography. This type of book is (as I think Toynbee said) just 'one damned thing after another' and will usually contain reams of conversation repeated verbatim as though the writer had a genuinely photographic memory or had taken a tape recorder with him or her to every luncheon and every meeting they'd ever had. I doubt if I could recall accurately conversations which I had yesterday, let alone conversations which took place several decades ago. (When I use conversations in this book I am not suggesting that the words used are absolutely accurate. I merely aim to convey the flavour of what was said. And none of the individuals involved is identifiable.)

Type B starts with some well-known, exciting piece of click bait from the writer's history (usually dug out by a ghost writer) and then in Chapter Two the book reverts to type and follows the sort of pattern described in Type A.

Readers of the first two volumes of Memories will be aware that I have not followed either of these blueprints. Some people have minds like filing cabinets. Mine is more like the drawer in the kitchen which contains everything for which no one can think of a proper place; the drawer that is full of paper clips, bits of string too short to be useful but preserved nevertheless, rubber bands, bottle openers, toys from Christmas crackers, odd gloves and used up tubes of glue, broken sunglasses, a new watch strap that has never been fitted, a screwdriver and some foreign stamps on a piece of paper torn from an envelope. (When new homes are built they should be equipped with a drawer like that – just to make the incoming occupants feel welcome and comfortable.)

And naturally this, my third volume of autobiography doesn't fit into any known category either. It is offered as a buffet rather than a formal sit-down four or five course meal. I hope you found it entertaining, information and revealing. This book is an autobiography but it is neither a Type A nor a Type B. It is a type of my own design; a type which rests on my observation that although most biographies and autobiographies tend to suggest that our lives flow from the beginning to the end, just as lives tend to flow in novels, films and plays, that isn't how life works out. Or at least mine hasn't so far and this far in I can't see much change coming. Our lives are a series of episodes connected by our hopes, our reactions, our fears, our personalities, our long standing relationships and by recurrent events and characters who pop in and out, sometimes expectedly but mostly unexpectedly.

I'm generalising, of course, and I can already see that there are exceptions.

Some people plan their lives with commendable precision. They know exactly what they want to do and they know the sort of person they want to do it with. They drive their lives forward with confidence and the apparently certain knowledge that when they are

30 they will be doing this and when they are 40 they will be doing that and when they are 50 they will have achieved this and that. Others, of course, hang around waiting for life to happen. 'I'll just get on with paying the mortgage, mowing the lawn, filling in the tax form and then see what life brings.' There is a danger that they will waste their lives on the administrative debris.

But these two groups are exceptions and most of us, I suspect, go through life, buffeted by the mildest of breezes, often choosing educational courses and careers and homes and partners on whims and fancies; drifting here and there within society's framework without ever considering ourselves to be drifters at all. We may like to think we have made rational decisions but often we have not. Our lives are often changed by moments or events far more than they are controlled by thought or planning. Life is about crossroads and making decisions but most of us have less rational control over our decision making than we like to think we have. The choices may seem small, and the decisions peripheral but the consequences are often life-changing and very consequential.

I doubt if anyone in the world of traditional publishing agrees with me (and to be honest I don't much care, or as Rhett would say `I don't give a damn') but it is my belief that thoughts and attitudes are as important as actions and that disappointments and failures are as revealing and as interesting as successes and triumphs. And, for the reader, it is, I suspect, educational to know how much of any individual's life can be credited to luck, how much to talent and how much to created opportunities. Incidentally, in the interests of freedom of choice, true democracy and the elemental anarchy which should be an essential part of all our lives, if you feel unhappy with the order I've selected the memories in this book, please feel free to read them in any order you like or, with the aid of a pair of scissors or a sharp penknife, to rearrange the book to your liking.

After I had written my two previous volumes of autobiography (cleverly and innovatively titled 'Memories 1' and 'Memories 2') it occurred to me that perhaps I ought to have included more about my career in medicine – particularly in view of the fact that health care in general, and general practice in particular, have changed dramatically in my lifetime.

I realised that although I had written a good deal about specific parts of my life (in seven diaries and two volumes of memories) and had written about my experiences as a doctor (in fifteen volumes about life in the village of Bilbury and three books under the name Edward Vernon) I still had a good many stories to tell about the patients I'd met, both while I was practising in hospital and as a GP and, indeed, after I had officially retired from general practice.

And so I decided I would write more about some of the patients I had met; making this an autobiography which would partly be about other people but which would, help me explore my thoughts, feelings and influences.

(You may, at this point, wonder why I don't just write a straightforward autobiography. Start at the beginning, take the reader through each stage of my life, throw in a few photographs and then finish up with some sort of grand summation about the meaning of life. But if you've read any of my other books you will probably know me well enough to know that was never going to happen.)

These are stories from the days when real-life GPs were available 24 hours a day and 365 days a year. No secrets have been shared or compromised in this book. All the names and details have been changed so completely that no one (not even the individuals concerned) will ever be able to identify any of the people described in this book.

And so, to sum up, as with the previous volumes of Memories, this book, another instalment of my life in bits, is a collection of largely disconnected memories. They are in no particular order or importance. They were written in quiet seclusion at Bedside Manor, a haven 'Far from the madding Crowd's ignoble strife'.
Bilbury, Devon
Summer and Autumn 2022

My early life

In my previous volumes, I forgot to say anything about my education and if the books in this series are to be considered any sort of autobiography I need to correct the omission. The story of my education is really quite uneventful and I shan't be in the slightest bit upset if you decide to skip to the next disjointed memory and leave this section for an evening when you are having difficulty in getting to sleep. But it has to be done, so let us both grit our teeth and we can get through this together.

If you want the short version here it is: I learned to read and write, I went to three schools plus a medical school, which I suppose makes four, I learned other stuff I have mostly forgotten, I left school. You will note that I learned to read and write before I went to school. I did this because I was desperate to read the words in a comic called the Dandy.

That's the short version.

Here, now, is the slightly longer version.

I began my education at a church school in Bloxwich, which I first attended when I was four-years-old. (I was born just round the corner in a maternity hospital which was then known as the Bloxwich Maternity and Child Welfare Hospital but which has become Bloxwich Hospital.) The school building has long gone and the school may have also disappeared. At the time, Bloxwich was in Staffordshire but the boundaries were changed years ago and I have no idea where they've put it. So it is possible that everything has disappeared. It still seems odd to me that the authorities should be allowed to move whole towns about as if they were abandoned motor cars.

I stayed at the school in Bloxwich for two years until my parents moved from a prefab into a house backing onto the park in Walsall, which was also in Staffordshire but which has also been moved to some other manufactured county. I'm pleased to say that unlike Salzburg it hasn't changed country, but it has apparently moved. I only know this because on a previous occasion a book jacket of mine contained the information that I was born in Walsall, Staffordshire and this attracted letters of complaint from concerned citizens letting me know that Walsall was no longer in Staffordshire. My reply then, and now, is that it was in Staffordshire when I was born and I cannot see that its current whereabouts should be any of my concern. Wherever it is, I just hope it is warm and well looked after.

I wasn't at the school in Bloxwich for long but I remember that school with some fondness. Our classroom was a church building and we wrote and did our sums on pieces of slate, writing with slate pencils which bore only a superficial resemblance to the stationery items which you and I now think of as pencils, and we used damp cloths to remove our primitive scratchings. No one believes me when I mention this but it is true. I learned my tables while I was there. Together with our teacher we chanted our twelve times table with joy and pride. In those days teachers seemed to enjoy teaching and to take pride in their work. It was, as far as I can remember, a happy time and a pleasant and perhaps slightly misleading introduction to the educational experience.

In Bloxwich, my parents and I lived in a Prefab (common parlance for a prefabricated building) which had walls not much thicker than cardboard. As a result we were very cold in winter and very hot in summer. My main memory of our time there, and my first clear memory of my life, is being woken up to look at the innards of a television set on our tiny kitchen table. I didn't know it was a television set at the time, of course. My Dad had built the device with a cathode ray tube, a variety of valves, bits of wire, solder and so on – all bought from a local store. I was, and am, in absolute awe of this achievement, not least because the chances of my ever being able to build a television set from scratch are about the same as a ten-year-old boy deciding to have a lie-in on a Christmas morning. When I first saw it, our television set had no case – there was just a small cathode ray tube and a mass of components behind it. The BBC (the only channel at the time) was showing some sort of variety show and tiny people were dancing on the screen.

When I was about six we moved to a smart detached house which had good sized gardens, front and back, two greenhouses and two huge concrete air raid shelters. There were even two sets of steps down to the garden. The previous owner had been a builder with a taste for symmetry. He left without leaving a forwarding address and for years afterwards we received mail from companies trying to sell him building materials. For some reason unknown to me their promotional packs always contained blotting paper which I found extremely useful throughout my school career. My parents must have scrimped and saved to afford the deposit to buy the house. The house cost them a couple of thousand pounds and is now worth the best part of a million. That's inflation. I checked on the internet and the air raid shelters are still there. I'm not surprised. They were built in the 1930s to withstand German bombs so I suspect they'll need a lot of knocking down.

The house backed onto a park with trees, and the whole was rather grandly known as Walsall Arboretum. In the summer the fair and the circus used to park there. The circus was best because if I stood on the top of one of the air-raid shelters I could see the animals being exercised and I remember the giraffes used to play football with the riggers. The fairground played bright music for hours every evening.

My second school, which I started to attend when we moved to the house with the two air-raid shelters, was known as Chuckery Mixed Infants School in Walsall. I seem to remember that there was a large sign over the entrance which said 'Mixed Infants', carved in stone. It confused me for a while and in these days of blame, recriminations, lawsuits and damages I could probably now claim that I was traumatised by the bewilderment I felt, traumatised so much indeed that my life has been ruined and my pain can only be relieved by the payment of substantial damages from whomsoever was responsible for that 'Mixed Infants' sign. I was definitely very happy at that school too and I had a lot of exercise because I walked there in the morning, I walked home at lunchtime, I walked back after lunch and then in the afternoon I walked home again. It was a long journey for a small boy and it required me to cross several roads – one of them a ring road which was extremely busy even in those days. All this was done without the aid of zebra crossings or white coated pensioners holding metal lollipops.

In the playground we played with marbles, hopscotch, tops, cricket, football, conkers (in the season) and toy racing cars. We swapped stamps and collected cigarette cards. At Christmas we were given small toys or bars of chocolate by the educational authority. I preferred the toys and always thought the bars of chocolate showed a lack of imagination on someone's part, but the school gave us something and that was nice. Occasionally, one of the teachers would pretend to be Father Christmas, but I wasn't fooled.

At weekends and in the holidays I spent my free time building Meccano models when it was raining, and when the weather was good I experimented outside in the garden (using the flat roof of one of the air raid shelters as a workbench) with a chemistry set which contained explosives, acids and all sorts of toxic and dangerous goodies. I could make potent gases and coloured smoke and burn holes in the concrete. These days, university students are probably not allowed to play with the stuff I had in my chemistry set back in the 1950s. Friends of my parents lent me a fort, complete with soldiers and a toy cannon which fired ball bearings with great ferocity. I doubt if the cannon would be legal these days. My Dad built me a wooden garage and a wooden farm.

The 1950s were good and simple times. Rationing was still in place for most of the decade (though, ironically, it had long ago been lifted in Germany) and I remember my Mum used to fill an ordinary egg cup with dolly mixture sweets once a week as a sugary treat. The dietary asceticism gave me a sweet tooth and built a destructive later craving for coconut ice and Chelsea buns.

My third school was Queen Mary's Grammar School, also in Walsall, which was in my day a bit of an exam factory – the sort of place which existed to ensure that every child collected the requisite number of certificates and obtained a place at some sort of institution of further education. The school seemed to me to measure its success by the number of pupils who were accepted at Oxbridge. I got a lot of exercise while at that school too. It was further away from home than the mixed infants but I either walked there or cycled there.

On one occasion I got knocked off my bicycle when a boy from another school stepped off the pavement in front of me. I narrowly missed having my head crushed by a bus. Apart from that joust with death I don't think I ever did anything memorable while at that school. The bicycle accident led to my first encounter with bad medicine. The doctor I saw after my accident wrapped up my knee very tightly and didn't do anything much else. Unfortunately, this meant that the knee became swollen and fixed. I was told I mustn't walk, bend the knee or do anything other than lie in bed or on the sofa. I did this faithfully, innocently believing that a miracle would mend my damaged knee. At regular intervals I went to the hospital to have vast amounts of fluid drained from the joint. Eventually, my parents took me to a private consultant who sorted out the mess that had been made, and helped me regain movement in my knee. If they hadn't done this I would probably still be lying on the sofa and visiting the hospital to have fluid removed and the bandage renewed.

I had spent all my pocket money on books ever since I'd had any pocket money and when I arrived at the grammar school I discovered that you could read books without having to buy them. I became the school's most enthusiastic library addict. The library had a modest but decent collection of orange Penguin paperbacks and other cheap editions and I discovered PG Wodehouse, Hilaire Belloc, Graham Greene, Leo Tolstoy, Charles Dickens and many other authors. When I'd read all the books in the school library I joined the public library and used to cycle there once a week and fill my saddle bag with books. In the summer holidays this pilgrimage became a two or three times a week event. I don't remember ever owning a bicycle lock and I don't remember anyone else locking a bicycle either. They were simpler days. It wasn't until my third year at medical school, when I acquired a Honda moped, that I owned a conveyance which I locked. (My Uncle Charlie, who was a tiny bit roguish and whom I loved very much, never ever locked his car but he told me that was because he was hoping someone would steal it and he could claim on the insurance. It was an old Citroen, of the style favoured by an early Inspector Maigret, and it is now probably worth a fortune.)

Sadly, I'm afraid I don't have much else to show for seven years at grammar school. I was a stage manager for the school's annual drama production and I was thrown out of the school Combined Cadet Force for wearing a blue mac while on parade in the rain. I always thought the cadets who stood there getting soaked were the stupid ones who deserved to be cashiered for having no wit or sense of self-preservation. I was never a prefect or even a sub prefect or a milk monitor and never aspired to these roles of high office. (I was never quite sure what the milk monitor was supposed to do but there was one and he is probably now working in NHS administration.) There were so many rules that no one could keep track of them. It was like the EU in that new rules were added every day and old ones were never rescinded. This meant that some of the rules were contradictory. I was never even appointed a blackboard monitor (the boy whose job was to wipe the blackboard clean as and when instructed) nor was I selected to take messages to the headmaster but I was responsible for some fairly reasonably sophisticated practical jokes which involved writing sophisticated but fake notices and fixing them to the school noticeboard. These caused much consternation among both staff and pupils. I did, however, collect the usual array of O and A level certificates as I passed through the school. As I understood it at the time the O level certificates entitled me to take the A level examinations and the A level certificates enabled me to go to university to take more examinations. Apart from the certificate confirming that I have the degrees of MB CHB from Birmingham University, I have no idea what happened to the certificates which I laboured so hard to obtain. My university degree certificate, confirming that I have a medical qualification, hangs in our gardeners' lavatory outside the house. It conveniently covers a small damp patch.

Right from the start I knew that I wanted to be a writer and while I was still at school I started writing short articles and stories and drawing cartoons for magazines.

People write for all sorts of reasons. They write in order to buy food. They write because they want to become famous. They write because they want to be incredibly rich and own a fleet of expensive cars and several huge homes. They write because they have a cause or a purpose and want to change the world. Or they write because they can't not write; it's just in the blood. That was me. I didn't start writing to get rich or anything else though there were (and are) things about which I felt passionate. But I wrote for the same unfathomable reason that some people collect train numbers and others build models of the Eiffel Tower with used matchsticks.

What else can I remember about my schooldays?

Sometimes I came home from school through the park (the grandly named Arboretum) and the park keeper would blow his whistle and shake his fist at me because cycling in the park was forbidden – even on freezing cold, snowy days when the park was completely deserted. I rode through the park because it was more fun, safer and quicker than cycling along the road. The park keeper, who wore a blue uniform and could be easily identified from some distance away, never caught me because I had young legs and lungs, and a bicycle, and he had old legs, with too many years in them, and a pair of heavy boots. He used to shout rather threateningly and generally behaved as park keepers were expected to behave in those days. Once, he hid in a bush and leapt out in front of me with malice aforethought. This, however, was a tactical error and he didn't do it again. I skidded to a halt in front of him and he stared at me, without any idea of what to say or do, silent and glowering. After a moment I dismounted, pushed my bike for ten yards and then remounted and carried on cycling. I think we both felt that his catching me wasn't in the proper spirit of the chase. He didn't hide in the bushes again but contented himself with shouting and blowing his whistle.

I gather that schools have changed somewhat in the last 60 years or so. These days, schools are designed to avoid upsetting pupils (or teachers) with history, facts or views which they might find startling or surprising. Instead, pupils are fed an easy to swallow diet of officially approved propaganda. Students who take examinations are allowed to see the questions in advance so as to avoid stress, remove the risk of failure and make modern teaching methods look successful. Originality and imagination are crushed before they have a chance to flourish.

My third school taught pupils to accept boredom, fear, discipline and injustice and in that I don't think it was any different to other schools. We were also taught there is sometimes a rough and ready relationship between effort and talent on the one side and success on the other. Excuses for failure were punished as severely as sins. The strong survived while the weak were battered into submission and acceptance and prepared for the statutorily approved lifetime of futility, disappointment, resentment and obedience. One or two teachers hit pupils over the head with steel rulers and threw objects at them. Some teachers could be quite ferocious about this – as though they considered the violence a perk of the job with pupils always in season, as it were. I don't think anyone was ever seriously hurt. My strongest memory of grammar school is that there were many pitched battles involving strong rubber bands and paper pellets which had been dipped in inkwells.

On the whole, I don't think there was all that much difference between English schools in the 1950s and 1960s and the schools which Dickens had written about so vividly a century earlier. It's always important to remember that schools were invented during the Industrial Revolution as a form of organised child care, enabling their parents to work full time in the newly built factories and preparing children for their own lifetime of structured devotion.

When I'd finished with school (or school had finished with me) I should have gone straight to medical school but instead I spent eight months working as a Community Service Volunteer in Kirkby, just outside Liverpool. When I arrived there, Kirkby was a new town which had a reputation for being a dumping ground for those considered too rough and ready to live in the city itself. If you consider this an exaggeration I would point out two things: the local police station was covered in thick riot netting and protected with barbed wire, and at night the buses from Liverpool to Kirkby were accompanied by police cars, ready to provide protection for drivers, conductors and, presumably, innocent passengers. I wrote about my experience as a full time volunteer in a previous edition of 'Memories' but I can summarise my time there quite easily. When I arrived in Liverpool one autumn, I was a fairly typical 18-year-old grammar school boy – polite, neat and half-full of respect for authority. When I left, early summer the following year, I had become a rebel; constantly questioning authority. Those months as a Community Service Volunteer changed my life more dramatically than all my years at school and university. Ironically, I fear that as I became more questioning in my outlook, the organisation which had sent me to Liverpool, Community Service Volunteers, seems to have become more bureaucratic and more attuned to the needs and wishes of the establishment. A few years ago CSV asked me, as one of their earliest batch of volunteers, to write something for one of their anniversary brochures. But they never used what I wrote and ignored my requests to find out what had happened to my words. I strongly suspect that the organisation realised that I was too much of a rebel to be the sort of person they wanted to be seen as representing the organisation in even the smallest and slightest of ways.

After my sojourn in Kirkby, I spent three months working in Switzerland in the hope that I would learn to speak German by simply being there. I don't know why I wanted to speak German. I have never been any good at languages and years of learning French (and acquiring an O level) had left me capable of buying a loaf of bread, ordering a cup of coffee and telling anyone prepared to listen,

12

the location of my Uncle's pen. (If you're interested it is in the bureau of my Aunt. Or was it the pen of my aunt that was in my Uncle's bureau?) I hadn't realised that the Swiss didn't speak German but spoke, instead, their own bastardised version known as Schweizer-deutsch. It was like going to the far north of Scotland to learn English. I met no English people there, hardly spoke to the locals (except to order food) and had a very quiet time. I stayed in a small boarding house where I was the only resident and spent most of my time writing articles and stories which I posted to magazines and newspapers back in England.

And then I went to medical school in Birmingham where there was more of the same.

We were taught to accept and never question the establishment, though I understand that things have got even worse. We were taught to learn, digest, regurgitate and never question. If I'd gone straight from school to university I may well have become one of the mechanically operated robots the medical establishment was turning out. But I'd arrived in Birmingham with my rebellious streak thoroughly awakened and I questioned everything and everyone. Not surprisingly, this did not always go down well and I was undoubtedly regarded as a maverick, an outlier.

While at medical school I started writing professionally and prolifically. I wrote reviews of many kinds for 'The Birmingham Post' and 'Times Educational Supplement' and somehow managed to find time to write four regular weekly columns. I also wrote articles and stories for a host of publications (including regular articles, for no good reason that I can think of other than that they used to send me money in return, for a magazine called 'The Teacher') and I regularly criticised the medical establishment (including the medical school's hierarchy) in national, regional and local press and various medical journals. Foolishly I used my own name for many of these and it wasn't long before, even when I used a pen name, the authorities guessed it was me.

As a medical student I needed to get around from hospital to hospital and I began my motoring career with a moped. Helmets weren't required for mopeds in those days. I loved my 49cc Honda. It would do 28 mph all day long and it would start immediately whatever the weather – even if it were covered with a foot of snow. I've owned many cars but, with the possible exception of a pale blue

1958 S1 Bentley, a few trucks and our beautiful Maserati I don't think I've ever owned anything which gave me such a sense of fun and freedom. It would run for ever and a day on half a tank full of petrol and mile for mile was probably cheaper to run than a pair of shoes. It was certainly cheaper to run than the classic Bentley which had a seemingly unquenchable thirst for both petrol and oil. When the moped engine eventually blew up (possibly because whenever I rode it I tended to keep the throttle fully open until I'd completed my journey) I bought a car for £30 (paid with a cheque) from a friendly fellow who sold second-hand cars from a bombed site in the heart of Birmingham. His only office was a small temporary workman's hut – just big enough for the two of us. It was pouring with rain the day I bought the car and if there had been a shop selling umbrellas nearby I would have bought an umbrella. That had been my first choice. The purchase of a motor car had been an impulse buy occasioned by the need to get back to my flat before I drowned. If climate change had been as well marketed at the time as it is now, the weather that day would have been used as evidence of a coming apocalyptic cataclysm. I knew as little about cars then as I do now and bought it simply because it was large and blue. If MOTs had been introduced the garage which sold me the vehicle hadn't heard of them and nor had I. My first car was a very large Humber and it did less miles to the gallon than a Formula I car. On a trip, with much downhill coasting, I could squeeze four miles of travel out of a gallon of petrol. As I drove the Humber away from the bombed site it was raining. I turned on the wipers and they flew across the road into the oncoming traffic. I found that if I stuck my head out of the window I could pretty well see what was ahead so I never got round to replacing the wipers. The battery was tired and useless and because I couldn't afford to replace it I always had to leave the car parked on a hill. When I tired of the Humber breaking down (and I soon knew every local RAC repairman by name) I took it back to the garage where the salesman swapped it, without a moment's hesitation, for a small Ford van which had very little bodywork but an enthusiastic engine which produced a good deal of blue smoke. If there had been an award for the production of blue smoke that little van would have won first prize every day of the week. The exhaust gases leaked into the van and so I could only use it for very short journeys before I became sleepy and nauseous. I'm not sure that would be allowed these days. The windscreen wipers sort of worked (which is to say that they moved from side to side but without affecting the raindrops on the windscreen) but the handbrake came off in my hand when I tried to use it for the first time. I threw it into the back of the van where it remained for the rest of the van's life. The steering wheel was loose and detachable (allowing me to offer it to passengers with the words 'would you like to drive now?') and the back of the van fell off one day. (Actually it only half fell off, but the metal was so rusty that I was easily able to tear away the rest of the bodywork with my bare hands). The battery worked, which was nice, and the lights worked, unless it was raining, but the indicators did not work whatever the weather. But hand signals were still popular in those days so I simply stuck my hand out of the window and waved it about if I intended making a turn. If I had a front seat passenger and I was turning left they would stick out an arm to notify following traffic of my intentions. I once led a regal procession, containing the Queen Mother and every local dignity, through the city Birmingham and all the way to the Queen Elizabeth Hospital. Police on motorbikes tried to move me out of the way but there was nowhere for me to go and they soon choked on my van's blue smoke and had to drop back.

Looking back over a lifetime of motoring, I can honestly say that the dealer on that bombed site was the most honest car salesman I've ever had dealings with. He didn't lie to me, he didn't hide anything and, although he may have been operating on the edge of whatever laws existed at the time, he gave pretty good value for money. Even in the 1960s, £30 wasn't a lot to pay for a car. And when I became tired of the Humber's eccentricities and tantrums, he immediately swapped it for another vehicle without asking me for more cash. How many second-hand car dealers would do that these days? I may have been unfortunate but my hard-won experience is that it is safest to assume that however charming they might be, all car dealers (and all estate agents) will have only a tenuous understanding of the truth. Even car dealers selling very expensive cars seem to be as mean with the truth as anyone else. I once bought a classic Silver Cloud Rolls Royce which had, said the salesman, been re-sprayed on bare metal. When the new paint bubbled and peeled off, the previous colour appeared and then came off too. I sent the patchwork car back on a low loader and, overcome with shame and the prospect of unwelcome litigation, the garage, at the time one of the most reputable dealers in Rolls Royce and Bentley motor cars, gave me my money back.

At the end of the five year course at medical school, I was punished for my various literary activities by being required to stay on for an extra six months 'to acquire maturity'. By this I assumed they meant they wanted me to be more compliant and obedient.

As punishment, I had to sit a special examination and was required to see and diagnose a couple of patients (I described one of them in 'Memories 2'). An outside examiner was brought in to assess my skills and knowledge. After a five minute viva voce he asked me why I'd been required to re-sit the examination, dismissed my flustered answer with a knowing smile and sent me on my way with a kindly pat on the shoulder. It had been a tough lesson in power and its abuse but I'm afraid that if the lesson was designed to turn me into a machine finished doctor it didn't work very well.

The warnings kept coming, though.

I remember a kindly registrar telling me that I would never have a successful career in medicine unless I stopped writing articles. Even a well-meaning ward sister took me on one side and warned me that although she agreed with my criticisms of the establishment she had heard whispers suggesting that if I wanted any sort of career in medicine I would be well advised to put the cover on my typewriter and the cap on my pen.

When I qualified and had completed the required hospital jobs (necessary to obtain full medical registration) I had two jobs before moving into general practice. Unfortunately, both jobs ended before they began.

First, I applied for a job with a large pharmaceutical company (hoping to obtain some inside information that I could expose) and was offered a large salary and a new motor car. Then, days before I was due to start work I was told that someone at the company had recognised my name as the author of articles which were considered not entirely complimentary about the pharmaceutical industry and some of its products. I was invited to sign a letter promising to stop writing articles and columns and most definitely promising not to write anything about the drug industry and most very definitely promising not to write anything about the company which had offered me the job. I refused. The company withdrew the job offer and, to my astonishment, actually paid me a fairly substantial sum in compensation. I seem to remember that the sum was, for some reason, tax free.

Second, I then applied for a job as an editor with the Department of Health because I thought it would give me an insight into how the department worked. I didn't see myself carving out a long term career as a civil servant but in those days London was a fine city and I was looking forward to working and living there for a year or so. I went to an office in Northumberland Avenue, just off Trafalgar Square, and was interviewed by a small man in a very small office. He wasn't a dwarf of any kind but he was so small that if he'd ever needed to use a walking stick he'd have had to reach up to grab the handle. I remember that like many small men he was deprived as far as humour went but well-endowed in terms of ego. I reckoned that if I got the job I could live in a room at my Club, just a few hundred yards away (which was probably cheaper than renting a flat), spend all my money in the second-hand bookshops which lined Charing Cross Road and take all my meals in one or other of the many restaurants in the vicinity. London was full of excellent museums, wonderful art galleries and great cafes and my plan was that when I'd tried all the cafes I'd work my way round the museums and art galleries.

I didn't get the impression that there were a good many candidates for the job but maybe the interviewer was taking his time and seeing just one candidate a day. He certainly didn't seem over-worked. His in-tray and out-tray were both empty.

To my mild astonishment, I was successful and was appointed to edit some of the journals which were at the time published on behalf of the Government. To be honest it didn't look like onerous work. My main task was to have been editing a 12-page journal which was published at what seemed like irregular intervals, sent out to GPs and almost certainly never read. You could have filled it with knitting patterns published upside down and no one would have ever noticed. It was a job which couldn't possibly have involved more than a couple of hours work a month. It sounded promising, especially with Lord's cricket ground in St John's Wood no more than a short taxi ride away.

Sadly, someone in the Department of Health recognised my name and I was fired a couple of days before I was due to start work. This time I was disappointed to see that there was no plan to give me any compensation for the job they'd offered me and then taken away. And who wastes time and money suing the Government?

I also applied for a job with the World Health Organisation in Geneva, Switzerland but I was defeated, partly by the extensive application form and partly by my suspicion (engendered, I think, by either the questions on the application form or the notes in the vast amount of accompanying material) that my ethnicity was likely to prove to be an insurmountable handicap. ('Tick which of the following languages you speak: Urdu, Berber, Flemish, Swahili, Icelandic'). I never got round to completing the form and so I never became Director General of the WHO.

I then applied for a full-time job as GP (which had always been my long term aim) with a practice where I'd worked part time as a locum while I was applying for the jobs mentioned above, and after a rather searing interview got the job as a replacement to a partner who was retiring.

I was a GP in the 1970s and 1980s and things were very different then. I had a single handed practice with one receptionist. I had no appointment system and, together with two other small practices, provided my patients with 24 hour cover. Patients or relatives could ring any time of day or night, 365 days a year, and speak to me or another local doctor. In this book I want to explain why I believe that things were better then (for both patients and doctors) and explore the ways in which the changes have dramatically and permanently changed medical care. Who knows, maybe in a few decades time someone in authority will look back on medicine in the 20th century and decide that things really were better then.

I have explained what went wrong and why I left general practice in my book 'Memories 1' so that saga need not delay us here.

And that's the story of My Early Life. It's not exactly 'David Copperfield' but at least it didn't take as long to write, it doesn't take as long to read and it doesn't take up much space.

How the NHS lost its way

Looking back over the last 60 years or so, it is my belief that things started to go wrong with the NHS half a century ago when appointment systems became more or less compulsory for GPs. Before that, patients had been able to see their family doctor simply by turning up at his or her surgery during the advertised opening hours. The 24 hour a day availability of doctors meant that patients who weren't well enough to visit the surgery, or weren't able to get there for any reason, could telephone for a home visit. And, of course, patients could telephone their doctor at any time of day or night, every day of the year if they needed advice. The system worked well. Patients enjoyed the comfort of knowing that their doctor was pretty well instantly available, and doctors enjoyed the professional satisfaction of providing a personal, effective service to the patients on their list.

When I first started out, appointment systems existed only in large practices with a number of doctors all working together. It was official policy to encourage doctors to work together in health centres, and doctors were under considerable pressure to see their patients by appointment. Looking back it is clear that this was all part of an overall plan to remove GPs' independence and to bring them into the 'body of the kirk', as it were. The NHS was still fairly young and the administrators were in the process of running the service the way they wanted it to be run. Lone GPs did not fit into their plan.

I ran two surgeries a day, and patients who wanted to see me simply had to turn up in the morning or the late afternoon. Because there were no appointments to be made, I could manage quite well with one member of staff who doubled as a receptionist and a secretary. She greeted the patients and fished their medical records out of a filing cabinet and she typed out my letters, put the stamps on and sent them off. On arrival, each patient was given a number torn from a roll of raffle tickets so that there could be no arguments about who had arrived first. Patients would ask around and find the person

19

with the number lower than theirs so that they'd know who to follow. The system worked very well and no patient ever complained about it. Indeed, I never met a patient who preferred having an appointments system to not having one. I never met a doctor who liked appointments systems either. The secretary/receptionist did everything slowly and methodically, as though it were the only thing in the world that mattered and the most important thing she would ever do. And she answered the telephone and took calls from patients who needed to be visited at home. She did have a tendency to panic if things got too exciting – if, for example, the telephone rang at the same moment as the doorbell.

My own experience (fairly widely shared, I believe) was that the introduction of appointment systems changed everything – separating GPs from the patients by an administrative system that was a nightmare for GPs to run and which provided new, unwelcome hurdles for patients to leap if they wanted advice. Much effort was made by the administrators to convince both doctors and patients that everyone would be better off in a health centre and with an appointments system. There was some bullying and in the end I don't think doctors really had much choice.

When I started practice I occupied my predecessor's old surgery and waiting room, renting the rooms and the furniture, and I was happy there although the rooms were small, and the furniture creaked wearily. My waiting room, I am proud to say, had the best magazines in the area. I had a patient who worked for the railways. His job was to sort magazines which were being sent, by train, from wholesalers to individual shops. He would pack up three copies of 'Blue Budgerigars Weekly', five copies of 'Unbelievable Stories' and four copies of 'Favourite British Canals' and tie them together with a piece of string before putting a label on the top magazine of the parcel – that would be the supply for Jack's Corner Shop at the corner of Acacia Avenue and Letsby Avenue. At the end of each train journey he always had a few magazines left over and he would bring me a selection of titles – most of which I had no idea existed. My patients were, thereby, treated to an eclectic and remarkable collection of reading matter. Most doctors used to supply their waiting room with magazines they had bought for their own delight, and so patients were left with nothing more exciting than a couple of magazines on golf and one on yachting. Mine had dozens of wonderful magazines to choose from – always up-to-date and fresh.

When my predecessor decided to move away from the area and to sell what had been both his home and his practice premises, I had to find somewhere new to work. I'd have bought the building if I'd had any money. I was living in an ancient and rather primitive flat at the time and running the practice from there would have been impossible. When I say that it was primitive I am perhaps overstating the case. There was running water (even if most of it came through the ceiling) and there was a plentiful supply of electricity.

Since having an appointment system had pretty well become a necessity, I joined forces with another local doctor (one of the four with whom I shared on-call duties) and we moved our two practices into a very modest terraced house in another part of the town. There were no facilities for car parking but one of the oddities of the planning system at the time was that doctors could open and run a surgery wherever they liked and there was nothing whatsoever that the planning officers could do about it. (I have no idea whether this has changed but I suspect it has not.) We simply informed the NHS (which sent out letters to all our patients), screwed our brass plates to the front door and filled what had been the dining room with our motley assortment of chairs so that it could be called The Waiting Room.

In addition to having new premises we also had to install extra phone lines and hire more receptionists to deal with the wretched appointment system. As far as I was concerned the new system was a chaotic disaster. Patients still sometimes turned up wanting to be seen immediately and I could never turn people away so my surgeries seemed to be pretty open-ended. It was by no means unusual for me to see 30-40 patients in a single morning or evening surgery. That's a lot of people to see and a lot of decisions to make.

And at more or less the same time, in the early 1970s, much the same thing was happening all over England.

GPs who had managed with just a surgery, a waiting room, an office and one receptionist were bullied or pressured into starting appointment systems and found that they needed extra staff to deal with the phone calls.

Doctors who had run their practice from their homes, often using their dining room as a waiting room, had to move into purpose built health centres and clinics and hire extra receptionists to handle all the telephone calls and to keep the appointments book. Doctors found that they had to merge with other local practices because of the cost of the new clinics and the extra staff.

The bureaucrats encouraged the development of clinics because they helped get rid of the traditional, lone GPs who had been difficult to control. As the clinics grew in size so the number of staff grew too. The dramatic increase in the number of receptionists meant that practice managers and personnel specialists had to be hired. When I first practised as a GP I managed with one member of staff – a receptionist. Today, my former practice has been submerged into an administrative giant – with literally dozens of employees. Modern practices are so big that they have to hire specialists in 'human resources' to manage the staff members who are employed. Every time a practice grows in size, the barriers between the patient and the doctor grow higher and wider and the relationship suffers still more. The days of the 'family doctor' have gone and have, I fear, gone forever. The changes which have been made will never be reversed. Patients no longer see the same doctor every time they visit a surgery or clinic. The bureaucrats aren't going to abandon their changes and GPs are unlikely to decide to start providing a proper 24 hour a day service for every day of the year. How many modern GPs would willingly work on Christmas Day and Boxing Day?

And as practices grew in size so GPs moved further and further away from their traditional role as family doctors.

Prior to the mid-1970s, doctors used to do pretty well everything themselves. District nurses did dressings and so on in patients' homes but they rarely did much in the doctor's surgery – calling in once or twice a week to discuss patients with the GP. Doctors took blood pressures, weighed patients, syringed ears and took blood samples. All these minor procedures helped to seal the relationship between doctors and patients. (The procedures were done with fewer problems, too. Today, doctors and nurses consider themselves too important to perform venepuncture and so blood samples are often taken by health care assistants who have no formal training, no knowledge and no skills. As a result, the phlebotomist goes straight through the vein – producing a huge bruise. A friend needs regular blood tests because of her pernicious anaemia but as a result of what I suspect is a mixture of technical ignorance and practical incompetence, her cubital fossa looks a battlefield.)

When doctors regularly visited their patients in their homes, they grew to know them as people and, in many cases, as friends. The chronically sick knew to whom they could turn if they were worried about a hospital appointment or if they wanted a consultant's advice interpreted. The GP was the patient's valued first port of call in any illness, and remained the patient's advisor throughout any illness. The GP was the guide and interpreter in the often impenetrable jungle that is modern health care.

But all that changed as practices became more bureaucratic and grew in size. As the number of single-handed, independent practitioners fell so doctors became remote figures; hiding behind teams of advisors and sub-specialists, teams of receptionists, telephone operators, human resources specialists, social workers, accountants and health care assistants as well as their desks. When new employment laws from the European Union were brought in, it was decreed that GPs should not provide a 24 hour service for 365 days a year (even though very few GPs had complained about the system and, as far as I know, no patients had ever expressed dissatisfaction).When GPs were offered a chance to work the same sort of hours as librarians and accountants, their union leaders leapt at the opportunity and GPs abandoned their long-standing professional sense of responsibility. There was reason behind this apparent madness, of course. The long-term aim was to bring GPs into the highly bureaucratic NHS machine and to change their position from independent contractors to employed cogs in a great machine. (Technically, GPs remained as independent contractors but in truth their independence had disappeared.)

A system which demanded that there be more female doctors than male doctors suited the changes because female doctors wanted fewer working hours and no weekend or night work. Doctors also found that by controlling their income they could dramatically reduce their tax liabilities. As a sop to tradition, patients in the UK were offered a telephone advisory system which appeared to be staffed by teenagers with few or no qualifications. In some parts of the country, one or two doctors were hired to provide a notional out of hours service but because these few doctors were each responsible for millions of patients, there was no chance of their being able to visit patients at home.

New laws were also introduced removing the traditional confidentiality which had always existed between doctors and patients and which had provided the bedrock for the sense of trust between the two. And GPs, now working part time at their NHS jobs, took on work for internet health companies. Patients who were unable to consult their own doctor found that they could, for a fee, consult a GP from another practice somewhere else in the country. GPs had created a demand for this new service by their own selfishness and greed.

There were changes to the way that nurses worked, changes in the way they regarded themselves and changes in the way that they were positioned within the health service.

The idea that nursing should be an academic rather than a practical profession was imported from America and leaders of the nursing profession demanded that nurses should be allowed to have far more responsibility; to make diagnoses and to prescribe treatments. Only those nurses who took degrees and acquired academic certification were allowed to rise through the ranks to become senior members of the profession.

Prior to these changes, hospitals had been simply run. Each ward had a ward sister (who was in charge of the nursing) and a ward clerk (who was in charge of looking after the medical records). Each hospital had a matron (who was in charge of all nursing matters), a secretary (who was in charge of administration) and an almoner (who looked after patients' social problems). Porters were hired to wheel patients around and to look after the heavy work. Nursing auxiliaries dealt with simpler, routine nursing work. And doctors (consultants and junior doctors) looked after diagnosing and treating patients.

Up until the 1970s, all this worked moderately well, to the quiet satisfaction of patients and staff, but things were changed dramatically and, it seemed, almost endlessly, by the introduction of many new layers of administration. This wasn't the first time there had been administrative changes. The NHS had been constantly changing ever since its creation and it seemed that the minute the staff had become accustomed to one system, so a new system would be introduced. The only people who benefited from these changes were the administrators who gradually took more and more control. They closed smaller hospitals because they did not fit comfortably into a new bureaucratic hierarchy which had been designed, more for the satisfaction of the administrators than the welfare of patients or the comfort of the staff. Nurses and doctors abandoned working practices which had been carefully devised, and the NHS became a battle ground where consultants fought bureaucrats for power. Inevitably, the bureaucrats won and the consultants lost. It was a rout.

In both general practice and hospitals, the bureaucrats had taken control.

Helped in their aim by increasingly powerful professional trade unions, which abandoned any sense of responsibility for patient care in favour of merely improving their members' earnings, the conspirators had successfully destroyed the National Health Service, removing all sense of morality from a system which had also become increasingly beholden to the powerful and corrupt international pharmaceutical industry.

What none of the unions realised, however, was that they had helped set up a system which was perfectly designed to ensure that individual professionals would, in just a few years, be completely replaced by robots and computers. Research has shown that computers make better diagnosticians than doctors, that robots are better at surgery than human surgeons and that robots make better, more caring and more reliable nurses than human nurses. The robot nurses can be programmed with enough caring to revive the valuable placebo response that used to augment medical treatment in such a powerful way. (At some point, however, the computers will need to be properly programmed. As I was writing this section, my wife Antoinette, who has breast cancer, was sent a standard letter by the part of the NHS which is looking after her cancer, inviting her to attend a routine breast screening session. Inefficient and tactless to say the least.)

Neither the medical nor the nursing profession has realised it yet, and the health care trade unions haven't cottoned on, but there is no future for human doctors or for human nurses. They will all be replaced by robots and computers. The new system, which eradicated home visits and night calls (difficult for robots to manage) and destroyed the traditional relationship between doctors and patients, has made this possible.

Sadly, the NHS today provides a far inferior service now than it did in the decades immediately following its creation. It is not difficult to argue that the NHS today provides a far inferior service to the NHS of 1950.

Sharing this truth has not made me popular.

I am reminded of the following lines lines by Thomas Gray: 'Where ignorance is bliss,'Tis folly to be wise.'

And, as I have discovered, it is folly too, to be honest.

Unforgettable patients

Two of my patients, Mr and Mrs Thomson, bought a seven acre plot of land. They couldn't afford to buy a house, or even a down payment on a house, so they decided that they would put a second-hand caravan on their piece of land, and live in the caravan until they could afford to build their home. And they would, assuming they managed to obtain planning permission, build their house on their seven acre plot. They knew exactly where on their plot they would build. The land was sloping but with the help of a digger they'd be able to erect the house of their dreams. It was never going to be anything ambitious but it was going to be home.

That was the plan.

They hadn't been married when I took over the practice but they were both my patients and after they got back from a five day honeymoon in Cornwall they brought me a slice of wedding cake which I thought was lovely of them. The cake was stale and solid enough to use as hard core for road mending but I said thank you very much, as you do, and wished them all the very best, and my receptionist's small dog, which she sometimes brought to work with her, ate the cake with great relish and so everyone was happy.

At the time of their marriage, he was a clerk in a local bank and she was a hairdresser working in a local salon. For the first twelve months they lived in the spare room at her mum's which wasn't the most auspicious start to their marriage because the spare room was the sort of room which used to be called a box room and even a single bed took up most of the space. The bride's brother occupied the larger spare bedroom and he couldn't move into the smaller bedroom because he had a large model train set which was laid out on four trestle tables. The train set was nigh on impossible to move and certainly too large to fit into the small bedroom.

The bank clerk hated the bank where he worked and the hairdresser hated the salon where she was employed (neither of them got on well with their bosses) and so they saved as hard as they could for a year, resigned from their jobs, bought the plot of land

and, in order to make some money, started to cultivate the land. They did some research and decided that in order to maximise their income they would specialise in a single crop and that lavender was the simplest and, for them, the most profitable crop to grow. More research convinced them that, serendipitously, the land they'd bought would be perfect for lavender.

Things went well.

Their lavender grew and they harvested their first crop successfully. They obtained a good price for it in advance – selling the entire crop to a company which made scented candles, soaps and little cloth sachets that old fashioned ladies liked to put into their drawers. They'd made enough out of the lavender to live but they still wanted to build their house, so Mrs Thomson made a few extra pounds by setting up as a part-time mobile hairdresser, cutting people's hair in their own homes, and Mr Thomson made a few pounds doing the accounts for a local plumber, a corner shop and a car mechanic who serviced cars in his garage at home. Mr Thomson said he made a great deal more money than he would have thought possible and the extra money was all put on one side for when they started building their home.

And then their world pretty well fall apart.

Two glum men from the local planning department told them that they couldn't park their caravan on their own land without obtaining permission. And when they applied for permission for their caravan, they were told that they couldn't have it. A cheerful soul in the planning department also took great delight in telling them that there was no way that they would ever be given planning permission to build a house on their land. They were given no reason, they were simply told that they couldn't.

They got round this setback by moving the caravan around a little.

Every month they hitched the caravan up to the battered old Land Rover they'd bought (and which Mrs Thomson used for her mobile hairdressing business) and moved it across the field to a new spot. This still wasn't terribly legal but every time they moved their caravan the council had to alter all the paperwork telling them that their caravan was parked illegally. The Land Rover was in very poor condition and broke down often but when it wouldn't work they always managed to find someone willing to move the caravan for them. Because I had a tow bar on the back of the truck we owned, I managed to move it for them two or three times.

And then, just when they were beginning to think things weren't destined to go their way, they had a little luck.

An old lady, Miss Fetling, who owned a cottage which bordered onto their land, decided, shortly after her 93rd birthday, that she wanted to move into a small one bedroomed flat in a building which was run especially for the older citizen. The old lady, who was also a patient of mine, was still as bright as the proverbial button but was, she said, beginning to feel her age and felt she needed to have a telephone and some people nearby. She was a lovely lady. I remember she once told me that she was alone but never lonely and that she thought this was probably preferable to being lonely but never alone. (The latter is, of course, a state of affairs common in big cities.)

Miss Fetling had worked as a secretary to a film producer, whose name I knew, and she had amazing stories to tell, which I much enjoyed, of her years at Pinewood and other British film studios.

GPs who do not talk to their patients, let alone visit them at home, never have these unexpected joys. I am not surprised most of the modern GPs hate their work and do it only for the money. How sad that is.

The building into which Miss Fetling moved had a resident concierge (though they didn't call her that, preferring something long and boring with the words 'management' and 'care' in the title) and her new flat was equipped with an emergency call button so that she could ring for help if she fell or felt unwell. The old lady regarded this move as merely another stepping stone in life. She was always optimistic and never thought of death. She had some of the belongings she didn't need straight away put into storage. It occurred to me that anyone in their 90s who puts furniture, clothes and ornaments into storage is clearly an optimist, with the right attitude to life.

The cottage which she was leaving, and which was now for sale, needed a good deal of attention because nothing had been done to it for years. The elderly tend not to bother doing repairs to their homes. A combination of tiredness, lack of funds and a feeling that the business of renovation can, with luck, be left to the next owner, means that missing tiles remain missing, gutters leak, window frames rot and the boiler struggles to do what it was installed to do. The only water supply came from a pump and a borehole, and sewage went into a septic tank which probably hadn't been emptied since George VI had been on the throne, if you'll pardon the slightly irreverent thought. The 'facility' was out of doors, at the bottom of the garden.

The cottage had no electricity, cooking was done over an open fire (which also provided the cottage with heating and hot water) and lighting was provided by oil lamps.

As you can imagine, Miss Fetling's cottage wasn't the property of the month as far as the estate agents were concerned and the only prospective purchasers were the couple who had been living in the caravan. They made a modest but fair offer, which the old lady happily accepted, and moved out of their now rather elderly caravan and into the cottage. Everyone thought they would put in electricity and have mains water and sewage connected but they didn't do any of those things. They decided that they rather liked the rustic lifestyle, which was cheaper than making changes, and having been living in a caravan for rather longer than they'd intended they decided that the cottage was definitely an improvement. I helped them by towing the caravan round to the cottage and parking it on a patch of rough grass beside their driveway. For reasons which I have no interest in trying to understand, they did not need to obtain any planning permission to park the caravan next to their cottage. Mr Thomson used the caravan as an office where he could do the accounts for the lavender business and the accounts he was paid to do.

As Mr Thomson, the ex-bank clerk, said: 'Sometimes life kicks you in the teeth, and sometimes life lifts you up and puts you on top of the world – the important thing is to accept whatever you're given with equanimity, whatever you feel about things there probably isn't anything much you can do about it.' It was something very like that anyway. It has been a year or two since he said it and I didn't make a verbatim note at the time.

In addition to not having a flushing loo, an indoor water supply or any electricity the cottage didn't have a telephone and since the new occupants decided that they too could manage without one, they chose not to have one installed.

This was fine until there was an emergency and then there were problems.

Mr Thomson had been on the roof of the cottage, trying to repair a section where half a dozen slates had slipped or been blown off, when he slid off the roof and landed painfully and awkwardly on a small paved area where the previous owner had, on sunny days, sat in an old easy chair and eaten her meals, read a magazine or done her knitting. The chair, which had, judging by the damage to the stuffing, been home to several families of mice, stayed out in all weathers, covered with an old piece of tarpaulin in the winter months.

Mrs Thomson, who'd been in the kitchen baking, heard the crash and rushed outside. At first she thought that her husband, motionless, was dead.

He wasn't dead but he was unconscious. He was bleeding badly from a cut in his leg and the positions of both those limbs made it clear that he had broken both a leg and an arm.

Suppression a natural inclination to scream, Mrs Thomson realised that she now had a huge dilemma.

She didn't want to leave her husband but, as you will remember, they didn't have a telephone (and mobile telephones were available only to millionaires driving in limousines) and the narrow, country lane on which they lived was a dead end and had no passing traffic. To see a car or van on the lane was a rare novelty and the only people using it were, generally speaking, people who were lost. The couple received very little mail so even the postman was an unusual sight. Because it didn't go anywhere the lane wasn't even used by local farmers.

To make things worse the lane was at one point narrowed by an old stone bridge.

The bridge crossed a stream which in summer dried to a trickle, but never dried completely, and in winter became a narrow torrent. The bridge was so narrow that only a car or small truck could possibly pass over it. The bridge certainly wasn't wide enough for an ambulance.

Mrs Thomson realised that she had no choice. She had to leave her husband where he lay and go to the nearest farm, over two miles away if you followed the lanes and, perhaps, a mile and a half away if you went across the fields, to ask if she could use their telephone.

Before she left him Mrs Thomson had the good sense to make

sure that her husband was breathing, and to tie a makeshift bandage around his leg, just above the bleeding point. I know first aid experts now disapprove of tourniquets but she did the right thing. If she hadn't stopped the bleeding, her husband would have almost certainly bled to death and whatever first aid procedures had later been recommended would have been of very little value.

I can only begin to comprehend the horror of her journey.

She decided to go across the fields, thinking that since it was a shorter journey it would be quicker. She ran and stumbled across one field after another. At one point she found herself stopped in her tracks by a thick hawthorn hedge. She found a spot where sheep had once broken through, removed some barbed wire and a piece of rusty corrugated iron that a farmer had used to block the gap, and carried on, scratched, cut and bleeding from hands and arms. No one ever realised more thoroughly the penalty one must pay for living in the country, and the extra penalty to be paid for not having a telephone. Several times she almost turned back, wanting to see how her husband was; to see if he had regained consciousness. She realised that she should have left a note to tell him that she'd gone for help.

All journeys, however terrible, must eventually come to an end of some sorts, of course.

Realising that an ambulance would not be able to reach their cottage she telephoned my surgery and luckily I was there. I had finished my morning surgery and was signing letters and prescriptions. I promised to get there as quickly as I could and told her to go back to the cottage.

The farmer put Mrs Thomson in his Subaru truck (I remember that Subaru trucks were at that time even more popular than Land Rovers with farmers – I suspect because they were cheaper to buy, more reliable and probably cheaper to run) and drove her to the cottage. Her husband, now awake, realised that she had gone for help and meanwhile he had had the presence of mind to unfasten the tourniquet for a minute or two to allow blood to flow into the rest of his leg. He knew enough about first aid to understand that if you leave a tourniquet on a limb for too long then the tissues, and the limb, will literally starve to death.

I arrived at the cottage no more than ten minutes after Mrs Thomson and the farmer had got there. A careful, immediate examination showed that Mrs Thomson's first assessment had been accurate: Mr Thomson had a broken arm and a broken leg and a gash, probably caused by the sharp edge of a piece of broken slate, which had torn through a blood vessel. The ground where Mr Thomson was lying was littered with shards of broken slate – and blood. The problem was that I had no idea what damage he had done to his spine, and although his abdomen seemed soft and wasn't painful, I didn't know what internal bleeding there might be. However, a quick examination showed that Mr Thomson didn't seem to have any nerve damage affecting his feet or hands. And there were no signs of any brain injury.

We obviously had to move Mr Thomson to the nearest hospital – around 20 miles away.

There were, it seemed, just two choices.

Either we called for an ambulance or we took Mr Thomson to the hospital ourselves. The ambulance was out because of the bridge and the farmer suggested that we telephone the police and see if they could arrange for a helicopter to be sent. Mrs Thomson pointed out that the area around the cottage was heavily wooded. And neither he nor Mrs Thomson could think of a flat piece of land where a helicopter could possibly land – even if one could be arranged. All the local fields were steeply sloping. Even the plot which Mr and Mrs Thomson had selected for the house they had never built was sloping and would have needed a considerable amount of work.

'An ambulance will never get across that bridge,' pointed out the farmer. 'We'd have to put him in my truck, take him as far as the bridge, carry him across the bridge and then put him in the ambulance.'

'If we're going to do that then we might as well take him all the way to the hospital,' I said. 'Besides, it will be quicker. To call an ambulance means someone going back to the farm to use the telephone. Then we have to wait for an ambulance to arrive.'

'Is it safe to move him?' asked Mrs Thomson. 'What if he's damaged his spine?'

I decided that it was a risk we had to take and that there was a way to minimise any danger.

After I had given Mr Thomson a hefty dose of morphine, the farmer and I removed one of the internal doors from the cottage and unscrewed the door handles. (The farmer did the technical stuff – my contribution was to find the screwdriver.) We then carefully slid the door under the injured Mr Thomson, using the flat piece of wood as a makeshift stretcher. I then lowered the tailgate on my truck (which was slightly longer and cleaner than the farmer's) and we lifted the door, together with Mr Thomson, so that it lay on the truck's flatbed and horizontal tailgate. Mrs Thomson sat in the bed of the truck with her husband, so that every few minutes she could unfasten the tourniquet and let some blood through into the tissues. There wasn't any way to tie the door and the man to the truck so we just had to hope that gravity would be sufficient.

The trip took 40 minutes and it was, as you can imagine, a nightmare of a journey. I had to drive very slowly along the lanes, which were bumpy and winding, but when we got onto the main road I could drive a little faster. Half way to the hospital, a police car saw us and, not surprisingly perhaps, waved me down. After I'd explained why I had a man lying on a door in the back of my truck the police car gave us an escort to the hospital and radioed ahead to let the Casualty Department know that we were on our way.

When we arrived at the hospital, a doctor and two nurses met us with a couple of porters and a trolley.

Happily, Mr Thomson was no more badly injured than had first appeared. He was given a couple of pints of blood and his arm and leg were set and plastered. Three days later he was home.

While her husband was in bed in hospital, Mrs Thomson set in motion the process for having their cottage fitted with a telephone. She was delighted to discover that they could have a telephone fitted without the need to have their cottage connected to the electricity supply.

That was a home visit, 1970s style.

Fads and fashions

It sometimes seems surprising just how much things have changed in less than a century. I have no doubt that it seems bizarre to young people today that there were houses without electricity when I first worked as a GP. The 1970s don't seem very far away to me but I suspect that to many today they seem as far away as the 1920s appeared to me when I was a boy.

Until I went to Kirkby, Liverpool as a Community Service Volunteer I'd lived a fairly stable, middle class life but my experiences in Kirkby had opened my eyes to a wider world.

Our experiences make us who we are and how we do what we do. Would Lowry have painted more pictures if he had not been a rent collector? Would they have been the same pictures? I suspect not; because his experiences made him who he was as an artist. And so on.

I remember meeting a couple who had wondered why their mattress seemed alive. It wasn't bedbugs. It was mice, who had made a nest there and were bringing up their offspring between the springs. I knew families who struggled to cope with the heat in summer and who opened all the windows to survive, not because the weather was hot but because they didn't know how to turn down their central heating. I met families living in rat infested properties who didn't know what to do and so just lived in terror – especially at night – covering babies and small children with wire netting to keep the rodents at bay. I knew a single woman who had found an abandoned baby on a bus. The baby had been wrapped in old newspapers and a blue blanket. The woman kept the baby and brought it up as her own. I doubt if I ever met a better looked after child. (It wasn't easy convincing the bureaucrats that they were at fault and had lost all the inevitable paperwork.) I knew old people who lived in high rise buildings and who didn't ever leave their flats because the lifts didn't work, or because they were too frightened of the gangs and the dogs. They were, quite literally, prisoners in their own homes.

In Liverpool as a volunteer, and then later, when I became a GP, I could initiate help for all those people.

The elderly imprisoned in their homes could be helped by arranging for young volunteers to take in the shopping, or escort the elderly to the shops. And as a GP I could get the lift repaired by screaming at the council and telling the usual, indifferent, uncaring clerk that if my patient died I'd put the building manager down on the death certificate as the cause of death. Nothing pushes a bureaucrat into action faster than that.

General practice isn't just about prescribing antibiotics, arranging vaccinations, handing out sick notes and referring patients to hospital consultants. Or it shouldn't be.

I remember a patient who had distorted vision in one eye. He was constantly nauseous and couldn't see. I bought him an eye patch until the eye problem could be sorted out. He could then see perfectly well with his one eye. He was as grateful as if I'd saved his life with a heart-lung transplant.

A man who had a stutter had discovered that if he sang he lost the stutter. I went with him to the hospital because he was frightened that the staff would laugh at him or tell him off if he sang his symptoms.

And I'd bet good money that you could find all those things happening now, today, if you looked for them.

But, sadly, modern GPs don't do home visits of course and never get to know their patients or understand their fears and frailties. They are too self-important to venture outside their cosy, convenient, purpose built health centres and their human barriers of receptionists, health care assistants and practice nurses. They are too busy filling in forms to bother about the people. There isn't anyone apart from GPs to look after those who need looking after; to be their protector. Social workers rarely leave their meeting rooms. They discuss 'cases', and make decisions about policy but they rarely do things.

Trends, fashions and fads come and go and it is vital to understand that many of the things we now believe to be true, and take for granted, are likely to be regarded as fanciful and absurd by future generations. Everything is, of course, changing ever faster.

In the 1970s and 1980s, there were still homes which had an outdoor lavatory. The posh ones had a water closet and a roll of loo paper hung on a piece of wire taken from a coat hanger and hung on

36

a nail. The poorer ones had a sentry box shaped loo at the bottom of the garden. The sentry box contained a seat and some roughly torn squares of newspaper stuck onto a rusty nail fixed to the back of the door. Beneath the seat there was an earth closet. The young of today regard these as laughably primitive (which they assuredly are) and probably think that such things were last seen in the 15th century. I may be getting on a tad, and you might not want to sell me life insurance, but I'm not that old and I remember such things very well. I even remember homes in which patients took their regular Saturday night bath in a tub placed in front of the fire. The hot water came from kettles and large saucepans.

One important lesson I've learnt, is that medicine (like almost everything else) seems to blunder from one idiotic enthusiasm to another. So, for example, it was not all that long ago that doctors believed in leeches and blood-letting. A century ago bowels were an obsession and everyone in the world seemed to worry about constipation. The newspapers and magazines were crammed full with advertisements for remedies such as liquid paraffin, Californian syrup of figs and ordinary syrup of figs that presumably came from somewhere less glamorous than California. I remember there was a 'medicine' available over the counter (without a prescription) called Dr J.Collis Browne's elixir which sold very well. That wasn't surprising since at the time it contained morphine in quite decent quantities. The makers of Horlicks invented a condition called 'Night Starvation which their product was invented to cure. A product called Phyllosan was advertised everywhere to 'fortify the over 40s', as though anyone over 40 was decrepit and ready for the knackers yard.

When I was a GP I had patients who had no electricity in their homes. I remember taking a consultant physician to see an elderly couple who lived in a terraced cottage. In those days, hospital consultants would do home visits if requested to do so by a GP. They received a handsome cheque from the NHS for their time.

(That particular consultant was, I remember, good at his job but he was what used to be known as a tartar and had a reputation for being rather obsessional and pernickety. I once saw him at a Test Match where, instead of enjoying the cricket, he was keeping a ball by ball record of every ball bowled. He had a large scorebook spread out across his knees. I have no personal knowledge of this but I am told that he was a keen concert goer who would take a copy of the score with him so that he could check that the orchestra were playing all the right notes, and playing them in the order the composer had decreed that they should be played. I remember he always wore a grey three piece suit, with a faint chalk-stripe, and a bright yellow bow tie which was, I'm afraid, one of those ready-made ones which come fitted with an elastic strap and a catch so that they can be snapped into place in seconds and never look droopy. His trousers were always supported by bright red braces, or suspenders as the Americans call them, to show that although he was reliable and solid he could also be brave and imaginative.)

The husband was having chest pains and the consultant asked where he could plug in his electrocardiogram machine. He was more than slightly surprised to discover that there was no electricity available. I'd forgotten there was no electricity and apologised profusely for this oversight. Eventually, we borrowed a long extension lead from a neighbour and plugged the electrocardiogram machine into one of the neighbour's electric sockets.

The thing is that every generation produces its own myths and fashions and only with time do we begin to realise the extent of our communal madness. It is only the older practitioners who can look at the latest fashions and fads with a duly critical eye, wondering which of them will last the course and which will be discarded and, in turn, laughed about as being as absurd as leeches or the privy at the end of the garden path.

I would put appointment systems into the same category as jars of leeches for blood-letting. Neither appointment systems nor leeches has ever done any good at all.

What proper doctors do (the importance of home visits)

Visiting a patient in their own home provides massively important information – especially if those patients also work at home.

Very early in my career as a GP I saw a patient who came to see me complaining of dizziness. Mrs Lapworth was exactly the same shape as one of those spherical dolls which always goes back upright when you try to knock them off balance. She was so big that if she'd stood still for any length of time she would have needed to apply for planning permission. And she always looked terribly fierce though this was simply a result of the way her eyebrows were shaped. When she looked at me I always felt I understood how an able seaman on 'The Bounty' would have felt if Captain Bligh had considered his main-brace splicing to be on the inadequate side of unacceptable. But her manner belied her looks; she was a very gentle, kindly sort of person.

Mrs Lapworth had high blood pressure and was taking tablets to try to bring it down to a satisfactory level. I'd warned her that the tablets might make her feel dizzy (by producing occasional low blood pressure) and that she should take care when getting out of bed, moving suddenly or driving.

I knew that she and her husband ran a shop together and since her husband was registered with another doctor in another practice, I didn't ask her about him and his health.

A week after I'd seen her, and started her on tablets for her blood pressure, I was called to see her at home. Her husband, who was the one who had telephoned on her behalf, told me that she had apparently fallen and although neither of them thought she'd broken any bones she was shaken up and would be grateful if I'd just check her over. He said she didn't really feel up to leaving home but that there was no real rush and that it would be fine if I'd go round as soon as I had finished my morning surgery.

When I got to their home it turned out that the shop they ran together was one of those corner shops which used to serve every community but which are now often being driven out of business by supermarkets. There were baskets of fresh fruit and vegetables stacked on the pavement outside and inside the shop every inch was utilised. There were newspaper and magazine racks, sections offering just about every type of canned food you could think of, shelves full of biscuits, display boxes full of chocolates and sweets and two shelves, high off the ground, stocked with alcohol and cigarettes.

I found out later that their shop was only a hundred yards or so from the local cinema and the couple sold cigarettes, soft drinks and chocolates to the cinema patrons. They did quite well with these customers because their prices were much lower than those in the cinema shop. I also found out that they stayed open in the evenings so that they'd get the second house business and that on Fridays and Saturdays they stayed open until nearly midnight and sold hot drinks and soup which, with entrepreneurial zeal and imagination, they prepared in their own kitchen and served in disposable plastic cups. These days they'd have been reported by some local busy body and closed down for not having the appropriate licence, but either no one from the council knew what they were doing or else they weren't breaking any local laws at the time.

It turned out that Mrs Lapworth had rather foolishly climbed the ladder to fetch cigarettes for a customer, and that when she'd reached up to pick out a packet of the brand the customer had requested, she'd suddenly felt dizzy and lost her balance. She'd started to come back down the ladder but hadn't quite managed it. She'd misjudged the position of the last rung and had fallen. She'd only been on the second rung of the ladder at the time of her accident and that was why she hadn't hurt herself too badly. They were right that no bones had been broken but it was clear that she was going to have some pretty substantial bruises on her left thigh, which had taken the brunt of the fall. I suspect that someone less well upholstered might have suffered more damage.

There was no need to ask her why she'd been up the ladder. Her husband was in a wheelchair and although he could move himself about quite well he couldn't possibly have reached the alcohol or the cigarettes.

'Why do you keep those things so far out of reach?' I asked.

'They're the ones that get stolen,' replied Mr Lapworth. 'We've had some trouble with children helping themselves to cigarettes, so we keep the ladder behind the counter to make them pretty impossible to get at.'

'Why don't you just keep the cigarettes behind the counter, so that they're out of the way?' I asked. 'If you did that Mrs Lapworth wouldn't have to go up a ladder anywhere near as often.'

'But there isn't any room behind the counter,' protested Mr Lapworth. 'Not with the ladder there.'

'Would you need to keep the ladder there if you didn't have to go up to collect the cigarettes and alcohol?'

Mr Lapworth laughed out loud. 'No, we wouldn't!' he agreed. 'We could just keep stock on those top shelves – things we only need once every week at the most.'

I helped bring the cigarettes and alcohol down from the top shelves (hoping none of my patients came in and saw me with an armful of cigarette packets) and stacked them behind the counter. I then put the ladder away where it wouldn't be any trouble.

Moving cigarettes around might not have been covered in any of my medical school textbooks, but it was excellent preventive medicine.

Patience, silence and the hand on the doorknob

Patience is possibly the most under-rated virtue for a doctor. I have always been painfully impatient, it's one of my worst and most irrepressible faults, but I knew that in the consulting room I had to make an effort to be tolerant and unhurried. Getting information out of patients isn't always straightforward. Many patients hide the important things they want to mention and will leave the consulting room or surgery without telling you what is really worrying them, unless you give them time and a little encouragement.

These days doctors may well have been taught a good deal about how to fill in forms, and the best way to satisfy health care bureaucrats, but they know painfully little about patients or human behaviour and too many have their fingers on the computer keyboard within seconds of a patient sitting down; anxious to tap in a quick conclusion, order a prescription and press the button to call the next patient. Doctors tend to talk too much and listen too little.

The problem is that doctors learn to see patients quickly (that's what they are encouraged to do by the appointments system – which introduced the idea of the five minute consultation) but you can only learn about a patient's signs and symptoms by listening.

Asking the wrong questions, and directing a patient in the direction that seems to fit the doctor's prejudices and immediate on the spot conclusion, is one of the reasons so many wrong diagnoses are made and why so many patients are made ill, or killed, by their doctors.

(I showed some years ago that iatrogenesis, doctor induced disease, is one of the three main causes of death, along with circulatory disease and cancer.)

It is my belief that a GP needs to know a great deal about human psychology, what drives people, when they are concealing something and so on. He or she needs to know as much or more about people than any psychiatrist or psychologist; he or she needs to be observant; and he or she needs to acquire skills that aren't ever taught and probably could never be taught. Without those skills the

GP will miss important signs and symptoms and patients will pay the ultimate price.

And in my experience, simple one word triggers (the traditional ones – when, how, what, where and why) have always been the most useful ways to elicit genuinely useful information.

And silence.

Never forget silence.

Silence is a dramatically under-estimated weapon in the doctor's armoury: just as useful as a stethoscope or a thermometer. If the doctor rushes his patients then he'll probably miss most of the things his patients want to tell him (or her, of course). I've never been trout or salmon fishing but from what I know of fishing, teasing the truth out of a patient can sometimes be similar to catching a game fish.

When newspapers and TV stations used to employ proper journalists, keen on finding the truth, it was well known that keeping quiet was the best way to obtain information. Most people dislike a silence and will talk to fill the space – telling you things that they perhaps weren't going to share. The very slightest of nods, or the raising of an eyebrow by a quarter of an inch, or a hint of a smile, can all help encourage a shy or reluctant patient to tell you what they're really worried about.

The judicious pause is a vital weapon in the armoury of any interrogator who is genuinely anxious to ferret out the truth. A silence will often trigger an honest, unguarded response – a fact or an opinion that might otherwise have remained hidden. Most people feel a desperate need to fill the silence. Interrogators working for the secret services use the same very simple technique when talking to defectors or captured spies. Over the years it has probably proved far more useful than water boarding or the removal of finger nails. Barristers sometimes use the silence, but they usually prefer to know the answers to their questions before they ask them and so the judicious pause would, for them, mean venturing into dangerous territory since you never really know what is likely to appear.

Tragically, modern doctors hardly ever use the judicious pause. A few decades ago, when general practitioners were much busier but had far more time to spend with and to talk to their patients, the judicious pause was used without thinking. Doctors knew that patients often kept their most important, private thoughts, memories, experiences and fears tucked away somewhere secret and that those thoughts, memories, experiences and fears were invariably of vital importance. Today's doctors are far too busy with pre-formed conclusions, prejudices and spoon fed pre-conceived notions to allow their patients to speak much at all, let alone to waste time in providing what is known, in radio parlance, as 'dead air'.

Tragically, the bottom line is that many patients hide their vital signs or symptoms and will only tell the doctor what they really want him to know if they are given plenty of time and encouragement. Time and time again I saw patients who would tell me about a patch of dry skin, or some other truly minor problem that clearly wasn't their real reason for coming to the surgery.

And then, as they headed for the door, I'd say something like: 'Is there anything else you want to tell me?'

And they'd turn and reply: 'Well, while I'm here, doctor, I wouldn't mind if you'd have a look at my left hand because I can't move three of my fingers...' or 'I didn't like to bother you but I suppose I ought to tell you that I've been passing a lot of blood recently.'

And then the alarm bells rang, like six fire engines screaming past the surgery window, and I'd ask them to sit down again and to tell me what else they'd noticed. And then we'd start the examination all over again.

I can't remember how many times I've only learned about a patient's real problem when they had their hand on the door knob and were ready to leave.

Cary Grant

I love true, curious stories about real people. I included several in my series of seven diaries but I've included one or two in this book in the hope that you haven't come across them.

Peter Bogdanovich, the film director and author, was interviewing an elderly, balding, frail, liver spotted film star called Cary Grant.

'My daughter is a huge fan of yours,' said Bogdanovich. 'May I bring her round to meet you?'

Grant gently said 'No'.

When Bogdanovich seemed surprised, Grant explained. 'I would much rather she remembered me as I was than as I am now,' he said.

What wisdom.

The removal man

I've never been a big drinker of alcohol, never drinking beer or lager, drinking champagne only when celebrating some date or event and hardly ever drinking any other wines. For decades I've largely confined myself to drinking an occasional malt whisky, favouring, for example, a glass of hot toddy made with Laphroaig and hot water in a Russian tea glass. It's a great way to recover, on a cold winter's day, after an hour or two in the garden or a brisk walk.

But I've always had a few bottles of alcohol in the house and when I was a GP I had more bottles of booze than at any other time in my life. Patients often used to bring me Christmas presents and the gift of choice was frequently a bottle of something designed to damage my liver. I usually received enough bottles of booze to last me through the year. I received book tokens, chocolates and home-made cakes too, but alcohol was the favoured gift and I like to think this was generic rather than personal.

Newspaper editors and TV companies were generous too in those days, though I doubt if the same thing happens much today. Budgets have been cut to the bone and a cup of coffee from a machine is probably as generous a libation as contributors are likely to receive. Back in the 1970s, food hampers and expensive bottles in fancy packaging were handed out like Halloween treats.

One year, when I moved house, I collected together all the bottles of alcohol in the house and put them into a single cardboard box – one of those boxes wine shops use, with the cardboard dividers providing some protection and preventing the bottles from smashing into one another. My collection of bottles fitted neatly into the box, with pride of place being taken by a rather splendid bottle of malt whisky which I'd been given by the producer of a TV show I'd worked on. It was a bottle of Cardhu, a malt whisky which comes in a very distinctive and unusual bottle. The producer and the programme's director had both signed the bottle, with an appropriately cheerful seasonal greeting. The producer's signature, and his greeting, were both in the purple ink that the producer invariably used. I doubt if many people still use purple ink. It used to be quite popular but these days it would probably be considered a little flamboyant, even decadent.

When the removal company turned up, I was pleased to see that one of the removal men was a patient of mine; a fellow whom I knew quite well because I'd been to his home several times to treat him, his wife and their two children.

The move went as smoothly as these things ever go, which is to say that there were the usual alarums and excursions as the removal men struggled to move beds and wardrobes down and then up winding staircases. I spent much of my time making cups of tea and handing round platefuls of biscuits. It was a hot day and the removal men stopped work at least once an hour for refreshments and sustenance. I remember that at one point I ran out of biscuits and had to pop to the nearest corner shop to buy fresh supplies. When they'd finished, and the furniture and the boxes of books and so on were all distributed around the new house, I handed out rather generous tips which more or less doubled the cost of the move.

It wasn't until a week or so after the move had been completed that I noticed that the box of booze was missing. It wasn't anywhere. All the other boxes had been safely delivered, but the box full of bottles was nowhere to be found.

I had my suspicions, of course.

The only logical explanation was that one of the removal men had stolen the box. It wouldn't have been difficult. The removers used a lot of old rugs and blankets to protect bits and pieces of furniture and it would have been very easy to cover up such an enticing box with a blanket and then 'forget' about it. If I'd noticed it they'd have been able to apologise, say they were glad I'd spotted the box and hand it to me with an innocent smile.

(Staff in nursing homes favour this trick almost routinely, I'm sad to say. They put the jewellery belonging to deceased patients into an envelope and then put the envelope into a drawer where it remains unless a relative remembers to ask for it. 'Oh yes, we were keeping it for you,' the staff will say. If, in a couple of months, the envelope hasn't been 'claimed' the contents will be sold and the money shared. By then it will be impossible for anyone to be expected to remember what happened to the jewellery.)

Three, or maybe four months, later I found out what had

happened to my box of bottles.

I was called to the home of the removal man who'd helped me move house. His daughter had a bad chest infection (not helped, I had no doubt, by the fact that both her parents smoked in their home) and I was sitting in an easy chair with her standing before me, so that I could listen to her chest when, out of the corner of my eye I noticed an impressive looking array of bottles. And among the bottles, in pride of place, stood a bottle of Cardhu, upon the label of which someone had written a note in purple ink. When I'd finished examining the little girl, had taken a starter pack of antibiotic medicine out of my bag and had written out a suitable prescription, I put my stethoscope away, closed my bag and stood up.

'Good collection of booze you have,' I said to the removal man.

He had the decency to blush and to look away.

'I see you like Cardhu,' I said, naming the bottle I'd been given, which was now sitting on his sideboard.

'Yes, doctor,' he managed to croak.

I reached out, picked up the bottle, examined it and put it down. I held the bottle long enough to be sure that he knew I'd seen the inscription. I didn't say anything, just nodded to him and left. It wasn't the right time to challenge him. But I wanted him to know that I knew he'd taken my bottles of alcohol.

A week later, my secretary told me that the removal man and his family had taken themselves off my list and had moved to another local practice. The local administrator always used to write to tell a doctor when his patients were changing doctors and moving to another practice. I have no idea whether they still do that.

'I wonder why they've moved,' she said. 'They're still at the same address and they always seemed very happy with you.'

I didn't say anything, but I was glad they'd moved. I really didn't want him on my list of patients.

A clean sweep

I had a number of patients who earned their living as professional entertainers. Two or three were television presenters and though none of the theatrical entertainers could be described as global superstars, most of them made a decent living – though there were also one or two who had what were, even then, called 'day jobs'. Their day jobs brought in enough money to pay their rent and utility costs and their evening work, in theatres and clubs, provided them with a little jam and cake.

Two patients were club singers, one was a comedian, one a session musician and another a magician who worked the clubs and pubs in the evenings and entertained children's parties on Saturday afternoons. He worked under two names, had two outfits and did entirely different shows. One of the club singers and the comedian were part timers, though both were successful and I think they clung to their day jobs just in the same way that children might cling to a comfort blanket.

Without exception these performers had all been close enough to success, to the breakthrough that would take them to stardom of one sort or another, to have a high point that they could look back on when the bookings were thin on the ground. All of them, without exception, still sustained hopes that one day they would break out and win the fame and fortune that they so desperately wanted and felt they deserved. Looking back on their careers, and the decades of disappointment, you could, if you were being cruel, describe their continuing expectations as a triumph of hope over experience.

No one in show business wants to spend their lives singing in pubs and small clubs. They all harbour and nourish the idea that one day something 'big' will happen. An agent, an impresario or a talent scout will be in the audience one night and will spot them and book them onto a big time television show. All the performers I knew attended auditions, they networked, they talk themselves up and they all carried around with them photographs and photocopied cuttings. They all had their Equity cards and worked occasionally as extras for

TV dramas and even more occasionally for films. In addition to being a singer, the only female would, for an additional fee, eat fire or do an exotic dance with a rubber python. (She explained that the more skills you have, and the more you are prepared to do, the more likely you are to get work. It apparently wasn't unknown for her to appear twice on the same bill, once as a country and western singer, dressed in a fringed buckskin outfit with boots, a hat and a pair of toy cap pistols in twin holsters, and then, under another name, as a speciality act – dancing with the tireless rubber snake.)

One of my patients, Mrs Yarrow, had been a member of an acrobatic group when she was younger. There were seven of them in the group. They pretended to be part of a large family but actually only three of them were related. Mrs Yarrow hadn't been part of the family; she was one of the outliers. She'd enjoyed gymnastics at school and had, quite literally, run away to join the circus. The troupe performed all over Europe but when the patriarch died (he was apparently run over by a twelve wheel lorry in Dusseldorf) the group disbanded and my patient found herself unemployed.

After a desperately unhappy year working as a shop assistant in Middlesbrough she got herself as a job as a professional wrestler and worked the clubs for several years before having to retire with a shoulder injury. By this time she had become engaged to a chimney sweep. They married and settled down.

When Mr Yarrow fell ill and could no longer sweep chimneys she tried to sell the business but failed and, having decided that sweeping chimneys couldn't possibly be all that hard, became one of the first female chimney sweeps in the country.

(Mr Yarrow suffered from terrible wind and indigestion and had a very poor appetite. He'd been investigated by the hospital several times and no one could ever find any reason for his problems. The obvious diagnoses had all been excluded. He had shrunk since he'd bought the clothes he owned and they were a size too big for him. His shirt collar was two sizes too large and he looked rather like a friendly and inquisitive tortoise peering out of his shell. He was a nervous man and I think that was the cause of his ill-health. When he gave up sweeping chimneys his health improved noticeably.)

Mrs Yarrow, was naturally quite muscular and her muscles hadn't turned to fat as they so often do with athletes. When she wasn't sweeping chimneys she always wore a flowery dress which looked

50

as if it might be a pinafore but wasn't. I visited them often and never saw her wearing anything else. I don't know whether she had several copies of the same garment or just washed it out overnight. When she was sweeping chimneys she wore a black three piece suit, which she'd altered to fit, and tied her hair up in a bun on top of her head.

'I'll always be poor, doctor,' she told me once. 'I've come to terms with that and it doesn't bother me. There will never be any limousines or yachts in my life. But I'll always be honest and I'll always be independent.'

After working as a chimney sweep for three or four years, Mrs Yarrow discovered a very profitable side-line and eased her way back into an unusual branch of show business.

A local couple who were getting married asked her to turn up at their wedding because, they said, it was good luck to have a sweep as a guest. They offered her a very generous fee to turn up in her chimney sweeping costume, with her brushes and with a few carefully applied soot smears on her face. They wanted her to appear in their photographs; standing with the bride and groom and then with the wedding party.

The local paper ran a story about her, complete with a large photograph and then a national tabloid interviewed her and she also appeared on the local TV news programme.

Suddenly, every engaged couple wanted her at their forthcoming nuptials and she was so booked up as a professional wedding guest that she pretty well gave up sweeping chimneys. Life had gone full circle and she was back in show business.

Malapropisms

Patients sometimes get a little confused when dealing with medical terminology. Here are some of my favourite malapropisms:

'My husband is important.' (She meant impotent, though he was an assistant bank manager which sort of made him important I suppose.)

'When he exercises he gets angrier.' (When he exercises he gets angina. He may have got angrier too, I suppose. But she definitely meant angina.)

'My husband suffers from premature emasculation.' (There was, of course, more truth in this than she perhaps realised.)

'I've got haricot veins in my legs.' (I don't know why but many patients get confused about what to call varicose veins.)

'I think I've got invented nipples.' (They were both inverted, of course. The easiest way to provide a temporary cure is by suction and there's one easy way to provide the suction. But it was never a remedy I felt able to recommend.)

'I've got a depraved trombone.' (She had diagnosed herself and thought she had a deep vein thrombosis. The diagnosis was accurate, even if the nomenclature was a trifle off centre.)

'I think I might have hello Peter. (He had alopecia and it was only when he pointed to the bare spots on his scalp that I knew what he was talking about.)

Alarm bells

I always dreamt of having a medical practice in an isolated village somewhere; a practice on an island would have been ideal. That way I could have taken on responsibility for the community. This wasn't a preference founded on ego, it was merely because it seemed to me that it would be easier to look after a relatively unchanging group of people who lived together in the same community. It would be easier to spot when outside influences were causing illness and it would be easier to track infectious diseases passing from family to family.

A doctor called Will Pickles, who practised in a fairly remote village in Yorkshire in the North of England in the early and middle decades of the 20th century, did amazing research showing how infectious diseases could spread. Pickles was influenced by two doctors, William Budd and James Mackenzie who argued that it was only the GP who had a real insight into disease.

I included a biography of Dr Pickles in my book 'My Favourite Books', which details over 100 of my favourite non-fiction books.

Dr Pickles realised that, as a country doctor, he had a special opportunity to study the spread of disease and at the age of 42, he began recording the incidence of infectious disease in his practice. He didn't have a computer, of course. He used a notebook. He tracked the spread of disease in his practice, jotting down details of meetings in the pub or at the local fete. If he knew that a disease had spread between individuals involved in a clandestine affair he would make a tactful, confidential note of that. And he did this for the next 25 years.

In the first 20 of those years he meticulously recorded 6,808 cases of infectious disease – including influenza, diarrhoea and vomiting, chickenpox, mumps, whooping cough, scarlet fever, hepatitis, lobar pneumonia and measles. Because he lived among his patients, and knew them well, Dr Pickles could trace the source and spread of epidemics in the dale where he lived. Dr Pickles himself wrote a magnificent book entitled 'Epidemiology in Country Practice'. It is a valued book on my shelves.

Pickles was one of the world's most significant epidemiologists and it is a tragedy that he is not more widely remembered with both respect and affection.

'A gypsy woman driving a caravan into a village in the summer twilight,' he wrote, 'a sick husband in the caravan, a faulty pump at which she proceeded to wash her dirty linen and my first and only serious epidemic of typhoid left me with a lasting impression of the unique opportunities of the country doctor for the investigation of infectious disease.'

And just as Dr John Snow (also largely forgotten but arguably the most important doctor in history) had so memorably arranged to have the Broad Street pump handle removed (to prevent the spread of cholera) so Dr Pickles had the handle chained to the pump. 'And there were no primary cases,' he declared in triumph.

Pickles believed that country GPs had a special opportunity because they 'tend to remain in one practice and to become part of their district.' The tragedy is that so few other doctors followed the example Dr Pickles set. It was his ambition that they would. 'The object of this book,' he wrote, 'is primarily an attempt to stimulate other country doctors to keep records of epidemic disease.'

So, why didn't they?

It was, I suspect, the abundance of boring bureaucratic paperwork that suffocated doctors and left them with no time for more valuable work.

But Pickles provided us with valuable information about the spread of a host of infectious diseases including chickenpox, dysentery and measles. It is our tragedy that his work has been largely forgotten.

For one reason or another I never did get to practice in a remote and isolated village (though there were very few of them left by the time I was in practice) and I never found myself working on an island (there were few enough of those to start with). And it's probably a little late to take on such a responsibility now, though I confess I do sometimes still think of it. Some people probably still dream of being train drivers or film stars though they know that time has passed them by. I dream of having a little medical practice on a small island with, say, 700 people living there. Antoinette and I could run our little medical practice, and the trials and tribulations of 21st century life would be miles away and forgotten. All would be well with the world.

Even old men can dream.

I worked in a small town and I always preferred to look after whole families of patients because it seemed to me to be best to look after the family as a unit.

Nevertheless I obviously understood how easy it was for families to be split between two different practices.

So, for example, if a couple who live in the same town get married the chances are quite high that they will be registered with different practices. And then what happens to any children they have? Will they be registered with his doctor or with her doctor? Or, as sometimes happens, will one child be registered with one doctor and another child registered with a different doctor?

This matters more than most people realise.

Occasionally, early on in my life as a general practitioner, I did suggest to patients that it might be advantageous if all the immediate members of a family were registered with the same doctor or, at least, with doctors working in the same practice. The doctor they chose didn't have to be me, of course. But the suggestion had never gone down very well. One or two patients probably thought, quite erroneously, that I was trying to get rid of them. And one or two probably thought, equally erroneously, that I was touting for patients. So I quickly abandoned that idea.

At its simplest level, if one child in a family has ringworm or nits, for example, the chances are pretty high that any other children will have the same problem. It is easier for one doctor to examine and treat all the children, and to do so at the same time so that the problem is eradicated and doesn't keep recurring. And if one patient in a family has a serious physical or mental illness it is easier to understand the problems faced by other family members, and to provide them with the appropriate treatment and support.

Sometimes, there is a real danger that a serious condition will be missed if patients in one family have two (or even more) doctors.

So, for example, consider the Dantons.

She was a patient of mine, and had been a patient of my predecessor since she was born. Her husband was a patient of another doctor at the other end of the town and he had been with that practice since he was born. They were both in their late thirties and had three children. Two of the children were registered with the other doctor and one was registered with me.

I had been treating Mrs Danton for some weeks and I didn't seem to be getting anywhere. Her first problem was that she had a miscarriage and lost a baby. It was her fourth pregnancy and the other three had gone very smoothly so this was something of a shock. When, a few weeks later, she complained that she was having difficulty concentrating and felt depressed it wasn't difficult to blame the miscarriage. Then she complained of joint pains and abdominal pains and occasional headaches. I could find nothing obviously wrong and asked a local consultant to take a look at her. He agreed that her problems were probably all related to the miscarriage.

Two weeks after her hospital appointment I was called to see her. She was in bed, tearful and complaining of abdominal pains. She also said that her arms and legs were aching so much that she couldn't bear to get out of bed.

The Dantons lived in a terraced house in a part of town I didn't know very well. I didn't go there often because I didn't have many patients in that area. There was another medical practice just a few hundred yards from the Danton's home. The houses, which looked as if they'd been built in the 1930s, but which might have been rather earlier than that, were neat and well-kept and the front doors and windows were all painted in different colours. Several of the houses had been altered slightly. One or two had had dormer windows installed, turning attics into rooms. All the tiny, front gardens seemed neat and tidy and it was a decent bet that on Sunday afternoons the area would have been alive with the steady buzz and drone of a dozen lawn mowers in action as back lawns were kept trim and neat.

When I rang the bell, the door of the Danton's home was answered by a man whom I correctly assumed was Mr Danton. I'd never met him. I introduced myself and he led me through the front room and into the parlour and opened the door which led to the staircase. Old terraced houses often had a staircase which could only be accessed by going through what looked for all the world like a cupboard door. These staircases were frighteningly steep and incredibly narrow. Indeed, they were so steep that quite a good many people used to come down backwards, as if they were descending a ladder. There were never any handrails or bannisters, simply because there wasn't room for such fripperies. I always felt as though I ought to be roped to someone, have a dozen carabiners on my belt and have crampons fixed to my shoes. A plump patient of mine who lived in one of these houses rubbed against both sides of the staircase when she went up or down the stairs. I followed her up and down the staircase once and worried quite seriously about how I would ever manage to remove her if she got stuck.

As I followed Mr Danton up the stairs he seemed to be moving with some difficulty. He told me, over his shoulder, that he was off work because he had pains in his legs. He worked in a local factory and his job involved a good deal of walking about. He said his doctor had made a diagnosis of fibromyalgia. He mentioned the name of his doctor but it was a name I didn't recognise. He pointed to the door leading to their bedroom and stepped back to let me go in ahead of him.

At this point alarm bells began to ring in my mind. It seemed strange, pushing rather hard at chance, that two previously healthy individuals in one family should both be ill with similar sort of symptoms. Previously, I hadn't known that Mr Danton was also ill. Mrs Danton hadn't mentioned it and because he wasn't a patient of mine it had never occurred to me to ask about his health. Once again, it became obvious that there were big advantages if all the members of one family living in the same home were registered with the same doctor.

Mrs Danton was lying in bed. She looked terrible. One of her children, a girl of fourteen or fifteen, was sitting in a chair in a corner of the room reading a comic. She was wearing a dressing gown over her nightie.

'Geraldine's off school too,' explained Mrs Danton. 'She's had tummy pains for a week. I thought it was her time of the month but she tells me it isn't. Perhaps you'd have a look at her for me while you're here.'

Geraldine, like her father, was the other doctor's patient.

And at this point the alarm bells were, at last, ringing very loudly.

When three people in the same family all fall ill, with similar symptoms, there just has to be a common causative factor. The chances of two members of a family being ill at the same time could just about be put down to happenchance – particularly when one member of the family had just had a miscarriage. But the chances of three members of a family all having serious symptoms at the same time were so remote that they could not possibly be put down to coincidence.

It didn't take long to work out that the house was probably the most likely culprit.

I looked around for mould and asked Mrs Danton if there was any damp anywhere in the house. She said there wasn't. Her husband, still standing in the doorway said that they'd decorated the bathroom, which had been a little damp, but that there had never been any visible mould.

I asked if any of the neighbours had been poorly. Both Mr and Mrs Danton said that they didn't know of any neighbours who had been ill, though a neighbour living three doors away had broken a leg in a cycling accident.

I opened the window and took a deep breath. There was no smell of chemicals or anything else likely to cause illness. It's not unknown for factory pollutants to cause health problems among householders in an area.

'Do you have gas in the house?'

Mr Danton said they didn't and that everything in the house was powered by electricity.

'Have you changed your diet recently?'

'Mrs Danton said they were eating the same sort of food they'd always eaten.

Suddenly, although it was a longshot, a possible answer occurred to me.

'May I take a look in your bathroom?' I asked.

Mr Danton, who seemed to assume that my request was personal, opened a cupboard and found a clean towel for me.

But I didn't need a towel or soap.

I knelt down, looked behind the pedestal supporting the sink and found one of the pipes. All the pipes had been neatly painted over.

'May I look in the kitchen?' I asked.

Mr Danton who had great difficulty walking, led the way downstairs into the kitchen. Once there I opened the cupboard under the sink. The pipes there hadn't been painted. They were grey. They certainly weren't made of copper. I took my pen-torch from my inside pocket. It was the torches I used to look down patients' throats. I shone the narrow beam at the pipe. And then I took out my penknife and scratched at the pipe.

Lead.

I was pretty sure that I had my diagnosis, though I'd never seen a case of lead poisoning before. Even in those days it wasn't a common problem.

'How long is it since you had anyone look at your plumbing?' I asked Mr Danton.

'I don't have any trouble,' he replied, misunderstanding. 'My Dad had prostate trouble. But I think I'm fine.'

'No, no, the house's plumbing.'

Mr Danton looked puzzled. 'We've never had anyone look at it. We don't have any trouble with it. It's just plumbing. We haven't had any leaks since we've been here.'

I explained that I would be taking blood from his wife and having it tested for lead poisoning and I suggested that he and his daughter see their doctor and ask him to do the same. I said I would telephone their doctor and talk to him so that he wasn't too surprised by the request. And I told him that no one in the family should drink water from the tap until we'd got the results back.

A few days later the diagnosis was confirmed. All the family were suffering from lead poisoning. The chances are that the miscarriage was caused by lead poisoning. The headaches, the abdominal pains and the limb pains were all a result of lead poisoning.

The Dantons drank bottled water for a while and used bottled water for cooking. They used their tap water for washing and flushing the loo – but nothing else. And they had to have their lead pipes replaced.

And they all recovered.

If the entire family had been patients of mine I hope I'd have spotted the link much sooner. And I'm sure that would have been the case too if the family had all been patients of Mr Danton's doctor. The fact that the members of the family were split between two doctors made the diagnosis more difficult.

And if I hadn't visited Mrs Danton at home, and met her husband and seen that her daughter was off school, I might have taken even longer to reach the diagnosis.

The joy of being old

There aren't many advantages to being old. But there are some.

I used to worry a good deal about water coming through the ceiling. When I was young I had half a roof blown away. So much water came in that the rooms on the ground floor were waterlogged. Everything in the house was ruined.

I developed a fear of leaks and, indeed, of any sort of roof trouble.

But the fears have eased somewhat now.

We have a roof valley which leaks in heavy rain. I deal with the leak by putting a bucket under the leak and catching the rainwater so that it doesn't soak the carpet too much.

The cast iron guttering along one side of our house crashed to the ground recently. It just fell off. The weight of the guttering was so great that it crushed a stout wooden garden bench that lay in its path as it fell. A solid bench became firewood in a moment.

I tried to get a roofer but no one would come.

So I shrugged and left it. The water pours off the roof but I really don't care. And when I walk round the other sides of the house I don't walk too closely to the walls just in case another stretch of guttering decides to fall.

We had leaks from two of our radiators. They're Victorian radiators and they've done good work for more than a century but they're elderly and failing. The water from the leaky radiators poured into downstairs rooms. We couldn't stand the thought of having workmen in the house for months to remove the old radiators and replace them with new ones. And we know that if two radiators have leaked then a third leak can't be far behind.

So we emptied all the radiators, turned off the central heating and bought half a dozen electric heaters.

I don't worry about any of these things now.

The joy of old age.

Women in curlers and Jimmy Young's wig

I used to do two or three week promotional tours of Britain and Ireland to promote my books. I did this at least four times a year when I had a new book out. It was customary for an author to tour with the hardback edition of a book but then to tour when the paperback edition was launched. Since I had at least two books published every year that means four book tours every twelve months. That's a lot of touring. The publishers arranged the interviews and booked the hotels. They also booked flights to Scotland and Ireland. I usually made my own arrangements if travelling by train or car and then submitted my expenses at the end of the tour. I've no idea whether or not authors do the same amount of touring now.

When I was touring most frequently, in the 1970s, 1980s and 1990s, I used to visit every national and local radio station and some national and most regional television stations. Gradually, as new local radio stations opened it became impossible to visit them all but sometimes it was possible to do one interview which was syndicated to a number of stations. I also used to record short radio pieces which were circulated to radio stations and used as inserts on a number of stations.

The upside was that I got to know a number of radio and television presenters and, when there was time, would go for a drink with them at their favourite local hostelry. Some (though by no means all) were fun to spend time with. The downside of visiting so many studios was that I had more than my fair share of embarrassing encounters.

At the TV studios in Birmingham I couldn't understand why the green room for artistes was full of catering staff who were making themselves at home, pouring themselves tea and eating all the biscuits. I didn't mind them being there at all. I was just puzzled. A researcher kindly explained that they were the cast members of a soap opera called Crossroads.

In Manchester I couldn't understand why the make-up department of the local commercial television station was full of such an odd looking bunch of people. I assumed they were all waiting to appear on the evening news, as I was, and I wondered how long the news programme lasted if we were all to be fitted in successfully.

Looking around, I amused myself by trying to decide why they were there. I decided that two of them looked as though they'd just won the pools.

One looked to be the sort of fellow who owned a 40-year-old piece of seaweed which forecast the weather more accurately than the Meteorological Office.

There was a bloke whose spectacles were held together with a bit of sticking plaster who looked as if he probably had a pet duck which liked to roller skate.

And a woman in curlers looked as though she'd perhaps got a relative who'd won a television talent contest.

When I quietly asked a make-up girl why they didn't offer to mend the bloke's spectacles with some invisible tape, she explained he, and all the other people milling around waiting to have make up applied, were the cast of a well-known soap opera called 'Coronation Street'. She was startled that I hadn't recognised any of them and I felt rather ashamed of my ignorance.

But one of my worst experiences was on a BBC radio 2 chat show hosted by a former singer called Jimmy Young. Mr Young was hugely popular, irrepressibly cheerful and quite friendly but I was tongue tied when trying to talk to him about whatever book I was flogging at the time. I sat about two feet away from him and just stared in horror at what must have been the worst toupee in tonsorial history. I was mesmerised by the awfulness of it. It reminded me of a story Peter Bogdanovich told about John Wayne. Bogdanovich was making a short documentary film about Wayne and the cowboy super star had forgotten to put on his hair. 'Shouldn't you put on your toupee?' asked the director. 'Oh, yes, I guess so,' replied Wayne, picking up his hairpiece from a nearby sideboard and just plonking it on top of his head without any regard for which way round it needed to be.

I do sometimes wonder why men bother to disguise their baldness with such badly fitting hairpieces.

If you think you need hair wouldn't you want to have hair that looked like hair? (That's a stupid question because the answer is 'obviously not'.)

In the stars

The astrology page in a newspaper or magazine is not usually taken seriously by editors or journalists, though it is well known that few pages in a publication are as widely and as regularly read as the astrology page. No editor of a popular print publication would put his paper to bed without knowing that somewhere at the back, just before the reader bumps into the sports pages, and somewhere in the vicinity of the letters page, the agony column and the puzzle section, there will be an astrology page. All of these features are essential components of what is known as 'the furniture' of the paper. Any decent editor knows that moving or changing 'the furniture' is a dangerous thing to do. And none of these items is more essential than the astrology column.

A good newspaper astrologer can make an excellent living by providing daily forecasts because his copy will often be syndicated to scores or even hundreds of other publications, not just around the country but around the world. After all, a prediction for the future can work just as well in Australia as in Britain.

Not a few of these professional astrologers got into their very specialised form of journalism by accident or good fortune, rather than by design. Indeed, I doubt if many of a country's top astrologers grew up planning a career in forecasting the future by birth date.

It is certainly true that in the past a very junior reporter would, if the regular astrologer was (through unforeseen circumstances) unable to provide the usual copy, be instructed to write something to fill the space. He would do this in addition to filing copy from the local courts, details of weddings and so on. If the usual astrologer remained absent (again, through unforeseen circumstances) the cub reporter would, if his copy proved successful, be hired as the replacement.

As I said, it was rare for editors or other journalists on a paper to take any notice of, or give credibility to, the astrology page. When you know that the predictions have been hammered out by a giggling 16-year-old in his lunch break, it is difficult to give them much credence. The astrology page was just 'there'; as indispensable as the crossword and just as relevant to the back end of the paper, but just there as a bit of fun. As far as the journalists were concerned the important stuff appeared in the front half of the paper; they cared most about the news, a little about the features and nothing at all the editorials – all of which fill the pages before the centre spread.

Sometimes, however, things didn't go quite according to expectations.

At one newspaper where I worked the editor once found himself summoned by the publisher with an unusual instruction.

It turned out that the publisher's wife was devoted to the astrology column in her husband's paper and responded to the advice offered therein as though it had been carved in tablets of stone and handed down by the Archangel Gabriel himself. She wouldn't get out of bed in the morning until she'd read the astrologer's thoughts for the day.

'Have you seen your astrology page for today?' demanded the publisher. 'In particular, the entry for Gemini?'

When he felt critical, or had found a bone worth picking, (both common occurrences) the publisher always referred to the paper as 'your paper' but when he felt satisfied, or had received a complimentary telephone call from the Prime Minister (an occasional but by no means rare occurrence), he referred to the paper as 'my paper'.

'Not in depth,' replied the editor, fearing the worst and wondering what might have slipped through the editorial net. He tried to think if someone had been sacked recently and might have altered the astrologer's copy in a petty act of revenge. Had someone put in something libellous or obscene? Despite the best efforts of the sub editors, such things happen more often than most readers realise – particularly when a sub editor has been sacked.

'It's gloomy!' complained the publisher. 'It's always bloody gloomy. If you're a Gemini, the end of the world is always just around the corner.'

'I'll sort it out,' promised the editor.

It turned out that the paper's astrologer had been dumped by his girlfriend (who was, of course, a Gemini) and, for absolutely no logical reason, had decided to make life as miserable as possible for anyone born under that birth sign.

Astrology columns are usually written at least a week in advance (there isn't the same sense of urgency as there is with, say, the football results) so the astrologer had to go through all the copy he had prepared and change his gloomy forecasts for Gemini to something more consistently upbeat.

The next morning's paper contained an optimistic, cheerful few lines and, for a while at least, peace returned to the editor's office.

The publisher's wife was happy. The publisher was happy. The editor was happy. And the astrologer kept his job.

C.B.Fry – a hero of heroes

When I was a lad I had a lot of heroes. Indeed, I have always enjoyed having heroes. But one who died when I was young always seemed to me to be truly Olympian.

Here, for those who haven't heard of him, is a small, short biography of C.B.Fry's achievements. He was, of course, an amateur sportsman – never paid for his efforts.

He played football for England.

He played in a Cup Final for Southampton.

He played Test Cricket for England (and captained the side). As captain he never lost. He also captained the Gentlemen cricket team. And never lost.

He scored over 30,000 runs in first class cricket with an average of over 50.

As a fast bowler he took 166 first class wickets at an average of 29.34 (making him one of England's greatest all round cricketers.)

He held the world long jump record.

He was the leading classical scholar at his college in Oxford. Later in life he read books in classical Greek for relaxation.

He was delegate for India at the League of Nations and wrote a speech which helped turn Mussolini out of Corfu.

He was invited to be King of Albania

He opened the batting for England with W.G.Grace.

He wrote a number of brilliant books including a great autobiography called 'Life Worth Living'.

He edited 'C.B.Fry's Magazine' for years. The magazine (about sport) is still an excellent read.

He wrote newspaper and magazine columns. His column for the 'Evening Standard' in London was credited with lifting the paper's circulation.

He founded a successful magazine for boys called: 'The Captain'.

He was a frequent and successful broadcaster appearing on programmes such as 'Any Questions' and the 'Brains Trust'.

He was so fit that in his seventies he could stand facing a

fireplace and then leap up, turn in the air and land on the mantelpiece facing his always appreciative audience.

He was Captain of the Training Ship Mercury and had the rank of Captain in the Royal Naval Reserve.

He wore a monocle with panache. (Not many people can do that without looking comical.)

He was a top class hammer thrower, shot putter, golfer and ice skater.

He played rugby for Oxford University.

Any one of those achievements (apart, perhaps, from the monocle wearing and the mantelpiece trick) would constitute the cornerstone of a highly successful career.

In addition, Fry stood as a candidate for Parliament but (almost unbelievably) lost by 219 votes. Two buses in Brighton and Hove were named C.B.Fry in his honour. And his ambition never faltered. In his 60s he went to America with hopes of becoming a Hollywood film star (as fellow England cricket captain C.Aubrey Smith had done).

If you're going to have a hero or a role model then you might just as well pick a good one.

Too many trophies but not enough wins

Mr Wilks was what is usually known as a 'bit of a character'. He was well enough off to merit the label of being an eccentric rather than being dismissed as a nutter or the village idiot. These days he would probably be diagnosed as suffering from one of those modern, fashionable diseases which consist of acronyms and nothing much else.

I can best sum up his character by explaining that in his early 70s he used an old-fashioned ear trumpet of the type made fashionable by Ludwig van Beethoven in the 19th century.

Mr Wilks kept the ear trumpet on a small table by his chair (he had arthritis in his knees and after he'd settled into his favourite fireside chair after breakfast he moved from that spot only for essential purposes) and he insisted that all visitors speak into it if they wanted to say anything to him.

Unlike the unfortunate Herr Beethoven, Mr Wilks wasn't actually very deaf at all. I once tested his hearing and to my surprise found that his hearing was pretty well normal for a man of his age. Before that I had asked him why, if he had difficulty hearing people, he didn't obtain a more modern hearing aid. He dismissed the suggestion with disdain.

The thing was that the ear trumpet was a prop. He had read somewhere that Evelyn Waugh, the novelist, had used one to discomfort visitors (particularly journalists who had come to interview him) so he adopted the idea for much the same reason, though as far as I know he wasn't visited by journalists or interviewed by anyone. The people most likely to be inconvenienced by having to shout into his ear trumpet were workmen, tradesmen and relatives.

Apart from his wife (who steadfastly refused to use the ear trumpet) the only relative of his whom I ever met was his brother Nigel, a bowling ball of a man who had served in the Royal Air Force during World War II and had been near to Hiroshima in Japan when the atomic bombs had been dropped there by the Americans. His waistline had last been seen in around 1952 and had, since then, been on the missing list. During the War Nigel J had risen to the rank of captain and had, unusually, retained the use of that rank after the war. He used to get terribly upset if a receptionist forgot his title and referred to him as Mr Wilks.

Nigel, was also slightly eccentric, though he had rather more justification for his singularity than his brother, and he used to come to see me once a month for a check-up.

As bald as the bowling ball he resembled in shape, Captain Nigel was convinced that he was suffering from radiation sickness occasioned by his presence in Hiroshima. Before I'd met the Captain I had known very little about radiation sickness but, in his honour, I studied the subject and made appointments for him to see various specialists. Neither I nor they had ever been able to find any signs or symptoms of radiation poisoning and the lack of hair on his head was partly due to genetic male pattern baldness (his brother was also bald) and partly due to his shaving the part of his head that wasn't naturally bald.

Nigel, had been given some compensation by the Government, and was totally obsessed with the idea that he was being killed by radiation sickness. Every time he had anything wrong with him he insisted that the problem was a result of the bombing of Hiroshima. I never managed to convince him that the varicose veins in his legs, and the indigestion he suffered after eating hot curries, were not linked to his war time experience. When I retired from medical practice, Nigel was still as strong as an ox and looked set fair to continue for several decades.

Nigel's brother, however, was not so fortunate or so long-lived. He died one Sunday of a massive heart attack. 'One minute he was shouting at the television, and the next minute he was dead,' his wife told me. We both suspected that the latter probably had something to do with the former.

After Mr Wilks died I went round to see his widow. It was a few days after he'd died and I wanted to see how she was coping.

Some bereaved people are inconsolable. I knew two people who, although apparently quite fit and well, died within a week of the death of a long-term spouse.

However, Mrs Wilks was alone in the house but she seemed to be coping well enough. She was smartly dressed and had her make-up done.

(Although relatives, friends and neighbours often recommended and expected them, I didn't usually prescribe tranquillisers or sleeping tablets. In my experience drugs of that nature didn't solve anything – they merely delayed the grieving process and the sadness. When the pills were stopped the grief and the depression appeared and seemed less natural, less explicable, and more lasting. If it seemed appropriate (and the patient didn't already have a penchant for taking too much of the stuff) I did sometimes suggest a night cap of something alcoholic. When I was a house officer in hospitals in the 1970s I was allowed to prescribe Guinness or sherry for the patients on my wards. I found both to be much safer and infinitely more acceptable to my patients than sleeping tablets.)

'I've just been packing up some of his clothes,' she told me, nodding towards a couple of black bags that were neatly tied and sitting in the hall way. 'I was just going to call a taxi because I don't drive and I don't think I can manage them on the bus.'

She made me a cup of tea and we sat down in their small, neat living room. She opened a packet of biscuits and poured the biscuits onto a plate.

'You must be very proud of all those trophies.' I said, pointing to the glass fronted cupboard that was full of silver trophies and cups. 'Each one is a memory I expect.'

'Oh those,' she said, and laughed.

'He must have been quite an athlete,' I said. 'I asked him once what they were all for but he changed the subject. I assumed he was just modest and didn't like to talk about them.'

'He didn't win them,' she said. 'None of them was really his.'

I didn't quite know what to say.

'He bought them all,' she said. 'If you look carefully you'll see they're all arranged so that you can't read the inscriptions. Two of them were won by a women's hockey team.'

I stood up and looked at the cabinet. She was right, of course. None of the inscriptions was visible.

'I hate them,' she said. 'He bought them at junk shops. I don't know why. He felt the need, I suppose. He bought most of them from that junk shop down near the railway station. We both got to know the owner quite well.'

'So, what will you do with them?'

'I'll take them back to the junk shop,' she replied after a moment.

71

'Maybe they'll give me something for them.' She paused and sipped at her tea. 'Maybe some other dreamer will buy them.'

When we'd finished tea, and had a couple of biscuits each, I put the black bags into the back of my car and put the trophies into a third black bag. They clanked a good deal. None of them was silver or even silver plate. They didn't look worth very much in monetary terms. I drove her to the nearest charity shop, where she dumped the clothes, and then took her to the junk shop.

'You can leave me here, doctor,' she said. 'I need to do a little shopping. I need to get something for my tea.' She looked at me and for the first time there was a tear visible. 'I haven't got used to cooking for one,' she said.

'Are you going to be OK?' I asked her, softly.

She looked at me and nodded. 'Oh, I'm going to be OK, thank you, doctor,' she said. She moved to go into the junk shop and then she paused and turned back. 'He wasn't a bad man, you know,' she said. 'He was just a little vain, I suppose.' She wiped her eyes. 'But he wasn't a bad man. We were married 47 years, you know.'

I nodded and told her to ring me if she needed anything.

I didn't see her for a while but nine months later she married the man who owned the junk shop.

So I suppose, in a way, she got the trophies back again.

The wrong diagnosis

I am constantly surprised by the apparent lack of empathy shown by many doctors. I honestly don't understand how it is possible for doctors to be as completely lacking in understanding and compassion as they frequently are.

Let me explain.

A few decades ago, in my forties, I had a persistent, nagging pain in my back. It had been there for several months and it was just about in the region of my right kidney.

I managed to convince myself that it was nothing more than a muscular backache caused by crouching over a keyboard. But then I noticed two additional symptoms. First, I started feeling constantly 'full' — as though I had just eaten a large meal. And, second, I found that my bladder needed emptying more often than I found entirely convenient.

I plucked up all my courage and made an appointment to see my general practitioner.

He took a routine urine sample.

And found blood.

The next step was a hospital appointment.

He didn't need to tell me his provisional diagnosis.

And it wasn't a good one.

At the hospital, the ultrasound pictures showed a kidney that had a huge lump on the side of it. More specialist X-ray pictures confirmed that there was something wrong. My kidney looked as though it were auditioning for a role as the hunchback of Notre Dame.

Unhappily the radiologists couldn't get a really good view of my kidney. Their view was obscured by large bubbles of inconvenient gas lurking around in the coiled nooks and crannies of my intestinal loops.

They confirmed my fear: renal cancer. And they told me I needed urgent surgery to have the kidney removed. There were, I was told, two local surgeons. One was quite good but had the bedside manner of a tax inspector. The other had a pleasant manner but wasn't very good at surgery.

I told them I was planning to fly to Paris that evening. 'Should I cancel it? I asked.

'Oh no,' said the radiologist. 'You go off and enjoy yourself. We'll sort this out when you get back.'

I often think that groups of medical students should all be given a blood test and told 'One of you has a serious life threatening problem but there is a mix up so we can't tell you who it is at the moment. We'll redo the tests and tell you in a week.' The students would then learn something more important than the course of the long saphenous vein or the names of the twelve cranial nerves.

At my insistence I was given an appointment to go to another, larger, city hospital for a scan.

The radiologist at the large city hospital laughed when he saw me. (Unbeknown to me, we had worked together at another hospital.) 'You think you're going to die, don't you?' was his greeting. I said I did. He then told me that there was nothing wrong with my kidney. It was, he assured me, misshapen but perfectly healthy. He said that Napoleon Bonaparte had a similar misshapen kidney.

I had narrowly escaped having a kidney ripped out.

No one knew why I was getting pains, or why there was blood in my urine, but I didn't have kidney cancer.

So I went to the airport and took the plane to Paris, as planned.

On the plane flying over the Channel the pain in my back got much, much worse.

And I suddenly realised what was wrong.

The gas that the radiologist had spotted in my intestines had expanded because of the change in air pressure and it was the gas that was causing my pain.

And it was the gas that was making me feel 'full' all the time.

And it was the gas pressing on my bladder which made me need to urinate frequently. And it was the gas which was pressing on my kidney which was causing the bleeding.

There was only one explanation for this apparently bizarre set of circumstances: I had irritable bowel syndrome: one of the commonest, least understood and least well treated of all modern diseases.

Apart from making my diagnosis I learned two things.

74

First, too many doctors just don't understand how frightened and alarmed patients may be when given scary news. They don't bother trying to sugar coat the bad news. And they don't take the trouble to offer some hope.

Second, a completely false diagnosis had been made as a result of a series of routine tests. If I hadn't insisted on a second opinion I would have had a perfectly healthy kidney ripped out. And I may be old-fashioned but I've always liked my kidneys to stay where God put them.

Oh, and I was so relieved that I didn't have kidney cancer, and so convinced that my own diagnosis was correct, that I didn't see my GP or the hospital doctors again. And they didn't care enough to make any effort to get in touch to do any more investigations.

A lovely jumper

Some of the patients a doctor sees live alone and have very little in the way of human contact.

If they have no relatives living locally or alive, and if their spouse has died, they may go for days without speaking to another soul.

In a shop or supermarket they are often the individual who wants to chat for a moment with the assistant, but equally often they get rushed away by an overworked assistant or by the presence of other, impatient shoppers queuing behind them. I always try to be extra patient when I am behind an elderly shopper who wants to exchange a few pleasantries with the assistant on the till. When I ran a publishing business in the 1990s we had a free telephone service. I paid for all the incoming calls. We had a number of customers who would ring up regularly for a chat with the staff – often staying on the telephone for an hour or more. This cost me a small fortune but it seemed a useful public service. And the callers would sometimes buy a book – helping to offset the cost of the calls!

I remember one patient of mine, Mrs Anderson. She was in her mid-seventies and quite fit. She used to come into the surgery every couple of months to collect pills for her arthritis. She was taking a fairly low dose of aspirin, a drug which I thought then (and think now) is one of the safest and most effective drugs for the treatment of inflammatory disorders and chronic pains. She knew she could have telephoned the surgery and asked for a repeat prescription but she liked coming in to see me and she always had a long chat with my receptionist.

Slim, and always neatly dressed, Mrs Anderson always raised her voice a little at the end of every sentence, turning everything she said into a question. It is something people do when they have little or no confidence in themselves or what they're saying; pleading for agreement and approval but leaving the way open for disagreement and disapproval.

At the end of one of her visits, after I had handed over her prescription and been reassured by her that everything with her was well, she picked up her shopping bag, stood and headed for the door.

'That's a lovely jumper,' I told her.

She paused, looked down at the jumper, as if uncertain about what she was wearing and then looked up at me, smiled and thanked me.

'It's the perfect colour for you. It suits you.'

'My daughter-in-law bought it for me last Christmas,' she said. And then she hesitated.

I could tell she wanted to add something so I didn't say anything else but just sat and waited. You can always let a patient know it's time for them to go if you pick up the next patient's medical records or fiddle with your pen but I sat stock still.

'Thank you for noticing,' she said, beaming. There was then a long pause. And then she nodded, very slightly, and left.

These days, of course, most people are careful to avoid making personal remarks. They're terrified of saying something that might be considered sexist or inappropriate.

But the little things we say and do are often far more significant than we realise.

An apparently throw away remark about some item of clothing or a new hairstyle can mean that someone feels that they've been noticed as a person rather than as just a number.

A flowery pinafore with scalloped edges

I have no evidence for this, and I have no idea if it still the case, but I suspect that every school used to have a creepy, nauseatingly correct pupil who was regarded by teachers and parents as the 'perfect' young man or woman.

He, or she, was the one who became a prefect – maybe even Head Boy or Head Girl. He was never late, never scruffy, never impolite and always the perfect pupil. He or she was the one who was, it was generally agreed, destined for great things. There would, it was confidently assumed (rather than merely predicted) be years of success ahead. The only question was: would the success come in politics, business, science, sport, the arts or a mixture of all of those?

Maybe there would be a couple of Olympic gold medals, and selection for a national side in any of a number of sports. There would be films, perhaps, success on the hustings, a Nobel Prize nomination, unimaginable wealth and a chest load of honours and titles culminating, no doubt, in a peerage.

The pupil destined for this glittering future, this unending collection of life's glittering prizes, was the one all our parents compared us against.

'Look at Reginald,' they'd say. 'Why can't you be more like Reginald?' (Or Elspeth, or whoever it might be.)

After I left school I forgot about our 'Reginald', of course.

And then, one harsh, dark winter's day, a patient came into my surgery. I had never seen him before but I knew the name and, strangely, I knew the face. He was what was officially termed a 'temporary resident'; someone passing through; staying in the area on holiday. He'd run out of the pills he took for his high blood pressure. He showed me the empty bottle, with his name and the dosage written on it.

I recognised his name on the bottle and on the form the receptionist had given me, but he clearly didn't recognise mine. And I recognised him because the supercilious sneer was still there, though it was duller now. He now had a small, bristly moustache and, as though labelling himself in memory of his greatest days, was wearing the Old Boy's Club school tie. He was losing his hair, the remains of which had been dyed, and he had dandruff on both the shoulders of his very cheap suit. He had a paunch.

`And what do you do for a living?' I asked him, when I'd made a note of his date of birth, the address where he was staying locally and his home address. His home address was in Blackpool.

I always asked patients what they did for a living and how they spent their free time. You'd be surprised how often these simple questions provided vital information. A man who spends his days standing up is more likely to develop varicose veins than one who spends his days sitting down. A man who spends his days sitting down is more likely to develop backache. A sedentary lifestyle makes heart disease more likely. And so on and so on.

He told me he had been a clerk in his local tax office but that after he'd been made redundant he and his wife had opened a small boarding house in Blackpool, where they lived.

Schadenfreude, enjoying delight at someone else's failure or humiliation, is inherently a mean emotion.

But for a moment, the briefest of moments, I saw him serving fatty breakfasts in a run-down lodging house. He was, in that frozen moment, wearing a grubby, flowery pinafore with scalloped edges. He had a tea towel draped over one arm and while one guest wanted the brown sauce another was moaning that his bacon was burnt and inedible.

I took his blood pressure, gave him a prescription for his pills and told him he should lose a little weight.

Against the grain

I was always in trouble at school, and at university too, but I never meant to get into trouble. It seemed to happen naturally.

On my first day at grammar school the music teacher, wanting to find out how much we knew, gave us the names of ten composers (Beethoven, Mozart, Schubert and so on) and told us to write down three compositions by each of them. I didn't know much about music so I simply wrote down 1st symphony, 2nd symphony and 3rd symphony by each name. It seemed a fair bet that they'd have all written at least a couple of symphonies. I came top in the test but was reprimanded for being unoriginal. I thought this was unfair.

I then joined the school's combined cadet force (or CCF) though this wasn't in the slightest bit voluntary. We were given a test to see which of us should be considered as suitable to be appointed as non-commissioned officers. We were put into a coach, given a questionnaire, taken to a village an hour or so away from the school and released with instructions to find the answers to the questions we'd been given. It was, we were told, an initiative test.

While my colleagues rambled around the village looking for gravestones and landmarks and discovering who lived in which house and so on I simply wandered into the village shop, which was also the Post Office, bought essential supplies and asked the lady behind the counter to help me complete the questionnaire. This she did in five minutes or so – answering all the questions.

I then took my supplies of sweets and pop (purchased as a supplement to the picnic lunch my mother had prepared for me), found the meeting place where we were supposed to be picked up by the coach, and sat in a local wood reading a book and watching the wildlife – particularly the squirrels.

(As an aside, I should mention that since I learned to read I have never left home without at least one book stuffed in a pocket. I love books. I love writing them. I love reading them. I love collecting them. Books are, for me, the most effective way for anyone to communicate with, and establish a rapport, with any number of total strangers – but doing it one at a time. A good book can take me into another world where I can forget this sometimes awful world. A good book can entertain me, inform me, amaze me or educate me. Or all of the above. I can read a book at my own pace. I can read it indoors, out of doors or in the bath. I can put it down, leave it and go back to it when I'm ready. I can write my own notes on the margins. I am constantly surrounded by books and I never leave the house without at least one stuffed into my bag or my pocket. All my jackets have pockets which have been stretched out of shape by having books pushed into them. I would no more dream of boarding a train or an aeroplane without two or three books than I would dream of travelling without my shoes. I always take a book with me when I visit the dentist, go to the doctor or have a luncheon appointment. You never know, the person with whom you are supposed to be having lunch might be late – giving you the opportunity to read a few more pages.)

I came top in the initiative test because, thanks to the lady in the sweet shop, I had more correct answers than anyone else.

But once again I was reprimanded when I openly explained how I'd done so well.

'If that lady in the sweetshop had been a German spy you would have been shot!' a furious Major (who was also our Latin teacher) shouted at me.

I pointed out, politely, that we hadn't been told to pretend that we were in Germany and that I had simply done what I'd been told to do. I think I may have used the word 'initiative'. Once again my copybook was blotted. I was never promoted beyond the rank of Private.

In my first few days at medical school we were given a multiple choice questionnaire and told that we would get one point for every correct answer but have two points deducted for every incorrect answer. Looking through the questionnaire and hearing my colleagues moan at the difficulty of the questions I decided that I would probably do best if I didn't try answering any of the questions. So I left the questionnaire entirely blank, took out a book, and waited for the end of the lesson.

Two days later our results were announced. I had come top with a score of nought. The second place pupil had a score of or around minus thirty something.

Inevitably, I was punished. This time I was accused of cheating because I had not answered any of the questions.

Pointing out that I'd merely followed the rules and had succeeded in coming top did me no good at all.

Things like this happened to me throughout my academic years.

I wasn't trying to be clever or trying to cheat but simply using my brain and my initiative.

You'd think that was what teachers wanted you to do, wouldn't you?

But it isn't and they don't like it.

When I left medical school I swore that I was finished with formal education and would never again take any examination of any kind.

And I haven't.

The language of flowers

Back in the early 1970s, just after I'd qualified as a doctor, I produced a new version of the Victorian classic 'Language of Flowers'. My version sold, I seem to remember, for 15 shillings or 75 pence a copy. This tiny volume received a good deal of publicity in gardening and countryside magazines, sold out, reprinted and sold out again several times. I didn't get rich. But I didn't lose money. I didn't do it for money. I did it because it is a beautiful little book and I wanted to share it with others. I rather doubt if any copies still exist.

After 'The Language of Flowers' I gave up publishing. I was rather busy running a general practice, looking after several thousand patients and, filling in forms to keep several thousand bureaucrats happy. I was also writing books, columns and articles and making television and radio programmes. For some reason I seemed to accumulate columns. I cannot remember the number I had but off the top of my head I can remember having an eclectic collection of columns with scores of publications as varied as the Sunday Scot, Weekly News, Hospital Times, Medical News, Sunday Independent, Glasgow Evening Times, Nursing Times, Nursing Mirror, North Devon Journal, Over 21 and Slimmer magazine in the UK and with magazines in America, South Africa, Australia and Ireland where I wrote a column for 'Ireland's Own' for what seemed a lifetime and a half. Some columns lasted for years and years and some lasted until the publication folded. I wrote two syndicated weekly columns which were printed in scores of newspapers and which lasted for decades. The trick with writing a column is not to exhaust your material in the first two or three weeks. Only later did I start writing columns for national newspapers.

After I retired from general practice I decided that rather than going into private practice (which requires more natural social graces than I can muster) I would concentrate on writing books. I wrote several dozen novels and non-fiction books for large, traditional London publishers. I was represented by a literary agent working at one of the smartest and most fashionable London agencies and the idea of publishing my own books never crossed my mind.

But then, for a variety of reasons (which I have explained in the earlier books in the 'Memories' series) I became an independent publisher. Or, as the book industry prefers to describe it, I became a self-publisher.

I am, I confess, puzzled by the widely held notion that there is something rather odd or distasteful about an author publishing his own work.

Indeed, I am convinced that the author/publisher will, in the future, become a figure in the same mould as the actor/manager of the theatre was in the 19th century, and the actor/director is in the modern cinema.

Turned down

The fact that a publisher rejects a book doesn't mean that the book is no good or will not sell. It could just mean that the publisher has returned the book without even looking at it (let alone reading it). Or it could mean that the publisher or the reader who did look at the manuscript is a moron who would find earning a living sticking tickets onto parked cars an intellectual challenge. George Bernard Shaw reported that he sent his first book 'to every publisher on the English speaking earth that I had ever heard of'. The book was rejected by them all. Thomas Pirsig's classic bestseller 'Zen and the Art of Motorcycle Maintenance' was rejected by 121 publishers. I think John Creasey lost count of the number of publishers who rejected his first book.

Many authors whose books went on to become major bestsellers published their books themselves in frustration. Beatrix Potter published 'Tale of Peter Rabbit' herself and did quite well with it. The translator of 'The Rubaiyat of Omar Khayyam' published the book himself.

Many years ago I wrote a book titled 'How to publish your own book'. That book is long out of print but I included a list of many great books which had been rejected by publishers – often not once or twice but dozens or even many hundreds of times. Here is an updated selection of books which were rejected by publishers:

Eric Ambler: The Ability to Kill
Jane Austen: Northanger Abbey
Samuel Beckett: Molloy
Arnold Bennett: The Old Wives Tale
Peter Boulle: The Bridge over the River Kwai
William Burroughs: Naked Lunch
James M. Cain: The Postman Always Rings Twice
Agatha Christie: The Mysterious Affair at Styles
Collette: Claudine in School
Cyril Connolly: The Rock Pool
Joseph Conrad: Freye of the Seven Isles

Len Deighton: The Ipcress File
Charles Dickens: A Christmas Carol
J.P.Donleavy: The Ginger Man
Arthur Conan Doyle: A Study in Scarlet
F.Scott Fitzgerald: This Side of Paradise
Gustave Flaubert: Madame Bovary
Anne Frank: The Diary of Anne Frank
William Golding: Lord of the Flies
Kenneth Grahame: The Wind in the Willows
Gunter Grass: The Tin Drum
John Grisham: A Time to Kill
Thomas Hardy: Tess of the D'Urbavilles
Frank Harris: My Life and Loves
Joseph Heller: Catch 22
Ernest Hemingway: The Torrents of Spring
Thor Heyerdahl: Kon Tiki
James Joyce: Ulysses
D.H.Lawrence: Lady Chatterley's Lover
John Le Carre: The Spy Who Came in from the Cold
Jack London: The Law of Life
Anita Loos: Gentlemen Prefer Blondes
Konrad Lorenz: Man Meets Dog
Norman Mailer: The Naked and the Dead
Somerset Maugham: The Razor's Edge
Herman Melville: Moby Dick
Grace Metalious: Peyton Place
Henry Miller: Tropic of Cancer
Vladimir Nabokov: Lolita
George Orwell: Animal Farm
Anthony Powell: A Dance to the Music of Time
Marcel Proust: Remembrance of Things Past
George Bernard Shaw: Man and Superman
Upton Sinclair: The Jungle
C.P.Snow: The New Men
Laurence Sterne: Tristram Shandy
Irving Stone: List for Life
Henry David Thoreau: Walden
Anthony Trollope: Barchester Towers
H.G.Wells: The Time Machine

T.H.White: The Book of Merlin
Oscar Wilde: Lady Windermere's Fan
William Butler Yeats: Poems
Leo Tolstoy: War and Peace

I still find it astonishing, and scarcely believable, that publishers turned down all those great books. But they did.

Other authors whose work was rejected include Graham Greene, Alexander Dumas, James Thurber, William Faulkner, Erle Stanley Gardner, Paul Gallico, Robert Graves, Zane Grey, John Irving, Henry James, P.G.Wodehouse, Rudyard Kipling, William Saroyan, Dr Seuss, Neil Simon, Gertrude Stein, Walt Whitman and Thomas Wolfe.

A gentle bump

For years I've owned a series of trucks, in addition to more usual motor cars. Trucks always have four wheel drive fitted and they have high clearance off the road so they're excellent on rough ground or on snowy, muddy or wet roads and tracks. I used to have a country practice with farms and cottages to visit and in winter a truck was immensely useful.

One truck I owned came with a tow bar fitted so that I could fit a bicycle carrier on the back.

(I bought it, I remember, from a car salesman who owned his own small garage. He was a very good salesman and always managed to trick me. I once bought a bright orange Saab from him. He assured me that orange was a very popular, fashionable colour for car. When I tried to sell it back to him a couple of years later he offered me a rock-bottom price, claiming that no one would want to buy a car that was such a terrible colour. The only good thing about the orange car was that it was very easy to find when I left it in a large car park. I was, at that point in my life, remarkably and rather pitifully naïve. Sadly, I don't think much has changed in that respect.)

Now the thing about trucks is that they tend to be quite long and the view when reversing isn't always quite as good as one might like – the rear view window in the cab is quite a long way from the rear of the vehicle and in those days trucks didn't have reversing cameras fitted as they often do now.

And I sometimes forgot that there was a tow bar sticking out of the back of the truck.

While parking beside the road one day I struggled to get into a space which was only just long enough and, while reversing into the space, I felt the back of the truck touch the car which was parked behind. It wasn't a hard bang, more of a kiss really. A motorist in Paris would have regarded it as routine parking. The minute I felt the touch I edged forwards a foot or so.

As luck would have it a man was sitting in the passenger seat of the car. He leapt out of the vehicle, ran to the front and bent down to inspect the damage. I got out too and joined him. He was short and bore an uncanny resemblance to a young version of Peter Lorre, the actor. Most people find short people more easily likeable than tall people. Short people like short people because they aren't tall and tall people like them because they're short and usually unthreatening. But this fellow didn't look likeable at all. He had far more hair than Peter Lorre ever had. It looked as though it had been cut and styled by a blind sheep shearer suffering from chronic and untreated Parkinson's disease. I realised that this probably meant that it was a very expensive haircut.

'I hardly touched it,' I told him, rather defensively, peering at the front of his vehicle. The only damage was a very tiny indentation in the number plate, obviously caused by the round metal part of the tow bar. You could only see it if you held your head a certain way and looked for it.

'There might be some damage to the engine,' said the man. 'Or the gear box. Or the suspension. You might have damaged the chassis.'

I went slightly cold thinking that this was escalating. An almost invisible dent in a plastic number plate had, in the space of about five seconds, turned into a fractured chassis. I was waiting for him to complain that he had developed whiplash and possibly permanent brain damage. I opened my mouth and shut it again. The words which I'd been about to air were the sort of words you are likely to hear when a grown man in bare feet stands on a sprinkling of Lego pieces. Those words. Not suitable for airing when there are children or delicate clergymen within earshot, or when you're trying to placate a man with pound signs hovering above his head.

'Do cars have a chassis these days?' I eventually asked, after a pause to bowdlerise my thoughts.

'You might have punctured the radiator,' he said, naming another car part of which I had heard. I was pretty sure that he was right in thinking that the radiator is usually to be found towards the front end of the vehicle.

As an aside, I should mention that I never used to hide my ignorance about motor cars. And then Antoinette pointed out that if I continued to tell garage mechanics that I didn't even know how to open the bonnet of whatever car I was driving then they would treat me like a cash machine. (It was and is true, however, that I don't usually know how to open the bonnet of a car though I did once own a 1958 Bentley S1 which drank oil like rugby players drink beer. I was forced to know how to open the bonnet in order to replenish the constantly diminishing supplies in the oil tank or whatever it is called. I used to buy oil by the gallon.) These days I do make a small effort to know some of the important terms relating to motor cars since I understand that if I don't I can hardly complain if they tell me that my aluminium double tappet washers are dangerously worn and need replacing with some incredibly expensive ones only available from a Korean specialist, and that if I want the car back before next Easter I will have to pay for the parts to be air-freighted at incredible expense.

Anyway, to get back to my story about the truck, the tow bar and the dented number plate.

I took my wallet out of my pocket and removed a £20 note. 'The only damage is to the number plate,' I pointed out. 'The damage is hardly visible but this should more than cover the cost of a new number plate.'

Just then a woman appeared. She was carrying two bags of shopping.

'Oh hello, doctor!' she said brightly.

Her husband explained what had happened.

'Oh, put that away!' she said, when she spotted the £20 note and realised what was happening. 'It's my car and I don't care if you bend the number plate in two and knock it sideways. It might stop me getting another speeding ticket.' She put her bags into the car boot.

'Sorry, doctor,' said her husband. 'I didn't realise you were the doctor!'

'That's OK,' I said. 'I'm sorry about the bump.'

'We've never actually met,' the husband said. 'I joined your practice when I married Daphne.'

I took his proffered hand and shook it.

'I was meaning to pop in and see you next week,' he said. 'I've gone a bit deaf in my right ear. I think it might need syringing. My other doctor used to do it once a year or so.' As he spoke he turned slightly and offered his ear up for my examination.

I peered at the ear though, of course, without an auriscope I couldn't see whether the ear contained any wax or not. In fact I couldn't see anything other than the fact that he had an ear. I checked the other side of his head. There was another ear there.

'Pop in and see me next week,' I told him. 'I'll sort that out for you in a jiffy.'

'Splendid,' he said, looking quite pleased with the way things had turned out.

As, indeed, was I.

The underestimated power of the placebo

Everyone has heard of witch doctors casting spells. It is well known, and well documented, that seemingly healthy individuals have died within weeks or even days of being cursed by a witch doctor of some kind. The power of the mind is difficult to under-estimate. A man or woman in a white coat can be, unwittingly, just as powerful as a witch doctor dressed in feathers and performing a mystical dance.

The word 'placebo' has been used since 1811 to denote a medicine given more to please than to benefit the patient. It is perhaps a rather unfair definition, for though the placebo may have no active effect it may nevertheless have a definite and useful psychological effect. An alternative name sometimes used is 'dummy tablet' as the constituent of a placebo is traditionally nothing more than lactose or starch. As well as being used to treat patients, placebos can be used to test patients and to test other remedies. Sir William Gull, a 19th century physician who, annoyed and disturbed by claims for many treatments said to be useful for rheumatic fever, published a tongue in cheek paper extolling the virtues of mint as a cure. He selected mint at random but was amazed to see that his mint water treatment became fashionable and apparently effective.

At medical school I'd never heard the word 'placebo' mentioned and there certainly had not been any mention of the way that apparently powerless pills can have a useful, practical effect in medical practice. But, after I qualified, and my reading strayed outside the medical school curriculum, I read a great deal about placebos and started hunting through the medical journals for more examples of the effectiveness of this type of healing.

I found that the medical literature was absolutely full of references to placebo power. The science of the placebo had all really started, it seemed, during the Second World War when an American army medical officer had run out of morphine while treating injured soldiers. Rather than admit to the soldiers (many of whom were in terrible pain) that he had nothing to give them the doctor found some vials of plain water and gave those by injection. To his amazement the water proved to be as powerful a painkiller as morphine. The soldiers' pains were eased though they'd been injected with nothing more powerful than water.

In the years which followed, the power of the placebo was investigated quite thoroughly by many experts. In 1946 a researcher called Jellinek found that out of 199 patients who complained of having a headache, 120 lost their headache when given nothing more powerful than a sugar tablet. It was shown that 30 per cent of patients with severe, steady, post-operative pain got relief from placebos. And according to a report in the British Medical Journal in 1970, no less than 60 per cent of patients suffering from angina had fewer attacks when given placebo tablets and told that their attacks would be less frequent.

I found that although placebos were hardly mentioned in the medical literature they were used (knowingly or unknowingly) more often than any other drugs. They were often sneered at and their use was often dismissed as unethical. This seemed strange since they benefitted patients enormously and had few or no serious side effects.

In the Journal of Mental Science in 1957, Trouton wrote that for medical purposes placebos should be red, yellow or brown in colour, bitter in flavour, and either very large or very small. Another paper published in 'Scientific American' in 1955 came to the same conclusion. From other studies it was concluded that green tablets or capsules were better for depressed patients while yellow tablets or capsules were better for anxious patients. Capsules were usually found to be far more effective than tablets. And so I concluded that a large, green and yellow capsule should be ideal for most patients. It was, therefore, no coincidence that when I was a GP I regularly used a large, green and yellow capsule which contained a selection of harmless vitamins as a placebo. I had great success with it.

Work done in Liverpool in 1964 showed that many patients were dependent upon the shape of their tablets. Patients were given amphetamine tablets, placebo tablets shaped like amphetamines and an amphetamine of a different shape. The placebo shaped like the amphetamine seemed to be better than the amphetamine which did not look like an amphetamine.

The efficiency of placebos can be startling. It has been shown that

93

30% of patients with severe, steady post-operative pain get relief from placebos. From this information it is clear that the effectiveness of a drug must be the effectiveness of the inactive qualities of the drug plus the effectiveness of the active part. No less than fifteen different studies on 1,082 patients have shown that placebos have an average effectiveness of 35% when given to patients with pains (including angina and headache) and nausea and with psychological problems such as anxiety. Any new drug which has a less than 30% effectiveness is no better than a placebo.

Surprisingly, perhaps, many patients who take placebos, and benefit from them, also suffer the sort of side effects usually only associated with active drugs. In the 'Journal of the American Medical Association' in 1955, Beecher reported 35 different toxic effects suffered by patients taking placebos and in the 'Medical Times' in 1963, Pogge noted thirty eight different types of side effect – the commonest being drowsiness, headaches, nausea, constipation, vertigo, dry mouth and a lack of appetite. Other patients have had dermatitis and some have even become addicted to placebo tablets which theoretically have no active constituents. Placebos have been reported to have observable physical effects – stopping sweating and even causing pupil constriction.

Some of the trials showing the effectiveness of placebos are fascinating. I found details of a clinical trial reported in the 'Canadian Medical Association Journal' in 1967.

Medical students were told that they were taking part in a clinical trial but unknown to them they were all given placebos. Some were given a green and yellow capsule containing nothing but sugar. Others were given a red and white capsule, against containing nothing but sugar. Those who took the red and white capsule took significantly longer to do simple arithmetic afterwards than they had before and between them the students reported a total of 44 side effects. More of the students taking the red and white capsules suffered side effects than of the students taking the green and yellow capsules. When the trial was concluded and the students told that they had all been given placebos, some simply would not believe it. They insisted that the capsules they had taken must have had some active ingredient.

The action of the placebo was discussed at length by a writer in the 'Prescribers' Journal' in 1968. Dr Harman from St Thomas's

Hospital, London wrote that even doctors when ill require and react to placebos. They want to believe that the tablets will help. On the other hand some patients never react when given placebos. For example, severely depressed patients may not react whereas anxious patients usually do.

Some experts condemn the use of placebos as unprofessional but both general practitioners and hospital doctors have used them. As one author put it: 'the hospital doctor, who is backed by a temple of healing which is nearer the seat of power than the wayward shrine of the general practitioner may find that the placebos he uses are exceptionally effective'.

As Knowles and Lucas wrote in the 'Journal of Mental Science' in 1960: 'The placebo response may well be an important component of many established treatments both physical and psychological and does in itself constitute a means of therapy'.

According to the 'British Medical Journal' in 1970: '60% of patients were found to experience an appreciable reduction in the frequency of attacks of angina by means of suggestion and placebos were as effective as 30mg of codeine in inhibiting the cough reflex'. Other reports have suggested that as many as 40% of all the mentally ill may respond to placebos. According to one British GP, seven out of ten British doctors prescribe placebos for unhappiness. Family doctors in Britain have estimated that up to a third of their patients have nothing wrong with them and are simply unhappy. Other GPs reported that up to two thirds of all the patients they see have nothing physically wrong with them.

That gives some idea of the extent and importance of placebo prescribing. It has been reliably estimated that 30 to 40% of NHS prescriptions are, effectively, for placebos even if neither the patient nor the prescribing doctor is aware of this. Sadly, drugs such as benzodiazepines are often prescribed as though they are placebos – when they most certainly are not.

It is of course a prerequisite of the placebo prescriber that the patient should believe in him and the treatment he prescribes. If the prescriber does not clearly seem to have faith in the drug he prescribes, then the patient will be unlikely to respond favourably. Even more important perhaps is the image of the whole medical profession. As a Norwegian doctor has put it: 'The placebo effect over and above the pharmacological effect will depend upon public

95

trust in doctors and the pharmaceutical industry. And anything which can destroy that trust will immediately reduce the effect of all drugs in practice'.

The one area where placebos still have an officially accepted place is in the testing of new drugs. It is usual either to test a new drug with a placebo or with the drug usually and widely accepted as the best available treatment. The problem with choosing the best available treatment is that this is always rather subjective and it is common for those performing a test to trial against a drug that is known to be dangerous. It is easy then to say that the new drug causes fewer side effects. Placebos are used because they are (wrongly) regarded as totally ineffective.

What is perhaps rather worrying is the fact that so many drug companies seem to be advertising and marketing products which do not even have the level of success one would expect with a placebo. If a placebo has a 30% to 40% activity, any pharmacologically active product should be better than that. Some studies have been published showing a placebo result of only ten to fifteen per cent, compared with which the drug under test did well. In such trials one must be suspicious of the techniques employed.

Recent studies have shown that some widely prescribed anti-depressant drugs (which invariably may have horrendous side effects) are notably less effective than a placebo.

And there has even been research which has shown that patients with heart disease, who had been considered suitable subjects for open heart surgery, recovered after going through an operation in which all that happened was that their chests were cut open and then stitched up again. The surgeon didn't touch the heart at all but the patients improved massively and because they hadn't been through the trauma of open heart surgery they recovered far more speedily. That's how powerful the placebo response can be!

A study of 200 patients, some of whom had stents put in to help them deal with angina and some of whom only thought they'd had stents put in, found that the placebo group were just as well after their non-existent surgery as the patients who had had (potentially dangerous and debilitating) surgery.

Another experiment, reported in the 'New England Journal of Medicine' in 2014, involved patients who had knee surgery for the repair of a torn meniscus. Half of the patients had actual surgery done to repair the tear and the other half of the patients went through a fake procedure. They were taken into the operating theatre and anaesthetised and bandaged but no operation was performed. The two groups recovered equally well. The surgery was of no real value whatsoever.

A review published in the 'British Medical Journal' studied 53 clinical trials which compared the results of real surgery with placebo surgery. In 39 of the trials the placebo group noted improvements and in 27 of the trials the results for the patients who had 'real' surgery were no better than the results for the patients who had no surgery at all – but who thought they had been operated on. It is clear from this work that much surgery (which comes with considerable risks, of course) is unnecessary and, indeed, unethical.

And then there is the equally solid evidence showing that the way a doctor talks to a patient can have a tremendous effect on the result of the treatment he offers. The doctor in a white coat can have just as powerful an effect on a patient as the witch doctor in a startling feather based costume. If a doctor convinces a patient that the treatment he is offering will work then the chances are much higher that the treatment will work.

As I pointed out in my book Mindpower, although the colour, shape and size of a placebo tablet affects its efficacy, nothing governs the power of a placebo quite so much as the enthusiasm with which it is offered to the patient.

So, if a doctor gives a patient a placebo tablet and says something like: 'Try this, it might help you a little', the chances of the placebo working are relatively slight.

If, however, the doctor hands over the placebo tablet with an enthusiastic comment such as, 'Take this. It's the most powerful and effective drug on the market. It will help you', the chances of the placebo working are increased enormously.

It is even possible for doctors to influence the sort of side-effects patients are likely to get simply by what they say.

So, if a doctor handing over a pill (whether or not it is a placebo pill) says: 'Watch out. This pill may produce a rash and make you feel drowsy', the chances are very high that the patient will complain that the pill makes him feel drowsy and gives him a rash. Our bodies respond, it seems, not simply to what is in a tablet but to what we expect it to contain.

Nor is it just tablets and pills and drugs that operate the placebo effect. We associate the placebo effect with pills simply because we associate doctors with pills, but in fact the placebo effect can work in a thousand other ways too.

So, for example, if a surgeon who is about to operate on a patient says, 'I'm afraid that when you wake up you'll be in a lot of pain and probably rolling around in agony', the patient will probably wake up in a good deal of pain. (That sounds like a silly thing for any surgeon to say but I've known it done.)

Whereas if a surgeon who is about to operate on a patient says something like, 'When you wake up you will feel much better and calmer and we will make sure that you do not suffer any pain', the patient will probably wake up free of pain and discomfort – whether or not they are given painkillers.

To give another example, if a doctor sees a patient who complains of a pain in his neck and says, 'I can help get rid of that pain for you with a little massage', the patient's pain will quite probably disappear after a little massage. It probably won't be the massage that will have got rid of the pain. It will be the fact that the doctor has promised the patient a cure.

By now, of course, it should be fairly clear that if a doctor can have this 'healing' effect, there is nothing at all to stop non-qualified practitioners from producing a similar effect. And that, of course, is just what happens. Many of the alternative practitioners who have a remarkably high degree of success with patients depend very much on the placebo effect. They help their patients get better by being enthusiastic and optimistic.

In order to create the placebo effect, nurses and doctors need quiet self-assurance that is built on confidence and transmits relief and hope to the patient. But too many of today's medical professions exude instead the self-satisfied arrogance that is more traditionally associated with investment bankers and barristers.

These days the use of placebos is frowned on by the medical establishment and by many who claim to represent patients' interests. The reason is quite obvious: placebos tend be generic or very cheap and nowhere near as profitable as many of the drugs they can be used to replace. The fact that placebos are often far more effective than infinitely more expensive and dangerous products is of no interest to the medical establishment which was long ago bought, lock stock and syringe barrel, by the pharmaceutical industry. The supercilious frowns of disapproval are sometimes accompanied by sneers because for reasons which have nothing do with health care or patient welfare it is considered improper and even unethical to use a placebo. I think this is madness. Placebos have been proved to produce a massive response in patients – especially when prescribed in a confident, reassuring way which also takes advantage of the doctor's own placebo effect.

Why is it ethical to prescribe a potential dangerous drug which produces a mass of unpleasant side effects and can kill, and which has, maybe, a 2% chance of improving a patient's condition, but unethical to prescribe a safe medicine which is incredibly unlikely to do any lasting harm (though even placebos can inspire temporary side effects) but is pretty well guaranteed to produce an uplift in the patient's health of 30% or even more?

When I was working as a GP I regularly used placebos and although I used a number of different products I had two favourites.

One was a vitamin product called Allbee with C which had the benefit of being a large, coloured capsule. It may have changed but at the time it was, I think, yellow at one end and green at the other end. (Patients would sometimes ask which end of the capsule they should put into their mouths first.) The capsule's size and colour made it a perfect placebo, and since it was an excellent and safe combination of vitamins (the range of B vitamins and vitamin C) it made a good vitamin supplement. It had the added advantage of being quite cheap and, therefore, no strain on the NHS's financial resources.

The other placebo I used regularly, and which was particularly effective with older patients, was called Alkaline Gentian Mixture BP and known and prescribed as Mist Gent Alk. This came in a liquid form, was dispensed in the traditional brown or green bottle, and looked and tasted like 'proper', old-fashioned medicine. When possible I preferred the pharmacist to put the medicine into a green bottle which, I always thought, gave it a more dramatic and powerful appearance. I always used to prescribe the medicine with specific instructions to the patient on how and when the medicine should be taken (repeated in the instructions to the pharmacy so that the advice would appear on the label).

There always used to be a strong tradition that medicines should taste unpleasant if they were going to work properly and I'd have liked to have found a placebo medicine with a more unpleasant taste or at least a bit more of a sting to it but I could never pluck up the courage to ask the pharmacist to produce a medicine containing even a flavouring of strychnine or arsenic.

I had tremendous success with these medicines and only rarely did they fail to work effectively though problems sometimes arose. Once, I remember, I was away for a day and one of my partners dismissively, and I think rather tactlessly, told a patient who asked for her regular bottle of medicine for her nerves that it was just a useless placebo and would do her no good at all. He refused to prescribe the Mist Gent Alk which had worked very well and instead, prescribed a benzodiazepine tranquilliser which caused her all sorts of problems for years afterwards.

Despite the professional scepticism, I successfully managed to treat a number of patients who were suffering with anxiety and depression and if I were young enough to go back into practice today, I would use placebos regularly. Maybe I would, at last, be able to persuade a pharmacist to help me find a really horrid tasting medicine to put in an old-fashioned green bottle.

I even found that it was possible to use a placebo to counteract the very real side effects associated with some medication. So, for example, a patient who needed to take a medicine which caused terrible nausea was cured of the nausea when I added a placebo to her therapeutic regimen. That's another advantage of the placebo. You can give it together with other medicines without having to worry about there being an adverse interaction.

The joy of simple tasks

Antoinette, my wife, needs regular blood tests. And because she had surgery for breast cancer, and had her lymph nodes fried with radiotherapy on that side, the blood must always be taken from the other arm. Every time she has blood taken she comes home with a badly bruised arm which gradually gets worse and becomes increasingly painful. This is because the women delegated to do the blood taking aren't doctors or nurses and aren't properly qualified or trained to be in charge of a needle. (I've had blood taken by one of these amateur phlebotomists and although I have very easy veins to attack she made a terrible mess of the job – leaving me with an enormous bruise.)

Many modern GPs are far too self-important to do jobs which they believe can be delegated to someone else. And, amazingly, it seems that practice and district nurses appear to have decided that they too are important to do the practical chores which used to be dealt with by GPs.

Doctors, I fear, are becoming increasingly like dentists – most of whom fall out of love with their career after about two or three years of work. Most of the dentists I've known have loathed their jobs and found something else to do with their energy. One built a massive model railway track in his loft. Another played golf several times a week and was Captain of his local club. A third played bridge at international level. And a fourth raced go-karts at least twice a week.

Now GPs are out of love with their unsatisfactory working lives and many of them are finding the need to do the same thing. Now that doctors don't do home visits or night calls there is no joy in the work; no real sense of purpose or community.

And the doctors and the nurses who consider themselves too important to perform essential tasks such as blood taking are not just betraying their patients, they are also missing out on another aspect of the very essence of primary practice.

You'd have to travel a long way these days to find a doctor who actually takes blood pressure readings himself. And I wonder how many doctors will still lance a boil, cure a subungual haematoma by pushing a hot paper clip through the nail or syringe a patient's blocked ears? How many doctors still put in stitches when they are needed? And how many remove stitches when they are ready to come out?

I always found that these simple tasks helped to cement my relationship with my patients. Few patients are as grateful as the patient whose ears have just been successfully syringed and cleared of the wax that was causing temporary deafness. Why should children have to sit in an Accident and Emergency department for hours to have their stitches removed? It takes seconds and should be as painless as any medical procedure can be. I used to tape the used stitches onto a card and give them to children who wanted to be able to show them to relatives and chums. I bet the health and safety watchdogs would have had hysterics if they'd known.

The same again, please

People are always fascinating, even when their lives seem fairly ordinary, even humdrum.

I had a patient who worked in a bank as a clerk. He was married with two children and lived in a neat, semi-detached house on a fairly new estate. He drove a small Volkswagen motor car and took his family to Spain every year for a two week holiday.

He came to see me when he was 40 and told me that he was fed up with his life and wanted a change. He talked of travelling round the world, or buying a boat and sailing round Britain or simply setting off with a rucksack and becoming a modern super-tramp. He was obviously having a mid-life crisis. He'd suddenly realised that his life was passing him by.

I listened and talked to him and thought he'd settled down a little.

But two weeks later he left his wife and children and moved into a small flat above a carpet shop. He gave the car to his wife and resigned from his job at the bank.

For six months he struggled on, doing odd jobs and helping out in the carpet store whenever they needed an extra assistant. He gave most of his money to his wife, who was divorcing him for desertion.

And then he got himself a job at another bank, two hundred yards away from his old bank. It was a very similar job to the one he'd given up.

At the bank he met a divorcee in her thirties. She was much the same age as the wife he'd left and she looked not unlike her. She had two children and a smart, semi-detached house on a new estate.

They married and he moved into her house.

And, it seemed to me that he ended up pretty well back where he'd started. Faced with the world as his oyster he hadn't moved far. He came to see me to give me his new address.

He'd bought a new, second-hand car, too: a Volkswagen.

It was the same age, the same model and the same colour as the one he'd given to his first wife.

'Have you got your old car back?' I asked him.

'Oh no,' he replied. 'But I know this model. I feel comfortable with it.'

'Are you going away on holiday this year?' I asked him.

'I thought I'd take the family to Spain for two weeks,' he said. 'I know a good hotel I can rely on.'

I was puzzled for a while because his story reminded me of someone else.

And then I remembered the book 'The Maltese Falcon' by Dashiell Hammett. There's a character in the book (but not in the film of the same name) who is called Flitcraft. To the surprise of Sam Spade, the detective, Flitcraft walks out of one life and then into another which is pretty much the same.

Maybe I should have written a paper for a medical journal and described this as the Flitcraft Syndrome.

The man with one glove

I once had a patient who had only one hand.

Mr Edwards had lost his right hand while driving his car on a motorway in the North of England. It was a warm day when the accident happened. He'd been driving in the middle lane with the window open and his hand sticking out of the window, in that rather careless way people sometimes do on hot days, and a van had overtaken him in the fast lane. No one ever decided whether he had drifted out or the van had drifted in, or if it was just one of those unfortunate accidents for which no one was to blame. Anyway, the van made a terrible mess of his hand and it had to be amputated.

The police said it was a miracle that he wasn't killed because after his hand was hit by the van he went into a wobble, swerved inwards and just missed a twelve wheel lorry that was trundling along in the slow lane, minding its own business. The driver of the white van had no idea that he'd been involved in an accident and just drove on listening to music on his car radio. It was only thanks to the motorist travelling behind, who stopped, offered help and later made a report the police, that anyone knew what had happened.

All this happened about five years before Jerry became a patient of mine and by then he had acquired and become adept with an artificial hand. He could make a fist, clench and unclench his fingers and even hold a pen or a tool, though his writing with that hand was pretty incomprehensible and he'd learned to write with his left hand.

'I don't suppose you've got any patients who need just one glove, do you, doctor?' he asked me one day. 'I've two perfectly good right hand gloves at home that I'll never have a use for. It seems a pity to throw them both away.'

I was pretty sure that he was the only patient I had who'd lost one hand but I remembered that when I'd been working as a house surgeon in the South of England I'd known a patient who had lost one leg in an industrial accident. He had several brand new, unused and unwanted shoes for the right foot he didn't have. By one of those odd coincidences that happen far more often than you'd think possible, he was on the ward having his prostate removed when another patient was admitted to the ward after a motorcycle accident. He'd lost his left leg and the consultant surgeon who was looking after them both had introduced the two men to each other suggesting that they might be able to buy a pair of shoes between them.

We never found out whether this would have worked (if one preferred brown brogues and the other only ever wore tennis shoes there would have been an impasse) because one of them had large feet and took a size 12 and the other took a size eight. But it had been a nice idea.

'I'll ask around,' I told Mr Edwards, and mentioned it to both of my partners later that day. Word got around other practices and a month later I had a phone call from a doctor thirty miles away who had a patient who'd lost his left hand.

I put the two men in touch with each other and whenever one of them bought a pair of gloves he sent the glove he didn't need to the other.

Maybe one day someone will set up a national organisation for individuals with one leg or one hand. Modern computer programmes should make it much easier than it would have been back in the 1970s.

(You may have noticed, by the way, that even in these reminiscences I always refer to patients with their titles (Mr or Mrs and so on). I abhor the modern practice whereby doctors and nurses refer to their patients by their given names. I sometimes wonder how many doctors and nurses would like to be addressed by their given names. I wrote a novel titled 'Mr Henry Mulligan' about a patient who felt the need to stand up for his dignity.)

A sweet tooth

Miss Thelma Partridge was in her late thirties and single. She worked as a personal assistant to a high flying company executive and in a way that was not unknown then, but is far less common now, she devoted herself to her work and her employer. She had no hobbies or real interests. She didn't go dancing or to clubs or pubs. She didn't play any sports. She worked late when her boss asked her to work late and she worked weekends when she felt it was necessary to keep up with the work.

She came to the surgery complaining that she needed to go to the loo more often than usual. 'Only to pass urine,' she said, looking slightly embarrassed at using the word. She would never have called it 'wee' or used any other slang word or any colloquialism.

She said it didn't sting and didn't look or smell unusual. I tested her urine with a little paper strip. There was no sign of any infection and no sign of any sugar. She said she wasn't drinking more than usual and wasn't thirsty more than usual.

But she also said there was something else. She felt weak sometimes. Not all the time. Just occasionally her muscles felt tired – as though she'd been doing heavy work. And there was occasional tingling in her hands and arms.

All sorts of alarm bells were ringing but nothing particular stood out.

I listened to her heart and lungs. There was nothing abnormal. I did a neurological test. I found nothing odd.

I took her blood pressure.

It was high.

I was still no nearer to making a diagnosis. But the mixture of symptoms troubled me. I arranged for her to see a consultant at the hospital. He did blood tests and found that she had very low blood potassium levels.

And he diagnosed a condition called 'primary aldosteronism'. I'd never seen a patient with this so I looked it up and read about it in my textbooks. (I still had some of the textbooks I'd used at medical school and I'd updated the essential ones every year; buying the latest editions.)

Aldosteronism is a serious condition usually caused by some problem with one or both adrenal glands. The consultant wanted to do more tests. He said he thought she might need an operation if there was a problem with one of the adrenal glands. He wrote to me and said there was a drug called spironolactone that might help but he wanted to do more tests first. He said he wanted her to go into hospital for a few days – mainly so that one or two of the other consultants could see her. He said he didn't put his finger on it but there was something unusual about her. He said he thought there might be something else going on but he didn't have the faintest idea what it was.

On the day I received the consultant's letter, I called in at Miss P's house to see how she was and tell her what was happening. I wanted to make sure that she'd heard from the hospital since they wanted to admit her within a couple of days.

She opened the door wearing her dressing gown and said that although she'd got up she hadn't had the energy to get dressed. She was desperately worried about her work and one of the company's secretaries was bringing her some work to do. She took me into the kitchen to make us both a cup of tea and I couldn't help noticing that there were several packets of liquorice sweets on the counter next to the kettle. There were also some packets containing raw liquorice.

'Do you eat a lot of liquorice?' I asked, though it was a pretty stupid question since she lived alone and there was no one else to eat all the liquorice.

She said she'd taken to eating liquorice a few months earlier after a friend had given her a box of sweets for her birthday. The liquorice had reminded her of her childhood. She confessed that she often ate two packets of them a day – plus a stick or two of liquorice. 'I sit in front of the television in the evening,' she admitted. 'I eat them instead of chocolates or biscuits. I've always had a sweet tooth.'

I asked her when her birthday was. She told me.

'And did your symptoms all start after your birthday? The weakness and the urinary problem?'

She thought about it for a moment and confessed that everything had started after her birthday – after she'd started eating lots of liquorice.

I didn't have the faintest idea whether liquorice could cause symptoms which match those of aldosteronism so I telephoned the hospital and spoke to the consultant. He said he didn't know either but that he'd talk to a couple of colleagues and ring me straight back. I had a second cup of tea and waited. He rang back a quarter of an hour later and said that he'd confirmed that liquorice could cause all the symptoms of aldosteronism without there being any problems with the adrenal glands themselves.

'Ask her to stop the liquorice,' he said. 'It could be the answer.'

He sounded quite excited and said that if stopping the liquorice made the symptoms go away then if I didn't mind he'd like to write up the patient's history for one of the medical journals. I said I didn't mind at all and that since the patient wouldn't be named I was sure she wouldn't mind either.

So I told Miss Partridge what the consultant had said. She put all her packets of liquorice into a bag and asked me to take them away and dump them so that she wouldn't be tempted.

A few days later all her symptoms had gone. And in due course the consultant wrote a short paper for one of the medical journals.

If I hadn't called at Miss Partridge's home, and seen all the packets of liquorice, she would have probably either been treated with drugs or surgery.

And if she'd been put on drugs she would have needed to take them indefinitely.

He wouldn't hurt a flea

I was called one day to visit a man who wouldn't tell my receptionist what was wrong with him but would only say that he couldn't make it to the surgery. In those days we didn't allow receptionists to act like doctors and demand information from patients before allowing them to have any medical help.

The modern trend is for receptionists to act like qualified nurses working in the sort of triage unit that used to be favoured by M.A.S.H. units on the front line. Sadly, most of the receptionists who are given this authority have no more medical knowledge than the woman in curlers who lives next door but one to your Gran and always knows who is ill, who is dying and who is dead.

When I got there it was clear that the house had seen much better days. It was well back from the road, behind a high laurel hedge, and I'd never noticed that it existed. It had, I discovered later, been built in the late 19th century for a man who had a small company making drain covers. There must have been a big demand for drain covers because the man had clearly once been very rich. The wealth had lasted for two generations before slowly disappearing.

(Very few small family-run companies survive beyond the third generation: the first generation works hard, the second generation doesn't have the imagination or the talent but feels a responsibility to keep things going and the third generation takes the wealth for granted, enjoys the good life to which they have become accustomed and regard as a right, and doesn't want to work very hard. The wealth then slowly disappears.)

When the family home had been built it had probably been surrounded by a dozen acres of gardens and woodland. Today, there was just enough garden for a clapped out, rusting Ford Consul (without wheels), a prize winning display of Giant Hogweed and several stone statues. One, which stood on a stone plinth, was particularly striking. It was of a woman who had clearly lost her bath towel and was reaching out expecting someone to hand her another.

There was a large ornate brass bell push next to the door but the

110

bit you're supposed to press was dangling loose and I could tell that the bell wasn't going to work so I used the door knocker which was shaped like a lion's head and had once been painted black. There was no reply to my knocking (unless you count the dog which had started barking somewhere in the house) but when I pushed on the front door it opened readily. I went into the hall and called out the man's name. In response there was a feeble response from upstairs. The barking dog increased its noise level and added a sense of rage and urgency. I'd been bitten three times by dogs which their owners had assured me wouldn't dream of harming a flea so I waited to see if the dog appeared, reckoning that I could disappear back through the front door and close it before the dog could get at me. When no dog appeared I went further into the house, leaving the front door open for a possible quick getaway, and made my way up the stairs.

I found my patient lying on top of his bed wearing only a pair of grey Y fronts (which had probably started life as white Y fronts) and a heliotrope pyjama top. He was a big man, built I suspect by the same people who put Sydney Greenstreet together. There was a scruffy looking, blood stained bandage wrapped around his left calf. He was a terrible colour and he was sweating.

'I caught my leg on my bicycle pedal,' he said, as I unwrapped the bandage. His claim was about as convincing as if he'd said he'd cut himself shaving. There were two wounds, both of which were badly infected, and they had clearly been made by teeth belonging to a fairly large dog.

'Whose bicycle was it?' I asked him, as I examined the wounds. They both looked awful. The edges of the wounds were an inch or an inch and a half apart and there were clear signs of infection. He was going to need an anaesthetic and the wounds were going to need to be cleaned before they could be sewn up.

'It was mine,' he replied. 'I left it in the hallway.'

'Yes, I heard it barking,' I said.

He looked at me, thought about denying it, and then abandoned the replacement lie he'd been planning to offer me as an alternative.

'What sort of dog is it?' I asked.

'An Alsatian. Wouldn't hurt a flea.'

'But it bit you. Mind you, you're not a flea, of course.'

There was a long pause and then he nodded.

'When did it happen?'

'Last Friday. Four days ago.'

'Did you clean the wound?'

This time he shook his head.

'You just put the bandage on?'

'My wife did. She works at the hospital. She said it just needed bandaging.'

'What does your wife do at the hospital?'

'She works in the canteen,' he said. 'Mostly behind the self-service counter.'

'Lots of practical medical experience then, I expect?'

He looked rather sheepish but didn't say anything.

'Why didn't you come and see me as soon as it happened? Or go to the hospital?'

'I didn't want them to put my dog down,' he replied.

'Why would they do that?'

'They always put dogs down if they've bitten someone.'

'Not necessarily. The dog usually gets another chance. Has it bitten anyone before?'

'No!' he said, rather too quickly.

I looked at him and waited. And waited.

'It bit me once before,' he said at last, when he could stand the silence no more. 'But it didn't mean to,' he added quickly. 'We were playing.'

'Wouldn't hurt a flea, eh?'

'Oh no. He's as harmless as a kitten.'

'All dogs are harmless until they bite someone,' I told him. 'If you'd come to see me when you were bitten I could have cleaned it and put some stitches in. But it's so badly infected that you'll need to be seen at the hospital. They'll need to clean out the wound and probably start you on intravenous antibiotics.'

'Am I going to die?'

'Not unless I kill you for being stupid,' I was tempted to reply. But I didn't. I just told him he wasn't going to die.

I'd have said that even if I'd thought he was going to die. Tell a patient that he's going to die and you dramatically increase the chances that he will. Besides, doctors never have a right to take away hope. I've seen enough miracles to know that they do happen.

'If I go to hospital will I have to tell them my dog bit me?'

''You'll have to tell them you were bitten by a dog,' I told him. 'But unless you choose to tell them, they won't know whether it was your dog, a neighbour's dog or a stray which attacked you in the park.'

'So I don't have to tell them it was my dog?'

'That's up to you,' I told him. 'Where's your phone?

'It's in the kitchen,' he replied.

'Where's the dog I heard barking?'

'It's in the kitchen.'

'I'll ring from my surgery,' I said. 'I'll ring the hospital, speak to your wife and tell her to come home straight away. There will need to be someone here to let the ambulance men into the house. And then I'll ring for an ambulance.'

'Will I lose my leg, doctor?' he asked, as I headed for the door.

'You deserve to have your head examined,' I told him. 'But you won't lose your leg.'

He didn't lose his leg but it was a close run thing. The infection was difficult to treat and he was in hospital for weeks. The surgeon who looked after him had to make the two wounds much wider, longer and deeper and eventually he needed a skin graft.

And the odd thing was that the dog died anyway. While my patient was in hospital his wife left the front door open and the dog escaped. It was run over by a petrol tanker.

Faceless but real

I found these paragraphs in my book 'Paper Doctors' which was published in 1977 by my first publisher Maurice Temple-Smith (who was a real gentleman, an old fashioned publisher who operated out of tiny offices opposite the British Museum):

'One of the reasons for our spending money on patients who are ill, rather than on people who are not yet ill, is that the man who has a chronic heart disease is real. When we are talking about candidates for open heart surgery we are talking about real, identifiable people. It is possible to go into a hospital and sit by the bed of a man who will benefit from an operation. It is possible to see him recover and see him to live on.'

'On the other hand the people who will benefit from campaigns to stop smoking, or cut down the amount of pollution in the air do not see real. We do not know who these faceless people are. You cannot go into a hospital and see the man who does not have bronchitis or who does not have lung cancer. And yet the men with chronic bronchitis and the men who will be saved from chronic bronchitis are just as real as the men with real heart disease. Each one of them has a family, friends, a job, a hobby and probably a mortgage. The point is that for the cost of a single open heart operation we can probably save a dozen men from getting chronic bronchitis.'

'On humanitarian grounds, therefore, it would be reasonable to spend more money on preventive medicine and less on curative medicine and research. There are also economic advantages to spending money on preventative medicine.'

The gas appliance showroom

Like most (if not all) professional authors I meet a lot of people who, when they know what I do for a living, tell me that they intend to write a book one day.

In my first diary, 'Diary of a Disgruntled Man', I described how I once met a man who, when he had asked me what I did for a living, said that it is his intention to write books when he retired in three years' time. He said he thought he might write novels and biographies and that it didn't matter whether he earned any money from his writing because he had a good pension to look forward to. I asked him what he did for a living. He said he ran a gas appliance showroom. I said wasn't it funny but it was my intention to run a gas appliance showroom in my spare time when I retired. He indignantly said it would not be possible for me to do this because his job required a good deal of knowledge and training and skill and other things he didn't go into but expressed with an airy wave of the hand. I said I felt sure I could do it and that I thought it would actually be very easy. I said I might manage several showrooms and would be happy to do it for very little money or even no money at all. He got very red faced, spluttered and said that if I did that I would be putting trained men out of work. He then stalked off in a huff.

On the nest

Several times during my life as a GP I was called out to see patients who had died while exercising in bed. All of the patients who had died in what is known colloquially as 'flagrante delicto' were male though my sample was not large enough to be used as evidence of any definite susceptibility of the male sex. Moreover, I suspect that there were other occasions on which the precise details of a patient's expiration were hidden from me by an embarrassed or diffident spouse.

On one occasion that I remember well, the death was notable for the fact that the deceased had succumbed while in what could most politely described as 'the wrong bed'.

I had only been a GP for a fortnight. I arrived at the flat to which I had been called to be met by a young woman who was fully clothed but who had clearly dressed herself rather rapidly. Her buttons weren't done up properly and her hair was awry. She was, however, wearing a goodly quantity of make-up and a powerful perfume. Her flat was small but neat and very clean. It was obviously well-looked after. There was a large vase full of flowers in the hallway. The flowers were silk, I remember.

She was, she told me, a patient of mine though I'd never met her before. She led me into the bedroom where a very overweight man, who looked to be in his mid to late fifties, was lying flat on his back on top of the bed. The coverlet had not been pulled back. He was wearing nothing but a towel which had been draped neatly over the area sometimes described as the nether regions. I examined him. He was clearly never again going to be concerned about his weight, the policies of the Government or earning a living. He was dead.

'Did you find your father like this?' I asked her, and even today, decades later, I still feel embarrassed at the naivety of the question.

'He's not my father,' replied the woman.

'Your husband then,' I said, after apologising profusely.

'He's not my husband,' she said. She paused. 'He was just a friend.'

'Is he a patient of mine?' I asked, though just why I asked this I didn't know then and I certainly don't know now. Before she could answer I asked another question. 'Do you know his name?'

'He told me his name was John,' she said. 'But I'm not sure.'

'Maybe we'd better look in his wallet,' I suggested. I was beginning to understand that this had not been a long-term relationship. I found his wallet in the rear pocket of his trousers which were, together with his jacket, neatly lain on a chair near to the bed. His shirt was neatly lain there too, but his underclothing and his socks were strewn about on the floor. There was no sign of his shoes.

'It says here that his name was Dennis,' I said, taking a credit card out of his wallet. I looked at several other cards and at his driving licence. They all carried the same name.

'Was he married?' she asked.

I looked again in his pocket. 'There's a letter from his bank manager which is addressed to him and his wife. It was dated two days ago.'

'So he was married?'

'It appears so.' I looked at the clock. It was 7.45 pm. It occurred to me that the man's wife was probably expecting him home for his dinner.

'His wife is going to be very upset,' said the woman.

'I would think so,' I agreed.

'He shouldn't be found here,' she said.

'Probably not,' I agreed.

'Will there be an inquest?'

'There will almost certainly have to be an inquest.'

'Is there anything you can do?'

'I ought to call for an ambulance,' I said, though I wondered whether I should simply telephone an undertaker. And then I had an idea. Two days earlier I had met the local coroner at a medical meeting. He had seemed to me to be very old. He was certainly well into his 70s.

I telephoned the police and asked if I could speak to the coroner. The police sergeant on the desk put me through to the coroner's officer – a policeman designated to work with the coroner. I explained who I was, but not why I was calling, and asked if I could speak to the coroner. I explained that I needed his advice. To my surprise the police officer gave me the coroner's home telephone number. I doubt if such a thing would happen today.

'Ah, he died on the wrong nest, did he?' said the coroner, with a half suppressed chuckle. 'Have you rung for an ambulance yet?'

I said I hadn't.

'But he's definitely dead?'

'Oh yes. He's definitely dead.'

'Don't do anything,' said the coroner. 'I'll arrange for someone to pick him up and take him to our morgue. We'll put him down as collapsed in the street and 'Certified Dead'. We'll need a post mortem before the inquest.'

Fifteen minutes later two policemen appeared. 'Is he dead, sir?' asked one of the policemen. I said he was. 'That's good, sir,' said the policeman. 'You found him collapsed in the street?'

'I did,' I agreed. He took my name and the address of my practice.

'We can't move him unless you've certified him as dead,' explained the policeman. 'It's a good thing that you're here.'

The four of us dressed Dennis as well as we could and then the policemen put the body onto a stretcher and took it downstairs to the street. They put him in the back of a plain police van and took him straight to the morgue. If I hadn't been there to confirm that he was dead, a doctor at the hospital would have had to certify him.

And that was pretty much the end of it.

The two policemen then called at the man's home address and told the widow that her husband had collapsed and died in the street.

The post-mortem duly showed that the man had had a massive heart attack and had died of natural causes. It was agreed that he was obese and that he drank and smoked too much. There was a very brief inquest and the case was closed.

Two days after the inquest the young woman in whose flat the man had died sent me a simple thank you card with a very nice bottle of wine. The card just carried the words 'In memory – thank you'.

The widow never knew where or how her husband had died.

The scary, staggering truth about the chemotherapy fraud

Over the years I have repeatedly found that all medical recommendations are best treated with a large dose of scepticism.

Nowhere is this more true than in the treatment of cancer.

Patients who are diagnosed with cancer find themselves in a state of shock. And yet, while in a state of shock, they find themselves needing to make a number of vital decisions very quickly.

One of the big questions is often this one: 'Should I have chemotherapy?'

Chemotherapy might improve a patient's chances of survival by three to five per cent though that modest figure is usually over generous. For example, the evidence suggests that chemotherapy offers breast cancer patients an uplift in survival of little more than 2.5%.

When you consider that chemotherapy can kill and does terrible damage to healthy cells, and to the immune system, it is difficult to see the value of taking chemotherapy.

I don't think it is any exaggeration to suggest that much of the hype around chemotherapy has taken the treatment into the area of fraud – far more fraudulent indeed than treatments which are dismissed as irrelevant or harmful by the establishment.

The chances are that the doctors looking after you – especially the specialist oncologists in hospital – will recommend chemotherapy. They may push hard to accept their recommendation. They may even be cross or dismissive or assume you are ignorant or afraid if you decide you don't want it. Cancer charities often shout excitedly about chemotherapy. But they are also often closely linked to the drug companies which make money out of chemotherapy – which in my view makes them part of the large and thriving 'cancer industry'. It is important to remember that drug companies exist to make money and they will do whatever is necessary to further this aim. They lie and they cheat with scary regularity and they have no interest in helping patients or saving lives. Remember that: the sole

119

purpose of drug companies is to make money, whatever the human cost might. They will happily suppress potentially life-saving information if doing so increases their profits. It is my belief that by allying themselves with drug companies, cancer charities have become corrupt.

Little or no advice is given to patients about how they themselves might reduce the risk of their cancer returning. The implication is that its chemotherapy or nothing. So, for example, doctors are unlikely to tell breast cancer patients that they should avoid dairy foods, though the evidence that they should is very strong.

The one certainty is that it is extremely unlikely that anyone you see will tell you all the truths about chemotherapy. The sad truth is that the statistics about chemotherapy are, of course, fiddled to boost the drug company sales and, therefore, drug company profits. And the deaths caused by chemotherapy are often misreported or under-estimated. So, for example, if a patient who has been taking chemotherapy dies of a sudden heart attack their death will probably be put down as a heart attack – rather than as a result of the cancer or the chemotherapy. There may be some mealy mouthed suggestion that the death was treatment related but the drug will probably not be named and shamed. Neither the chemotherapy nor the cancer will be deemed responsible. What this means in practice is that the survival statistics for chemotherapy are considerably worse than the figures which are made available – considerably worse, indeed, than whatever positive effect might be provided by a harmless placebo.

Here's another thing: patients who have chemotherapy and survive five years are counted as having been cured by chemotherapy. And patients who have chemotherapy and then die five and a bit years after their diagnosis don't count as cancer related deaths. And they certainly don't count as chemotherapy deaths.

A 2016 academic study looked at five year survival rates and concluded that in 90% of patients (including the commonest breast cancer tumours) chemotherapy increased five year survival by less than 2.5%. Only a very small number of cancers (such as testicular cancer and Hodgkin's disease) were treated effectively by chemotherapy. On top of this dismal success rate it must be remembered that chemotherapy cripples the immune system (now, at long last, recognised as important in the fight against cancer), damages all living cells, damages the intestines, can cause nausea and tinnitus, can damage nerves, can and does damage the bone marrow with the result that leukaemia develops,(staggeringly, iatrogenic myeloid leukaemia, usually known as 'therapy related' in an attempt to distance the disease from doctors, is, in ten per cent of cases, a result of chemotherapy), damages the heart and the hearing and will, in a significant number of patients, result in death.

It is true that chemotherapy may reduce the size of a tumour but in stage 4 cancer chemotherapy seems to encourage a cancer to return more quickly and more aggressively. The cancer stem cells seem to be untouched by the chemotherapy drugs.

Despite all this, the protocol in the treatment of cancer is to turn to chemotherapy and doctors are always reluctant to try anything else.

The Academy of Royal Medical Colleges, which represents 24 Royal Colleges, and a number of other important health bodies, has reported that chemotherapy can do more harm than good when prescribed as palliatives for terminally ill cancer patients. The colleges criticise chemotherapy advocates for 'raising false hopes' and doing 'more harm than good'. They concluded that chemotherapy drugs are unlikely to work.

On the other hand, I wasn't surprised to see a big cancer charity disagreeing with the 24 medical colleges and claiming that thousands of patients do benefit. My view, which I recognise is probably not shared by the majority of family doctors or oncologists, is that many cancer charities around the world are the unacceptable face of cancer care. It seems to me to be more concerned with making money and keeping the drug companies rich than in caring for patients.

Another report has concluded that chemotherapy can, in some circumstances, actually promote the spread of cancer cells. It was reported in 2017, for example, that when breast cancer patients have chemotherapy before surgery the drug can make the malignant cells spread to distant sites – resulting in metastatic cancer and sending the patient straight from Stage 1 to Stage 4.

Scientists analysed tissue from 20 breast cancer patients who had 16 weeks of chemotherapy and the tissues around the tumour was more conducive to spread in most of the patients. In five of the patients there was a five times greater risk of spread. In none of the patients was the tissue around the tumour less friendly to cancer cells and to metastasis. The problem, it seems is that cancer cells have a great ability to transform themselves and the chemotherapy, designed to kill cancer cells, may encourage the development of cells which are resistant to drugs, which survive the treatment and which form a new cancer.

The one side effect associated with chemotherapy that is widely known is the loss of hair. But that is, to be honest, the least of the problems. Chemotherapy kills healthy cells as well as cancer cells and the severity of the side effects depends on the age and health of the patient as well as on the type of drug used and the dosage in which it is prescribed. And whereas some side effects do disappear after treatment (as the good cells recover) there are some side effects which may never go away.

I mentioned the serious side effects a little earlier but here, as a reminder, is a list of just some of the problems that can be caused by chemotherapy drugs:

The cells in the bone marrow can be damaged, producing a shortage of red blood cells and possibly leukaemia.

The central nervous system can be damaged with a result that the memory may be affected and the patient's ability to concentrate or think clearly changed. There may be changes to balance and coordination. These effects can last for years. Apart from affecting the brain, chemotherapy can also cause pain and tingling in the hands and feet, numbness, weakness and pain. Not surprisingly, depression is not uncommon.

The digestive system is commonly affected with sores forming in the mouth and throat. These may produce infection and may make food taste unpleasant. Nausea and vomiting may also occur. The weight loss associated with chemotherapy may be a result of a loss of appetite.

In addition to hair loss (which can affect hair all over the body) the skin may be irritated and nails may change colour and appearance.

The kidneys and bladder may be irritated and damaged. The result may be swollen ankles, feet and hands.

Osteoporosis is a fairly common problem and increases the risk of bone fractures and breaks. Women who have breast cancer and who are having treatment to reduce their oestrogen levels are particularly at risk.

Chemotherapy can produce hormone changes with a wide variety of symptoms.

The heart may be damaged and patients who already have weak hearts may be made worse by chemotherapy.

And the other problem with chemotherapy is that it can damage the immune system.

And it is known that chemotherapy can damage DNA.

And does chemotherapy alter the nature of cancer cells? Can it, for example, trigger a change from an oestrogen sensitive cancer cell to a triple negative cell – much harder to treat?

And then there is that risk that chemotherapy might spread cells around the body.

Finally, there is increasing evidence to show that chemotherapy may hasten the death of a number of patients.

Drug companies, cancer charities and doctors recommend chemotherapy because there is big money in it. The least forgivable of these are the cancer charities which exist to protect people but which are ruthless exploiters of patients.

As always the medical literature is confusing but in the 'Annuals of Oncology' I found this: 'the upfront use of chemotherapy does not seem to influence the overall outcome of the disease'.

Most doctors won't tell you this, or even admit it to themselves, but cancer drugs are killing up to 50% of patients in some hospitals. A study by Public Health England and Cancer Research UK found that 2.4% of breast cancer patients die within a month of starting chemotherapy. The figures are even worse for patients with lung cancer where 8.4% of patients die within a month when treated with chemotherapy. When patients die that quickly, I feel that it is safe to assume that they were killed by the treatment not the disease. At one hospital the death rate for patients with lung cancer treated with chemotherapy was reported at over 50%. Naturally, all the hospitals which took part in the study insisted that chemotherapy prescribing was being done safely. If we accept this then we must also question the validity of chemotherapy. The study showed that the figures are particular bad for patients who are in poor general health when they start treatment.

Next think about this.

In the UK, the National Health Service publishes comprehensive guidelines on what must be done if chemotherapy drugs are spilt.

There are crisis emergency procedures to be followed if chemotherapy drugs fall on the floor. And yet these drugs are put into people's bodies. And residues of these dangerous chemicals are excreted in urine and then end up in the drinking water supply. (I explained several decades ago how prescription drug residues end up in our drinking water.)

It is hardly surprising that many patients being treated with chemotherapy report that their quality of life has plummeted.

The standard oncology approach to cancer is to give chemotherapy and then wait and see if the cancer returns. If it does then more chemotherapy is prescribed. The tragedy is that for so many patients chemotherapy will do more harm than good. Astonishingly, a quarter of cancer patients die of heart attacks – often triggered by deep vein thrombosis and by emboli and brought on by the physical stress of chemotherapy. But these deaths are not included in the official statistics – either for cancer or, just as importantly, for chemotherapy. It is no exaggeration to say that the establishment fiddles the figures to suit its own largely commercial ends – extolling the virtues of drug company products at every opportunity and never failing to throw doubt on any remedy which might threaten the huge cancer industry

Here's another thing you might not know.

During the lockdowns and concerns about covid-19, patients who were on chemotherapy were taken off their treatment. They were told that since their treatment would affect their immune systems they would be more vulnerable to the coronavirus. That's an important admission because the one thing we know for certain is that a healthy immune system is vital for fighting cancer.

Doctors probably won't tell you any of this but they won't deny it because it is all true.

The bottom line is that treatments described in clinical trials, paid for by drug companies and generally reviewed by doctors with drug company links, and then published in medical journals which accept huge amounts of drug company advertising, are the only treatments the medical profession accepts. There is much talk about 'peer review' trials but all this means is that another doctor or two, with drug company links, will have looked at the paper and given it their approval.

The word 'corrupt' doesn't come close to describing this whole incestuous system.

Anyone who wants to have chemotherapy should have it. I'm not trying to dissuade anyone from using whatever drugs they believe might help them. I'm only interested in providing unbiased, independent information which might help patients make the right decision for themselves.

But too often, I fear, patients beg for treatment, completely understandably, because they want something to be done and because they have been misled by the drug company inspired, and paid for, hype about chemotherapy. And doctors provide that treatment, even though a little research would tell them that they may be doing more harm than good. There are a very few cancers which can be treated well with chemotherapy – but they are very few and they are unfairly and unreasonably promoted as success stories by the drug companies and their shills.

The thing that is forgotten is that chemotherapy can badly damage the patient's body's own protections – and with some patients may, therefore, do infinitely more harm than good.

Every patient should decide for themselves – and discuss with their doctors the evidence for and against chemotherapy in their situation. But I think that all patients are entitled to be provided with the background information they would need to help that process of assessment.

Tragically, however, the ignorance about chemotherapy is, sadly, widespread and all pervasive.

How many women with breast cancer realise that their survival chances might be better if they took daily low dose aspirin and avoided dairy products than if they accepted chemotherapy?

Doctors don't tell them that because they have, as a profession, been bought by the pharmaceutical industry.

A sad, sad story

There was a story in the papers about a young mother who refused to have radiotherapy or take chemotherapy or, indeed, drugs of any kind.

Reportedly, the hospital refused to perform surgery unless she also agreed to have radiotherapy and chemotherapy.

I found this difficult to believe but several papers ran the story.

So the young woman gave up meat and she and her husband spent all their savings (a total of £70,000) on trying a variety of alternative treatments – none of which worked. The young woman is now dead, leaving behind a penniless husband and a young daughter.

What astonished me was the nature of the comments on the internet. They were, without exception, sneery, abusive and critical. They were also built on ignorance.

Now I can understand why a woman would refuse to have radiotherapy and chemotherapy (particularly chemotherapy) and if it is true, that the hospital refused to allow her to have surgery alone then that was unforgiveable, but my reason for mentioning this is not the death of the woman but the comments which were posted underneath the article.

Here is a representative sample of the comments I saw (I have removed the names or initials or false names of those who commented):

'Hard to feel any sympathy for the tree hugging pair.'

'They are convinced that following an alternative lifestyle is the answer to everything.'

'So their poor daughter is left without a mother, due to their ignorance. What's the betting the poor girl has not been vaccinated as well.'

'Stupidity is incurable.'

'Why do people think they know better than the doctors?'

'Without being rude she should have taken the free treatment.'

'No sympathy from me as this cancer could have been treated and she refused so their own fault.'

I felt sickened when I read those comments.

Sympathy?

None available.

Understanding?

Not present.

Compassion?

Entirely missing.

A young woman died, terrified and in despair. Her husband, now with a young daughter to care for, mourned.

And the doughty, so confident of themselves, denizens of the internet could do nothing but scoff and sneer.

I know the internet has given us some useful services. But I feel daily that we would be better off if Tim Berners-Lee had invented something else.

A salutary story

People often don't listen as well as they perhaps should. And too often, I'm afraid, people don't look at a problem from the other person's point of view. We're all guilty of this. We get stuck in one position and we can't see the situation from any other angle.

Mr Knight was in his early fifties when I became a principal in general practice. He was one of the relatively few people in the world who really had dragged himself up from poverty to wealth. Most of the people who claim to be self-made millionaires started off in life with at least one solid silver spoon in their mouth.

'I dragged myself up by my boot straps,' they boast, when being interviewed. But when you look a little more closely you find out that Daddy owned two factories, a couple of newspapers and a radio station and that their first job, at nineteen, was as managing director of one of Daddy's enterprises.

Mr Knight was a well-known figure locally. He had a successful business and he and his wife were often pictured in the local paper because they were involved with a number of local charities. His father had worked for the local coal board as a clerk. His mother had been an office cleaner. They'd lived in a terraced house with an outside lavatory and their only bath had been taken in a galvanised tub filled from kettles heated over the fire. I know this all to be true because his parents were also patients of mine.

I didn't see Mr Knight very often. He came once to have a passport photograph signed (GPs were on the acceptable list for this minor bureaucratic chore) and he had a couple of insurance medicals. And he once had a bad attack of flu that kept him in bed for a week.

That was it until he came in one day looking terrible. He was accompanied by his wife, a tiny woman, only a fraction above five feet tall. She looked as delicate and as fragile as a sparrow. They made a truly odd couple since he was well over six feet tall and built pretty much along the lines of an old-fashioned red British telephone box.

Mr Knight told me that he couldn't sleep and wasn't eating very well and that he felt tired and listless. He denied having any pains or any specific physical signs or symptoms and confessed that he wouldn't have come to the surgery if his wife hadn't made him come.

'Tell the doctor what's been happening,' urged his wife.

Mr Knight looked down at his hands for a while, as though searching for inspiration. The silence lasted and lasted. Eventually it was broken when Mrs Knight spoke again.

'My husband has a factory making parts for the car industry,' she told me. I nodded, I knew this. The factory was one of the biggest independently owned businesses in the area and employed over 200 people. 'Things have been difficult recently because the big car companies have started buying more and more parts from Asia.'

'Companies over there have much lower overheads,' explained Mr Knight. 'Their wage bills are a fraction of what we have to pay. They have lower taxes, their property prices are lower and they pass less for their raw materials.'

'Kevin has been worried sick for weeks now,' said Mrs Knight. 'He's lost weight and he's not been himself.'

'I've been very edgy,' her husband confessed. 'I lose my temper very easily.'

He wife reached across, took his hand and squeezed it. There were tears in Mr Knight's eyes. It was clear to see that they were a very close couple.

'I should have cut costs by making some people redundant but I didn't like to do that,' continued Mr Knight. 'Jobs are in short supply in this area and I can imagine how hard it can be for a 50-year-old man to find work when his skills are no longer of any value.'

'We haven't taken any money out of the business for eighteen months,' said Mrs Knight. 'We're not on the breadline. We've got a lovely house here and a villa in Spain but we're probably not as wealthy as people think we are.'

'The problem is that the unions have been pushing for a pay rise,' said Mr Knight. 'I've explained the situation. I've shown them the prices that the Chinese are charging. I've shown them our balance sheet. But they don't listen, they don't take any notice and they don't seem to see things from my point of view. I'm prepared to keep going and to try to turn the business round but we can't pay people any more than we pay them. If we do that then we'll just go bust. It's my business but I have responsibilities to shareholders too.'

'Now they're talking about a strike,' said Mrs Knight. 'The union says that if the company doesn't approve a 7% pay rise they're going to go on indefinite strike next week.'

They both looked at me, waiting for me to offer some sort of sticking plaster.

'I could prescribe sleeping tablets,' I told them. 'I could prescribe tranquillisers. But I'm not going to. Neither would help you think clearly and neither would help you make a decision. You've got a very real, practical problem which can only be solved by you.'

They both looked disappointed.

'It's perhaps time to think about yourselves and your own health,' I told them. 'What happens if the union does go on strike?'

'It'll be a disaster,' said Mr Knight. 'We'll lose some of our contracts. The big car companies aren't sentimental. They'll get the work done in Asia. They've been good to us because I know the buyers and we've got a good working relationship. But once we lose contracts we'll never get that work back.'

'Do the union people know that?'

'Oh yes. I've shown them all the paperwork. They think I'm just negotiating. I even spoke to a meeting the other day and explained why I couldn't pay them anymore than I am doing. But the work force didn't believe me. After I'd left they voted to go on strike.'

'What other options have you got?'

'A property company wants to buy the land where the factory is,' explained Mr Knight. 'They'll knock down the factory and build offices or a car park and maybe a supermarket on the ground floor. They've offered me a very good price.'

'Tell the unions,' I suggested. 'Explain that if they don't listen to you then the factory may close and all those jobs will be gone.'

They thought that was a good idea.

I didn't see either of them again but the following week's local newspaper carried a story on its front page about a strike starting at their factory. There was a picture of workers with placards outside the front gates. 'We'll stay out until we get a pay rise,' said one of the strikers, defiantly.

And the week after that the same newspaper reported that the Mr Knight had closed the factory and sold the site to a property

130

company. This time the picture on the front page was of a pair of gates, locked with a huge padlock. There was a CLOSED sign on the gates telling the world the name of the new owners.

I heard later that the Knights had sold their English home as well, and had decided to retire and to move to their villa in Spain.

I felt terribly sorry for the workers who had lost their jobs. I knew that many would probably not find work again. Several were outspoken in their criticism of Mr Knight. But in truth it was the union representatives who were guilty. They should have listened more carefully.

A little tighter please

When I was a senior medical student, and a junior houseman working in hospital, one of my jobs was to sew up new mothers who had suffered a tear while giving birth (or who'd had an episiotomy to make a little more room for the baby to be delivered and to avoid an otherwise, ragged and uncontrolled tear).

I'd sit at the business end, with the woman who'd just given birth, usually tired, euphoric and invariably surprising talkative. If I'd just been through what they'd been through my throat would have been too sore from screaming to allow me to say anything. As I sewed away almost every woman said the same thing: 'Can you sew me up quite tightly?'

On one occasion a woman who needed no stitches at all still made the same request.

It was, I suppose, the corollary of the male fear about size.

And there is, of course, no more potent fear than fear itself.

Under another name

I first used a pen name on a book when I was in my twenties.

I had written three non-fiction books ('The Medicine Men', 'Paper Doctors' and 'Stress Control') and I then wrote a novel called 'Practice Makes Perfect' about a young doctor in general practice.

My literary agents at the time, David Higham Associates, felt that I couldn't write fiction under the same name as I was using for serious medical books and insisted that I used a pen name for the novel. I don't know whether they thought that readers would be confused, that booksellers would be bewildered or that I might forget what I was writing. For simplicity I did what so many authors have done and simply reversed my Christian names. I became Dr Edward Vernon.

In so far as I was at the time practising as a GP, the book bore some resemblance to my own experiences but the similarities were incredibly slight – and deliberately so. I was too conscious of the risk of a libel action to base any of the characters on real people. I was, for example, well aware that James Herriot, the best-selling author of a series of books about a Yorkshire vet, had been involved in a tricky libel case with one of his own partners. And so the doctors, the patients and the situations were all invented. You could say, I suppose, that other than the plots and the people and the surroundings everything was true.

The first book in what I had always thought of as a series was bought by Macmillan in London and then Pan, an associated paperback imprint, bought the mass market rights. This led to a moderately embarrassing moment when I met the Pan editor who had purchased the rights. She hadn't realised that the books had been written under a pseudonym and was surprised to find that Vernon Coleman, the author of 'Stress Control' (for which she had also just bought the paperback rights) was also the Edward Vernon, the author of 'Practice Makes Perfect'. Both books were on the same list and one of them had to be delayed a month or two so that I could promote 'Stress Control' as Vernon Coleman and then promote

'Practice Makes Perfect' as Edward Vernon. I can't remember which book was delayed but there was a considerable amount of confusion; much of it mine. I subsequently found myself wandering around the country as Vernon Coleman and then, a little later, wandering the country as Edward Vernon to be interviewed by the journalists. This led to some confusion and embarrassment; all of it mine.

Tom McCormack, the American publisher of James Herriot's books bought the American rights to 'Practice Makes Perfect' and to the sequel (which became 'Practise what you Preach'). There was much excitement among my agents and British publishers for they knew that Herriot's books were massive sellers around the world. Tom McCormack flew over to London and I met him for a long editorial discussion at his very elegant hotel. I remember that the meeting was held in his room. I assumed this was done so that no one overheard us and rushed off and stole the ideas. The excellent Mr McCormack had a few suggestions, which I followed (including the introduction of a romantic interest) and then he flew back to the United States. There were grand plans for the books in America but things ended up rather fizzling out. I was told that Mr McCormack had broken a leg or an arm or some other limb while skiing and was away from the office when the first book was released. His company, St Martin's Press, did produce good-looking books and the reviews were excellent but the books never sold in the millions.

In the UK (as in the US) the books were published by Pan as non-fiction because the editors felt that readers would prefer to think that the stories were all true. This has subsequently resulted in website editors listing the books as non-fiction. Even when I have pointed out the error they have persisted. You'd think they might accept that I'd know whether what I'd written was real or not but it seems that as far as sites such as Wikipedia are concerned the author, the one person who you would think might know whether a book was a novel or an autobiography, is the only person in the world not allowed to comment on such matters. I used to be mildly irritated but to be honest I no longer care.

In my 20s and 30s, I often used pennames in magazines (sometimes because I had more than one article in the same issue) and I cannot remember most of the names I used (or which were put onto articles by editors without bothering to tell me). There were undoubtedly times when I didn't bother to tell the editors my real name.

The next time I used a pen name on a book was when I wrote a novel about the channel tunnel.

'Tunnel' was written in the late 1970s and first published in 1980 – before the final plans for the Channel Tunnel were drawn up and long before the actual Channel Tunnel was built. When researching the book I spent some time trying to work out where the tunnel should start, where it should end and what form it should take. I was and am delighted that the tunnel which was eventually built (after millions of pounds of research) bore a notable resemblance to the tunnel I 'designed' and 'built' for this novel. They started it where my tunnel started and the tunnel emerged in France exactly where I thought it should. And my design for the tunnel was the same as the one that was used. I was quietly pleased to have got that right. They should have me as the consultant. They'd have saved a lot of money. I also created the European Union (which existed at the time, but under one of its earlier pseudonyms).

I wrote the book 'on spec' (without a publisher's contract) and when I'd finished it I sent it to my agent, a woman called Anne McDermid. I can't remember whether she was at David Higham or Curtis Brown at the time. (I changed agencies when she moved from Higham to Brown.) She didn't think it was the sort of book I should be writing (I had just begun to establish a reputation as an author of hard-hitting medical books such as 'The Medicine Men' and 'Paper Doctors' and was already writing light, humorous fiction under the pen name Edward Vernon. I think the idea of my writing a disaster novel, and acquiring another pen name, may have been just too much for her to bear. Or maybe she just hated the book.)

So I retyped the front page of the manuscript and replaced my name with the pen name Marc Charbonnier. I then sent it off to a publisher called Robert Hale which produced a good deal of fiction. They bought it straight away, paid me money as an advance, consulted me on the cover and generally behaved very decently. I can't remember if I ever told them my real name but I expect I did. In those days, however, it was possible to pay cheques into a bank account even if the name on the cheque wasn't the same as the name on the account. This was very useful for writers who were using pen names. On more than one occasion, I do remember turning up at my bank with a fistful of cheques apparently made out to different people. (The cheques all went into my current account and appeared in my accounts, by the way.) This was just one of the many ways in which life was much simpler then.

Years later, I republished 'Tunnel' as a mass market paperback under my own name and serendipitously managed to take a terrific photograph for the cover. I happened to be in Paris when there was a real fire in the Channel Tunnel. There were signs from SNCF at the Gare du Nord telling travellers about the fire and warning that the Tunnel was closed. I took a photo of the empty station and the sign and used it for the cover of the paperback.

I also managed to take the jacket photographs for both the hard back edition and the mass market paperback edition of my novel 'Deadline'; and both of those pictures were taken in Paris. The photo on the cover of the hardback was taken inside one of my favourite haunts, the Café de la Paix, near the Opera in Paris. And the photo on the cover of the first paperback edition was taken outside the Gare St Lazare, in Paris where there is (or quite possibly was) a terrific sculpture showing a huge number of large clock faces.

Come to think of it quite a few of the photographs I used on my book covers were taken in Paris. One of the joys of independent publishing is that the author can take control of every aspect of a book's publication – including the book's cover.

Since the days of Marc Charbonnier I've used the name Edward Vernon a couple of times and, for one reason or another, I've used a variety of other pen names. I added them up while writing this book and to my surprise I've now written books under 18 different pen names. Some of the time I have used pen names to protect the books against the inevitable one star attacks from people who disapprove of my views about drug companies and so on. These people think it is fair to destroy a book they haven't read, or even looked at, because they disapprove of what they think the author might have said. I don't look at reviews anymore because some of the 'reviewers' (and I use the word in a very broad manner) will write the most outrageous lies and libels in attempts to kill off a book. And people complain about the oddest things. One so-called reviewer gave a book a one star review because she said I hadn't replied to an email she claimed to have sent me though I have no idea where she sent it or why she assumed I received it. Her complaint received several hundred votes of approval from people who obviously know better than I do what emails I receive, read and should reply to. Hey ho, the world is a strange place and the internet has made it ever stranger.

Some of the books I've written under pen names have done very well and I think of the authors as children – released into the world to find their way on their own.

He missed the bus

Benny Hill was for many years Britain's most successful and highly paid television comedian. His shows were massively successful and were shown in just about every country in the world. But Hill was notoriously parsimonious. He lived in the tiny house he'd occupied all his life and famously carried his belongings around in a plastic, supermarket bag. One day he arrived late at the TV studios where he was due to record part of one of his programmes. The producer was surprised for Hill was never usually late.

'What happened?' asked the producer, who'd had an entire studio full of actors, extras and crew waiting and unable to do anything for the cameras.

'My bus was late,' explained Mr Hill.

From then on the studio sent a limousine to pick up Mr Hill every time he was due to attend a recording.

I bet he was chuffed to bits because it meant he didn't have to pay the bus fare.

Reviews and reviewing

The aim of a review (whether of a book, a film, a play, a restaurant or a hat) is to judge how well the author, film-makers, playwright and cast, chef or milliner has succeeded in their aim, and to offer readers of the review an honest opinion on the item. If the review is published in a paid-for publication, the reviewer will also be expected to write the review in a way that will entertain the readers. All reviews are, by definition, subjective and, traditionally, it was always accepted that only a very small percentage of those who read the review would ever go on to read the book or watch the play but would nevertheless regard themselves as informed about the value and validity of the book (etc., etc.).

Reviewing has, however, been changed by the internet and the traditional role of the reviewer has been transformed.

Today, the modern review is too often about the reviewer than the object of the review and review space is frequently used to parade personal opinions, prejudices, hatred, professional jealousies, commercial expediency and complaints about the supplier, the printer and anyone else remotely connected with the alleged object of the review. It is as though a drama critic were to give a play a crushing review solely because someone stood on his foot while he was queuing for a bus to take him to the theatre. I've seen reviews in which the reviewer has complained about the quality of the packaging in which a book was delivered and reviews in which the reviewer has complained that the content of the book was not what they wanted – when the author had never promised or intended to include that material in their book. I wrote a book which received a bad review because it contained nothing about Gloucester Cathedral – a place I've never visited or claimed to have visited. A high percentage of reviews and ratings are delivered by people who have not read the book in question (or even seen a copy). The rules have changed and reviewers, who often have preconceived ideas, are allowed to use review pages to promote their own views or to libel an author with impunity.

When eBooks were first introduced, I expressed the fear that it would be all too easy for thieves to take an eBook, appropriate it as their own and sell it or circulate it freely. But as postage prices rose inexorably I found myself forced to succumb to allowing my books to be published in the eBook format, though it was with a great relief that I welcomed the availability of digital publishing for the creation of paperback editions.

My fears were proved correct, however, and several of my books have been stolen and distributed freely on the internet, sometimes with the thieves putting their own names on my work, publishing my work as 'their' book and collecting my royalties for themselves. It seems impossible to stop this happening. Things have got so bad that I have on numerous occasions had to provide old contracts and other paperwork to prove that I am the author of works of mine which have been on sale for decades. Writing books is what I do for a living (and have done for nearly half a century). Stealing my copyright is stealing away my livelihood.

And there is another problem. Malicious one star reviews are frequently posted by individuals who 'buy' an eBook, give a one star review, and then claim a refund for the book they've owned for ten seconds and probably never even looked at. These individuals tend to be insipid folk who regard life as a spectator sport and think of honour, integrity, honesty, freedom and self-respect as avoidable optional extras. Poorly educated they regard knowledge as an impediment to offering their opinions on almost every topic imaginable, regularly quoting other ignorant folk to support their own prejudices. Once they have found an author with whom they think they disagree, they tend to target all that author's books with abuse – determined to destroy both the books and the author, and very effectively killing both and damaging free speech in the process. These literary marauders, whose aim is to suppress, ban and censorship any ideas with which they disagree, will, taken together with copyright theft, and the campaign to abolish copyright altogether, lead to the end of books and original thinking.

I'm afraid I have very little hope for the future of authorship or, indeed, the future of books. Writers should be allowed to say anything (even to question the holocaust and to use 'banned' words) and they should be allowed to express extreme or dangerous opinions as long as they are not writing something libellous – in the sense of writing something untrue about someone.

Incidentally, if I could I would extend the definition of libel to include the dead as well as the living – this would dramatically improve the quality of history writing.

The surprise

I used to visit a couple who were both in their 90s. They were healthier, in body and mind, than many people half a century younger.

They couple had been married for over 60 years and were devoted to each other though people who didn't know them probably didn't realise that.

Mrs Templeton sometimes seemed to delight in criticising her husband, telling him off when he told stories she'd heard many times before and so on. But if anyone else criticised her husband in any way she became protective, indignant and as tough as a lioness defending her young. She would, metaphorically speaking, leap down the throat of the critic and pull out their livers. Metaphorically speaking, you understand.

Not that Mr Templeton needed that much looking after.

I once went round to their home and found him in their garden shed. He had cut a log in two along its length (not an easy task when the only tool you have is a rather blunt bowsaw) and had used a chisel to cut a groove in both halves. He'd sandpapered both halves so that they were quite smooth.

'What on earth are you doing?' I asked him.

He looked at me and winked. He then took a firework rocket from a paper bag, broke off the stick and then placed the rocket part of the firework into one of the grooves. He smeared glue all around the firework and fitted the other half of the log into position. He now had a log, which looked like an ordinary log but which had a firework inside it. When he'd done this he marked the log with a notch.

'What on earth are you doing?' I asked him again.

'Someone's been stealing our logs,' he said. 'This will be the last one they'll steal.'

John Milton

Publishers are notoriously snooty about how they treat their authors. This true story about John Milton sums up the relationship between publishers and authors.

When Milton's masterpiece 'Paradise Lost' was first published, the publisher put Milton's name on the title page in capitals: 'JOHN MILTON'. All in capitals.

The first edition was a disappointment bordering on a failure, though it eventually sold out.

Reluctantly, the publisher produced a second edition. This time Milton's name appeared as 'John Milton' – in lower case letters.

The second edition sold, but no more speedily than the first edition.

When the publisher produced a third edition he printed Milton's name thus: 'J.Milton'.

And on the fourth edition he printed Milton's initials only: 'J.M.'

Then the book began to sell.

The fifth edition had Milton's name published in full as 'John Milton'.

And by the time of the sixth edition, Milton's name on the title page was back to where it been originally: 'JOHN MILTON'.

As you can imagine, all these variations are of great interest to book collectors.

Swimming upstream

I find myself thinking a good deal about the way medicine has changed for the worse – and done so at quite a pace in the last decade or so. Doctors have leapt upon changes in their way of working with rare enthusiasm. Doctors used to be available 24 hours a day for 356 days a year. No more. These days they work shorter hours than your local library (if there is one). Your local friendly accountant is probably easier to contact. You could hire a flame thrower or a helicopter with less trouble than obtaining an appointment with your GP.

The odd thing is that the medical profession has a long history of resisting change, of protecting existing practices (however harmful they might have been) and of opposing innovative ideas which were later shown to save many lives.

For centuries doctors believed that blood-letting was a valuable method of treatment for almost all diseases. Using leeches and scarification blades to remove blood from patients was a standard treatment which was popular with the best informed health professionals (both physicians and apothecaries) well into Victorian times and the procedure was used for heart failure, headaches, fever, pneumonia, depression, broken bones and just about everything else imaginable – including, oddly enough, anaemia.

The stick-in-the-mud medical establishment opposed plans for better drains and they sneered at Dr John Snow when he said that people needed cleaner drinking water. The medical establishment opposed anaesthesia, the principle of asepsis and the use of vitamin C to prevent scurvy. Two Australian microbiologists, Barry Marshall and Robin Warren, were ridiculed when they suggested that the bacterium Helicobacter pylori might play a part in the development of peptic ulcers. Eight years later they were awarded the Nobel Prize. And poor Ignaz Semmelweiss went bonkers when his research on puerperal fever was ignored. There are hundreds, probably thousands, of similar examples of the medical establishment getting things completely wrong and promoting procedures which either did no good at all or caused serious harm.

Thomas Huxley once wrote that 'every great advance in natural knowledge has involved the absolute rejection of authority' and it was, of course, George Bernard Shaw who wrote that all professions are conspiracies against the laity, that all great truths begin as blasphemies and that all progress depends upon the unreasonable man.

Voltaire, who had a suitable bon mot or two for almost all circumstances said, very accurately: 'It is dangerous to be right in matters on which the established authorities are wrong.'

To a large extent the problem is that consultants in all fields of medicine have succeeded in establishing that they, and they alone, are the keepers of the sacred flame as far as their own small world is concerned. Neurologists will take no notice of suggestions, however logical and well-based, which come from outside their small (and often outdated) sphere of knowledge. Specialists live in ruts and protect those narrow, well established ruts with parental pride and determination.

Anyone who wishes to question the officially accepted view of some aspect of medicine must place his notions and his discoveries before the sceptical eyes of the specialists within that area. Unfortunately, of course, those specialists will be far more concerned about protecting the status quo (by which I mean their professional status and the profitability of the companies who provide them with free dinners and trips on the Orient Express) than with open-mindedly assessing something new which comes from outside their small circle of knowledge. They will react defensively if there is any criticism of their way of doing things.

The principle of 'peer review' (whereby any new notion or evidence must be assessed, before publication and acceptance, by those within a speciality) sounds like a good idea (and is in so far as it does act as a filter, preventing the acceptance of some of the more outlandish and criminally biased ideas) but the trouble is that the 'peer review' system means that anything truly original which originates outside the system will almost certainly be rejected. New ideas are blocked because they are new and anyone who dares to question the current way of doing things will be vilified, attacked, suppressed, silenced and ostracised. The result is that there isn't much science in medical science.

To all this must be added an often forgotten human factor: we have to remember that, for example, oncologists have spent decades learning about chemotherapy and other specialist areas of medicine. For them to have to accept the fact that their learning is now dangerously out-of-date (and that it is possible that chemotherapy does more harm than good) is nigh on unacceptable.

The other problem is that the institutions which govern the assessment and dissemination of officially accepted knowledge are to a very large extent in thrall to the pharmaceutical industry and the food industry. Moreover, research bodies are invariably dependent either upon government funding or upon money provided by large charities, and both of these are closely allied to the medical establishment and the various powerful industries which have a financial interest in such matters.

Big money can suppress inconvenient information very effectively. The corrupt power of the tobacco industry meant that it took decades for the evidence linking smoking with cancer to be accepted by governments and, more alarming, by the medical establishment.

I am not, by the way, suggesting that this uncomfortable phenomenon is confined to medicine. The failure to comprehend and accept the future when it is thrust into your face is something which is common among experts of every variety. A few years ago, Colin Wilson wrote an excellent book The Outsider, in which he analysed the careers and personalities of many great thinkers who had been ostracised. It isn't difficult to think of contenders. Just about all great artists, writers and inventors, people who revised the way we look at the world or the way we think about it, were criticised or ostracised for their beliefs. Galileo and Copernicus are obvious examples.

And a study of establishment thinking over the centuries shows that the experts are not infrequently embarrassingly wrong. In 1899, the Commissioner of the US Patent Office urged President William McKinley to close down the patent office saying 'everything that can be invented has been invented'. In 1943, the founder of IBM said 'I think there is a world market for about five computers'. In 1929, eminent financiers and economists queued up to announce that there would not be a financial crash. Western Union refused to buy the telephone when it was invented by Alexander Graham Bell – saying that there was no market for the device.

In a number of my books (including Paper Doctors, Betrayal of Trust, The Health Scandal and so on) I described how medical experts proved capable of making terrible diagnostic errors, persisting with useless remedies and denying the effectiveness of medicines which work.

The medical establishment does not like being contradicted – particularly when there are huge sums of money involved.

Thomas Jefferson wrote that: 'A little rebellion now and then is a good thing.'

And maybe we need more of it.

A parcel of books

When I first met him he was 96-years-old and heading steadily towards the receipt of a celebratory telegram from the Queen. He had been born in the 1880s and at the time of his birth his father (who was on his fourth wife) was 78. To my astonishment I realised that meant that his father had been born before the Battle of Trafalgar and before the Big Match between Wellington and Napoleon at Waterloo.

It's strange sometimes to realise just how close we are to what we think of as distant history.

I remember being shocked when I first learned that T.E.Lawrence, better known perhaps as Lawrence of Arabia, had died not all that long before I was born. When I was small I had assumed that Lawrence was some figure from the distant past, and probably not real at that. To a small boy Lawrence of Arabia was in the same sort of category as Robin Hood, the Green Knight and Lancelot.

Mr Robbins, my 96-year-old patient was a large man, imposing and elegant. He could have been an ambassador to a small country or a head waiter. You can't always tell what people have done with their lives just by looking at them. I once met a patient who appeared to have all the airs, manners and style of a high court judge. He had, however, spent his working life as a gentleman's gentleman, a valet, working for three generations of the aristocracy.

I remember that Mr Robbins had very bushy eyebrows which went up in the centre of his forehead, up towards what had once been his hairline, with the result that he looked constantly startled, not unpleasantly so, but just startled as though he had just seen or heard something rather surprising. He also had patrician, white hair, with what was left of it now combed straight back and nestling on his collar.

I found him fascinating to talk to. He had been a barrister, specialising in some arcane and doubtless profitable corner of taxation law though, thankfully, we never talked about that, and

148

sometimes talked in short speeches, seemingly not expecting me to comment.

'I have had a comfortable life,' he once told me, in a reflective mood. 'Always found life easy. I never tried hard, so never achieved anything much, certainly not as much as I should have done. My father always complained that I was born idle; always did what I needed to do and no more. I've always been careful and always behaved and consequently never had much to worry about. I always thought that worry was just interest on an un-payable debt. But these days I worry more than I ever did. I seem to worry about everything, perhaps because with age you get to know how easily and frequently things can go wrong. If I have to go somewhere I worry whether the taxi will arrive or if the train will be cancelled. So now I don't go anywhere much. It's easier than having to worry. But why should I go anywhere?' he asked, not expecting a reply. 'I'm already where I want to be.'

He and his wife, who was 92 and as sharp as a boy scout's pocket knife, lived alone in a rambling old manor house which had ill-fitting windows and ill-fitting doors and was, consequently, equipped with more than a reasonable assortment of draughts. A woman in her sixties came in every day to do shopping, cooking and cleaning. And a man who I knew was in his mid-eighties, because he too was a patient of mine, looked after the garden; cutting grass, pruning, trimming, lopping and doing daring things with power tools that always seemed far too heavy for him to handle safely. I once watched in horror as he climbed a tree to chop off a dead branch. He couldn't carry the chainsaw as he climbed so he tied the chainsaw to a piece of rope, took the rope up with him and then hauled the chainsaw aloft. I should have tried to stop him but he wouldn't have taken any notice and why should he have done?

I used to go and see the old barrister once a month to check his heart which had been, in his words, 'a bit dicky' for 30 years or more. He got palpitations regularly and sometimes his heart would fibrillate. He'd been tested thoroughly and no one could find a reason so he just put up with it. I don't think it troubled him a good deal. Two consultants had wanted to put him on pills but he didn't want to take pills so he didn't. Despite the slight and newly acquired tendency to worry, to which he confessed, he was fairly laid back and relaxed. I don't think he was a man anyone argued with. He said he thought a man could get used to anything if he just put it to the back of his mind and adjusted his life accordingly.

After I'd listened to his heart and taken his blood pressure we always had a cup of lapsong souchong tea and talked about books and authors. He loved books and his study, where he spent most of his waking hours, was lined from floor to ceiling with book shelves. The shelves were packed with books which he filed upside down, so that the upper spines were never damaged when a book was pulled off the shelf. He said he could read upside down as well as he could read things that were the right way up. It was a trick, he confessed, which he'd learned so that when being briefed he could read the notes in the file of the solicitor sitting opposite him. Most of the books were autobiographies and most of the autobiographies were travel books. He had an encyclopaedic knowledge of explorers and adventurers.

I turned up at his home one day and he immediately pointed to an unopened box on a nearby table. 'My wife will come in shortly to see if you think I'll make it to the weekend,' he said. 'While she's here I'm going to tell her that you've very generously bought me a box of books you thought I might like.'

Puzzled, I looked at the box of books. There was a label on the box with the name of a London firm of specialist auctioneers on it.

'You'd better tear the label off,' he said.

I tore off the label.

'My wife thinks I've got enough books,' he said in what he probably thought was a whisper. 'I love her very much and have done so for 50 years and change, but she doesn't understand books. How can a man have enough books?'

I nodded. I knew what he meant.

'She says I won't live long enough to read books as fast as I buy them,' he said. 'But that's not the point. I like having them around me. I like flicking through them and snacking on the contents.' He stopped again for a moment. 'She thinks I'm getting old,' he said.

I raised an eyebrow.

'When I reached 80 I realised that I was drifting unstoppably into the lower reaches of middle age,' he said. 'And I accept that I'm now about to move onto the next stage of my life. But I don't feel old so I can't be, can I?'

I agreed with him, checked his pulse, took his blood pressure and reassured him.

When his wife came in with a pot of tea, two cups and a pile of home-made madeleine cakes, we went through our little charade. (Despite the time of day, she wore a good deal of jewellery, most of which sparkled. The consequence was to me she looked for all the world as if she'd dressed up to go to a fancy dress party as a chandelier. At first I assumed that the jewellery was the sort of cheap stuff that is sold on street market stalls. It was only later that I realised that it was all real. And why shouldn't she wear it? I doubted if she got many chances to wear it at balls or dinner parties.)

He pretended I'd brought him a box of books and I pretended I'd brought them. He opened the box (which was packed with some ridiculously valuable volumes) and oohed and aahed and his wife looked at and smiled faintly. My battered truck was parked outside. She knew darned well that I couldn't have afforded to buy that boxful of books.

'My father had the same problem with my mother,' he said, when his wife had disappeared. 'He collected books too and spent far too much on building up his library. He had the bookseller send books to him in boxes labelled 'fertiliser'. My mother, who could be surprisingly earthy when the fancy took her, used to say it was all just my father's usual horse-shit.'

When I left he insisted on giving me a first edition of a biography of Macnair Wilson's biography of Sir James Mackenzie. It was one of the books he took out of the box.

'I ordered this for you,' he told me. 'I've already got a copy. Put it in your bag.'

I thanked him and managed to squeeze the book into my black bag.

A blush

I was a medical student performing my very first vaginal examination. No one had told me what to do. I knew nothing. You cannot believe how much nothing I knew. It was a ward for gynaecology patients.

I introduced myself to the patient. She was about 25-years-old and wearing a pretty blue nightie. She smiled, and looked a little nervous, as patients do when approached by someone in a white coat. She would have known I was a medical student because of the colour of my name badge. Actually, she would have known I was a medical student by the look of sheer terror I was struggling, and failing, to hide.

I drew the curtains around her bed and put a packet of disposable gloves, and various other bits of equipment down on the bedside table. I then removed my white coat and laid it on the foot of bed. I have no idea why I did this.

And then, for absolutely no reason that I can think of, I rolled up my shirt sleeves and removed my watch. Both shirt sleeves were neatly rolled to just below my elbows.

Why would I do that? What was I thinking? I have no idea. Maybe I'd watched a TV programme about vets and farm animals. I just don't know.

'I just have to examine you,' I said. 'Internally.' My shirt felt damp at the back.

I remember that the young woman in bed watched me with increasing alarm. 'How far up are you going?' she asked, nervously. She had gone very pale.

I blushed and couldn't think of a thing to say. I rolled my sleeves back down.

But I suddenly remembered that I am right handed and that my watch had been on my left wrist. I picked up the watch and put it back on.

'It'll be all right,' she said gently. She threw back the covers and pulled up her nightie.

152

There are moments which stay with us forever.

In the shadow of the Third Man

I told the beginning of the following story in the most recent editions of my book 'Bodypower'. But without the beginning, the rest of the story won't make a good deal of sense so if you have read something similar to the following few paragraphs in an edition of 'Bodypower' please bear with me for a few moments.

In the autumn of 1980 I went to Vienna. It wasn't the best time to be in the Austrian capital and it wasn't the warmest autumn in history. In fact, the weather was freezing cold and I'd made the mistake of taking with me a thin, English raincoat. The coat was fairly waterproof but not the slightest bit windproof and the wind cut through the material as if it weren't there. I walked with my shoulders hunched and my hands stuffed deep inside the coat pockets. Even so my fingers felt numb. I was so cold that I could hardly think; even my brain felt frozen. I was shivering.

I had walked to the area around the Prater Amusement Park (where the big wheel is situated – the one made famous in the film 'The Third Man' when Orson Wells and Joseph Cotton take a ride together) and it was dusk. The skies were dark with rain to come and in the early evening gloom the bright lights of the cafes seemed especially warm and promising. Vienna has cafés in plenty. London may have invented the café but the cafes of Vienna and Paris have carried on the tradition. I paused outside a particularly attractive looking café and through the open curtains I could see the dark wooden tables and chairs, the racks of newspapers neatly folded around wooden sticks and the plump, bosomy Austrian waitress hurrying about with vast cups of cream-topped coffee and slices of rich torte.

I went in, found a table near to the window and sat down. Inside the cafe it was cosy and comfortable. Old-fashioned radiators and a log stove gurgled pleasantly and the air smelt of ground coffee beans and rich chocolate cake. The waitress approached and smiled at me. I gave her my order, took my hands out of my pockets and tried to rub them together. They were white with cold and I could hardly move my fingers.

I cupped my hands, held them up to my face and blew on them. Slowly the feeling came back into them and slowly the colour returned. Gingerly I flexed and extended my fingers; gradually I regained the movement I had lost. As I watched my frozen fingers changing colour I suddenly became aware of something that was to change my life. I suddenly became conscious of the remarkable powers of the human body to adapt itself to cope with its environment. Outside in the bitterly cold autumn air the blood had left my fingers to reduce the amount of heat lost in order to try to maintain my internal body temperature. My body had been prepared to sacrifice my fingers to save itself. Inside, in the warmth of the cafe, the blood had rushed back into my hands. Once my body's internal thermometer had recognised that the temperature inside the cafe was warm my body no longer had to fight to keep me alive.

I felt the shivering stop and slipped off my coat. I picked up the coffee which the waitress had brought me and held my head in the steam rising from it.

I'd been qualified as a doctor for ten years and for most of that time I'd been working as a General Practitioner in a small town in central England. To begin with I'd enjoyed the work I did, but for several years I'd been growing more and more worried by the fact that too often I was finding myself interfering with illnesses when it seemed to me that my patients would probably get better by themselves if only I and they were prepared to wait.

Sitting in that cafe in Vienna, with my thawing hands wrapped around a steaming cup of coffee, I realized that the human body has far more extensive, protective and self-healing powers than we give it credit for. I realized that all of us, doctors and patients, tend to be too quick to rush for the medicine cabinet when things go wrong. I remembered a book I'd read when I was at medical school. Called 'The Wisdom of the Body', it was written in 1932 by a physiologist called W. B. Cannon, who believed that the body's abilities to protect itself from change and threat are comprehensive and far-reaching. And I remembered conversations I'd had with a friend, Tony Sharrock, who was convinced that too often doctors ignore the fact that in illness the body knows best.

I took out my notebook and pencil (for years I have never gone anywhere without both) and immediately wrote down the outline for

155

a book I knew I wanted to write. I called it 'Listen to Your Body' (though I later changed the title to 'Bodypower'). I wanted to try to teach doctors as well as patients that the human body has far-reaching powers that we ignore far too often. I wanted to try to persuade patients to learn to listen to their own bodies and to avoid interfering with their bodies unless absolutely necessary. I wanted to teach doctors that they should not always assume that whenever illness strikes intervention is essential. I wanted to show both patients and doctors that we all underestimate the remarkable healing powers of the human body.

It was one of those moments which happen rarely in our lives but which, when they do, are never to be forgotten. Sometimes, of course, those revelatory moments are so dramatic that they change the way people think. Isaac Newton sits under the apple tree and an apple falls. Galileo, in church, watches a clock pendulum swing. Fleming notices a change on a Petri dish. Rontgen spots the effect which will give us X-rays. I'm not comparing my revelation to those discoveries but you can, I hope, see what I mean. There are hundreds of such moments in our lives and most great and not so great discoveries can be traced back to a single incident or observation. The trouble is that most of the time we don't notice the revelation; usually because we're too busy doing something else (probably something unimportant).

I always think that a physician called William Withering provides us with one of the best examples of the importance of keeping our eyes open.

It is Withering who is credited with discovering the use of digitalis from the foxglove in the treatment of dropsy (the oedema caused by heart disease).

In 1776 William Withering, an English physician, described how he had learned about the effectiveness of the foxglove plant in the treatment of dropsy or ankle oedema, now known to be a major symptom of heart failure. Withering had learned about the usefulness of foxglove leaves from an old lady he had met on the way to Shropshire. On his outward journey Withering saw an old lady sitting outside her cottage. She had badly swollen legs. On his return journey he saw the same lady but now her legs were normal. He had the wit to stop and question her. He found that she had been treated by a local wise-woman with a herbal medicine made from the foxglove plant. (Many of these women, who were for most people the only 'doctors' available, were drowned or burnt as witches. The trials conducted by the witch finders were particularly cruel. Women suspected of being witches were dunked in the village pond, or some other suitable piece of water. If they drowned then they were innocent. If they didn't drown then they were clearly guilty and they were burnt.)

The drug Withering 'discovered', known today as digitalis, is still one of the most important weapons in the treatment of heart disease.

It seems that the foxglove had been known to be effective in the treatment of dropsy for several centuries. Withering's contribution was to evaluate the product and to describe in some detail the potential hazards that might be associated with the drug's misuse. He had no way of studying the drug's full effect, or of determining the precise way in which it worked, but his papers were among the first to include as precise an assessment as possible of a drug's potential pharmacological power.

When I was at medical school there was a small, out of the way library dedicated to William Withering. I think I was pretty well the only person ever to use it. It was a joy to have a whole library to myself.

Anyway, to get back to my story, a few days later I got back home full of excitement. I wanted to write the book and change the world.

Naturally, it wasn't quite that easy.

I sent the outline to my then literary agent with a letter that was bursting with enthusiasm. She was far less impressed than I had hoped she would be. She wrote back to me arguing that 'the serious illnesses people have nowadays simply wouldn't heal themselves, so there's a limit to how useful this process can be'. I was frustrated almost beyond belief. That was exactly the attitude I was so desperate to change.

The truth is that most illnesses are not serious but are treated as if they are. I insisted that the idea was relevant and valid and that the only way to put forward the idea was to write a book about it, explaining the remarkable self-healing powers of the human body and showing exactly how those powers could be harnessed.

With, I suspect, some reluctance my agent sent the outline out to one or two publishers. They returned it without any enthusiasm.

Throughout the early part of 1981 the outline was rejected as irrelevant, impossible or impractical by half the publishers in London.

But my life had already changed irrevocably. In the summer of 1981 I resigned from the National Health Service and decided to become a full-time professional writer. (I have explained why I resigned in 'Memories 1', the first volume in this series.) And the more time I spent researching material for the book I now called 'Bodypower' the more convinced I was that leaving general practice had been the right thing to do; I could not justify the work I was doing as a GP. As a practising doctor I just did not have the time to explain to my patients why I didn't always want to give them prescriptions. I needed to stand outside everyday practice in order to spread the philosophy that seemed to me to be so important.

I didn't really have much choice about leaving the NHS (they wanted me to break my unwritten contract of confidentiality with my patients) but leaving the NHS wasn't the wrench I'd thought it might be. I missed my patients desperately but I didn't miss the NHS bureaucrats. My last few months of existence as a GP were a constant battle.

It wasn't until 1982 that I found a publisher prepared to commission the book. I was having dinner with Jamie Camplin of Thames and Hudson to celebrate the launch of my book 'The Good Medicine Guide' when I managed to persuade him that the principles behind 'Bodypower' were not only sound but that they also merited a wider audience. Mr Camplin agreed to publish the book and the dream I'd had in that cafe in Vienna two and a half years earlier had been fulfilled. The philosophy I described in 'Bodypower' changed my life, and has influenced everything I've written about medicine since 1980. It has also influenced hundreds of medical writers, thousands of doctors and millions of patients. I'm proud that the 'Bodypower' philosophy is now widely acknowledged and accepted.

When new books are published it is customary for publishers or agents (depending upon who controls the rights) to send copies to newspapers and magazines in the hope that one (or more) will want to buy serial rights. What this means is that the publication will pay for the right to publish material from the book. The word 'serial' doesn't mean that more than one extract will be published. When a publication buys first serial rights they usually have the right to publish their selected extracts before the book is published. A publication which buys second serial rights usually has to wait until after the buyer of the first serial rights has taken and published what they want from the book, and they are usually only allowed to publish whatever they buy after the book has been published. (These rules vary and there are no hard and fast rules.) Sometimes a number of periodicals in a number of countries will want to buy serial rights and the amount of money paid will far exceed the amount of money that the publisher and the author can expect to make from sales of the book. For some reason which I never entirely understood, newspaper editors will pay a lot of money to take a few thousand words out of a book than they pay for a specially written article written by the same author. It is usually books by celebrities which attract the big money – particularly what are known as 'kiss and tell' books. The authors and publishers of political memoirs tend to make far more money out of serial rights than out of book sales. And, of course, if extracts from a book appear widely the demand for the book itself will be dramatically reduced.

Before 'Bodypower' was published, the first serial rights were bought by a British newspaper called the Sunday Mirror which, at the time, had a huge circulation, selling several million copies a week. A number of other publications, including several big selling UK magazines and a dazzling number of newspapers and magazines in other countries, also bought serial rights. Newspapers and magazines had much bigger circulations then than they have now.

The features editor of the Sunday Mirror at the time was a journalist called Robert Wilson who had published three science fiction novels and was, surprisingly, a fan of Nietzsche, the eccentric German philosopher and philologist. At that time, in the 1980s, most journalists working in Fleet Street drank a great deal of alcohol and many of them were chain smokers. Since they had seemingly unlimited access to expense money they could indulge these two hobbies at their publisher's expense. I think I only ever knew one smoking journalist who gave up his tobacco. The daily stress meant that they never had an opportunity to survive without a nicotine hit and most newsrooms were thick with cigarette smoke. The single exception smoked at least 60 unfiltered cigarettes a day (to help his nerves) and gave up cigarettes overnight. Six weeks later he had a massive heart attack and died. Your guess is as good as mine as to whether he would have died sooner or later if he had kept on smoking.

For a week or two I travelled to London regularly to talk to Robert about how best to utilise the book as a series of newspaper articles. Right from the start he realised that he could get several weeks' worth of material from the book, though even I do not think he realised just how much material he would eventually use.

The first week's serialisation was a huge success. The paper's circulation rose considerably and the paper's marketing experts insisted that it was the material from 'Bodypower' which was responsible. (Newspaper marketing departments look carefully at which parts of a paper are popular.) Naturally, the editor decided to promote the next week's serialisation very heavily. The paper bought TV advertising, had special T-shirts printed and promoted the book on massive posters stuck up on bus shelters and hoardings.

The serialisation went on for longer than anyone had expected and I confess it was quite exciting to see the paper's sales rising. On Saturday evenings I was often in London waiting for the first run of the paper to be printed and sold on the streets. In the pub which was patronised by the Sunday Mirror staff, the editors and feature editors of other tabloid newspapers would stare with ill-disguised envy at Robert as he boasted of the following day's extract and the boost to the circulation which they expected.

After the publication of extracts from 'Bodypower' had finished (the paper had published almost everything in the book – plus some extra material which I wrote especially), I wrote a number of articles for the Sunday Mirror, and Robert and I became good friends. I used to travel up to London by train and think up some feature ideas on the way. We would have lunch together and I would explain my ideas. He would commission them (for what now seem outrageous fees) and I would write the articles on the train journey home. A fee of £10,000 or £20,000 for an article wasn't exceptional. Things were different in those days. I gather that today, editors will expect to pay no more than £100 or £200 for a page article and even less for material published online. I strongly suspect that the fees were reduced to dumb down the editorial content and to ensure that experienced writers were replaced with teenagers. Newspapers used to have filing cabinets full of articles which had been bought but which were never used but Robert always used what I gave him and that pleased me more than the money.

Robert came to my house a couple of times (before he caught the train he packed his case with 200 cigarettes and a couple of bottles of gin to sustain him for the two and a half hour journey) and in London we had lunch together often. I would never drink more than a few glasses of wine but I don't have much of a head for booze and so I'd be woozy. Robert, on the other hand, would empty two or three bottles and seem totally sober. Head waiters and wine waiters everywhere knew him and smiled genuine smiles when they saw him. In posh restaurants he'd order steak and then ask for two slices of bread and make himself a steak sandwich. The first time he did this he asked my permission, which I thought was rather sweet.

I liked him very much and then one day he was fired by the Sunday Mirror. I think they were cost cutting, and hiring younger, more sober journalists saved huge amounts of money. They probably referred to it as 'letting him go to explore new professional opportunities'.

As an aside, it was, I believe, this policy which helped destroy the credibility of the press. Young people in any profession need mentors and the youngsters who find themselves with jobs on a national newspaper, and who are inevitably well endowed with the insolence of youth, are too likely to editorialise when they are supposed to be reporting. In 1909, Lord Northcliffe sacked a journalist (the editor's sister as it happens) for introducing her own views into an article in one of his papers. It is difficult these days to find a mainstream newspaper article which does not contain the views and prejudices of the writer. This is particularly true of articles published on the internet sites of newspapers.

I saw Robert a couple of times after that but he had changed a good deal. He kept working, writing travel articles for magazines and doing some editing, but he had lost his spark. The drink had begun to affect him. He developed the shakes and he was embarrassed and uncomfortable about the fact that his good days in Fleet Street had obviously gone for good. I tried to keep in touch but he didn't return calls and when he did he seemed diffident and didn't really want to meet. By then I had a column in another national newspaper and I think he found it difficult to accept that when we had a drink or a meal he no longer had a thick roll of brown drinking vouchers (ten pound notes handed out as expenses by the Sunday

Mirror's accounts department) stuffed in his pocket. He'd fallen on comparatively hard times and he was very proud. I don't think he wanted to be reminded of what had been his glory days. He was always impeccably dressed in an elegant two piece suit, dress shirt and tie but the suits became a little older and a little shabbier perhaps. He was the first man who ever hugged me. Whenever we met or parted he would throw his arms around me and give me a massive hug.

Today, I can't think about 'Bodypower' without thinking of Robert with great regret. In the end we drifted apart and lost touch and when I tried to find him after a gap of a few months I discovered that he had died. I'm not surprised. He drank and smoked far too much and he lived longer than most Fleet Street journalists. (At one time the average age of death among Fleet Street journalists was just over 40.)

Just before I wrote this piece for this book I found a quote from the legendary A.J.Liebling who was a staff writer on the New Yorker magazine in its heyday. The editor then was the equally legendary Harold Ross (about whom the even more equally legendary James Thurber wrote a wonderful book).

'I wish I had told him how much I liked him,' wrote Liebling about Ross.

And I knew what he meant.

I wish I had told Robert Wilson how much I liked him – not because of the boost he gave to 'Bodypower' (helping to make it my first Sunday Times bestseller) and not because of the number of times he hired me to write articles and not because of his smile, his stories, his wisdom, his wit and his warm humanity but because I just liked him, damnit. He could be like a little boy sometimes. Celebrities, particularly in the pop world, would telephone him to promote some film or record and he would be wonderfully excited when he'd put the phone down. 'Do you know who that was?' he'd ask, with a huge grin.

I liked him and I like to think he knew.

They don't make them like that anymore and now they never will. The world grows darker, the night grows longer and the end seems nearer when good people die.

And 'Bodypower'?

Well, I have regularly collected new evidence showing the

162

remarkable powers of the human body. There has been evidence from scientists around the world showing that the power of the body and the mind is greater than anyone could have dreamt a mere decade ago. We are influenced so much by everything we've seen or felt or thought. After all, dreams are just bits and pieces gathered from your personal psychological dustbin but you can learn a lot looking through someone's dustbin. I wrote a sequel to 'Bodypower' and called it 'Mindpower' and then wrote a sequel to 'Mindpower' and called that book 'Spiritpower'.

Researchers have shown that crying helps the body get rid of harmful waste material. It has been shown that tears shed because of emotional feelings, contain more protein than tears shed because of irritation. When you are upset and you cry your body is getting rid of unwanted and dangerous wastes. Researchers have also shown that during the last three months of pregnancy, and for the twelve months after a pregnancy has ended, a mother's lips produce sexually attractive chemicals designed to make her lips more kissable. Sebaceous glands along the borders of the newborn baby's lips produce similar chemicals and help ensure that the baby responds to its mother's kisses in an appropriate way.

Newspaper stories have supported the 'Bodypower' theory too. Soon after 'Bodypower' was published I read about a farm worker who had been involved in a horrific accident. He carried his severed arm for a mile in order to get help. His arm was then sewn back on by a surgeon at a nearby hospital. And I read of an 87-year-old widow who knotted sheets together and climbed out of her first floor window in order to escape from a fire. In both these cases the human body found resources that no one would have thought could exist.

Most exciting of all, perhaps, has been the response from the medical profession. When 'Bodypower' was first published the response from some parts of the medical establishment was cool. Doctors have for decades been taught that in order to beat disease they have to interfere with nature. The medical profession has grown in strength alongside the drugs industry; thousands of doctors have been taught that a doctor's first response to any illness must always be to reach for his prescription pad. But that has changed a little. Not enough, but a little. More and more often the medical journals now contain articles written by doctors explaining how they have discovered that it isn't always necessary to interfere when a patient falls ill; that the body can often look after itself; that the body's defence mechanisms and self-healing mechanisms are far more sophisticated than they had been taught and that the power of the human mind is far greater than anyone would have dared suggest just ten years ago.

In 1983 the philosophy behind 'Bodypower' seemed new and slightly frightening to many people. Some thought it threatening, a few even suggested that it was heresy to suggest that in 90 per cent of all illnesses there was no need for a professional healer, that the body could look after itself perfectly well. Today the philosophy described in 'Bodypower' is more widely accepted. It has not halted the march of modern interventionism but it has, perhaps, caused some of those who lead the march to break step. From the letters I have received I know that it has encouraged many to be prepared to take advantage of their bodies' own healing processes and to regard illness as something to be conquered in partnership with the help of healers (whether orthodox or alternative) rather than as something to be handed over completely to the professionals. Forty years after its publication there are still new editions coming out around the world and the book still sells thousands of copies a year.

Publishers, of course, haven't been quite so sympathetic. Three UK publishers let it go out of print when they'd sold all the copies they'd printed. I happily took the rights back and published it myself. 'Bodypower' was a big hit in the 1980s and 1990s but now, four decades later, it still sells over 2,000 copies a year in the English language alone and I'm still selling more foreign rights. Not many 40-year-old non-fiction books are still loved so much by readers. I'm proud of Bodypower and remember that freezing day in Vienna with increasing affection. I'm proud too that readers of an influential publication called 'The Good Book Guide' voted the book one of their 100 favourite books.

I fell in love with the theme and I suppose, in a way, I've fallen in love with the book.

Losing sight of the shore

'Man cannot discover new oceans unless he has the courage to lose sight of the shore,' wrote Andre Gide.

Maybe we need more courage in denying and rejecting our accepted ideas in order to make room for new notions.

Too many boxes, not enough receipts

Why anyone would want to be a GP without doing home visits is a mystery to me. And why they would prefer to be available for the same sort of hours (or, actually, for fewer) than a librarian or an accountant, is another mystery. It's a bit like becoming a racing driver and then vowing to spend all your time sitting in your racing car while it is parked in the garage. Or become a jockey and only sitting on the horse when he is in his stable.

I admit that I got tired doing night calls and visits. And I undoubtedly got crotchety. If I'd been up most of the night and had managed to get back into my bed at 6.30 am, hoping to get an hour's sleep before it was time to get up for the morning surgery, I would probably not be all sweetness and light if I'd then been telephoned by someone wanting to arrange for a repeat prescription for their skin cream.

After a very busy night on call I remember being called at six am by a girl who wanted a prescription for her contraceptive pills. She was going on holiday that day and had realised at the last moment that she was running out of pills. Her boyfriend became very aggressive when I'd suggested, holding in my weariness and my anger, that she meet me at my surgery premises just before the morning surgery started. He insisted that I visit because that was more convenient for them. And so I did so because in those circumstances it is easier to give in than to spend the next year and a half attending disciplinary hearings where I would have to defend my reluctance to visit the patient. I honestly don't think I ever lost my temper with a patient or a relative of a patient – not even with the selfish and the unreasonable – but this incident was probably as close as I got to showing my anger. Patients who are ill (or who just think they are ill) are always frightened and often edgy. The people who are just rude and demanding are just rude and demanding and best ignored. I always tried to follow the simple rule of treating all the patients I saw in the same way that I would like my own loved ones to be treated.

How often do things like that happen, how often are people that demanding and unreasonable? Not often; rare enough for me to remember. And when they are demanding and 'entitled' they always know the rules and regulations and they have the complaints procedure engraved on a piece of cold steel placed where their hearts should be.

Sometimes the nights and weekends were so busy that you'd eventually begin to wonder if there was anyone left that you hadn't seen. It's difficult then to remain professional. But you do it because it's what you've chosen to do. Some weekends in the winter I would literally lose count of the number of patients I saw – particularly over Christmas.

I'm very well aware that there can be a downside to providing a 24 hour a day service for 365 days a year. And I know very well that visiting patients at home can be inconvenient and even potentially dangerous. You'd probably be surprised to know how many feral dogs there are roaming around blocks of flats. And you'd be equally surprised to know how often the lift doesn't work in blocks of flats. This can be a pain when the block of flats is 16 storeys high and your patient (inevitably) lives on the top floor. It's even more of a pain when you have walked down all those flights of stairs and you remember that you've left your stethoscope behind.

Visiting patients who live in a deserted cottage on a pleasant summer evening can be fine but visiting those same patients on a dark, stormy night can be something very different. It can be doubly difficult if you don't know where to find the cottage. And even more tricky if the cottage is inaccessible in a car. And you have to cross a muddy field to get there. And there are cows in the field. Or a bull.

Of course, a dark and stormy night is nothing compared to hunting for a house which has a name and not a number on a foggy night. And if you want real excitement then you should try visiting somewhere you've never been before on a night when there is fog and snow. It's even better fun if you're driving a two wheel drive car without chains on the wheels. Doing home visits in town can be tricky in the day time when it has been snowing. I once parked a two wheel drive motorcar on ice outside a patient's house and came out twenty minutes later to find that the car had gone. A neighbour kindly told me that I could find my car on the front lawn of a neighbour seven houses away. The handbrake was still on when I found the car and the owner of the lawn was, fortunately, a patient of mine and very understanding about her flattened hedge and rose bushes. 'I'd been meaning to have that silly hedge taken out,' she said. After that I learned to park on snowy hills with my car in gear and the front wheels turned in towards the kerb. If there was no kerb I parked at the bottom of the hill and walked up.

But in the days when I practised I never knew a GP who would have had things any other way. Doing home visits and night visits was considered an essential part of being a GP. I once had an elderly partner who was hardly able to get in and out of his car. He still visited his patients at home though I remember that on one occasion his back and his hips were giving him so much trouble that he had to conduct at least one consultation from the bottom of a patient's stairs.

And I learned how to deal with the television set.

When I first became a GP I was shocked at the number of times I visited houses where the television was switched on and blaring away at full blast. Sometimes a member of the family would be watching it. And sometimes there would be no one watching. During any evening and on Saturday and Sunday afternoons there would often be a man in a vest sitting in front of the TV set. And in the mornings and weekday afternoons there would frequently be two, three or more children sitting transfixed on the floor a couple of feet away from the television set.

At first I would politely ask for the sound to be turned down – especially if I needed to examine a patient and listen to their chest.

One of my partners, a gentle man with rather more experience of such matters, laughed when I told him about a particularly annoying incident where I'd had to struggle to examine a baby while the father continued to watch a football match with the sound on full volume. In the end I'd had to conclude my examination in the hallway.

And he told me how to deal with the television set problem. (I should point out that I am talking about some time ago when television sets were rather different and had buttons with which the owner could control the colour, the contrast and the volume as well as the channel.)

'When you go into the room where there is a television set switched on you walk straight to it and turn it off. But you don't just turn it off – you struggle to find the right button. And you turn and press every button you can find. As you do this the owner of the television set will put down his can of beer and struggle to leave his armchair. But he will be too late. By the time he reaches the television set you will have changed every setting on the set. And it will take hours to set up everything correctly again. When you visit that house again you will find that the television set will have been switched off – and if it hasn't then the minute you walk through the door the man in the vest will have put down his can of beer and will be racing across the room to get there before you do.'

It was, quite possibly, the second best piece of advice about general practice that I ever received.

(The best piece of advice was to visit the local estate agency every six months or so and pick up a copy of a local map. They always have up-to-date maps which show the latest housing estates and planned developments.)

And, of course, some people are just plain, old-fashioned rude. I once visited a girl in her early twenties who had abdominal pain. When I entered the room her boyfriend was playing his guitar. (The word 'playing' is a euphemism for 'making a noise with' it.) As I struggled to examine her and listen to her answers to my questions the boyfriend, who seemed oblivious to my presence, continued to make noises which he may, or may not have, regarded as music. My requests that he at least go into another room were met with incredulity and then abuse.

You never knew what you were going to find when you visited someone else's home as a doctor. If an estate agent visits a house the place will have been tidied up and smelling of coffee or hotpot. If relatives visit, the magazines and books will have been put in their place and the toys will have been put away. But a doctor gets things in the raw and has to deal with the standard domestic confusions created by dogs and small children. You learn to tread over the toys on the driveway and cluttering the hall. You learn to be careful where you sit and you learn how to say 'no, thank you' very politely when you're offered a cup of tea in a dirty cup taken from the selection waiting to be washed up. (I had one patient who always tried to force me to accept a cup of tea. He was an impatient man who always made lukewarm tea because he never had the patience to wait for the kettle to boil. He also had an apparently unending supply of very stale biscuits. I can understand how someone could have one packet of stale biscuits but I could never understand how it could be possible to possess nothing but stale biscuits.) In the bedroom you learn to avoid treading on discarded clothing and slippers and you don't feel shy about asking for a fresh towel if you need to perform an examination requiring more than laying a stethoscope on a chest.

I visited a house once which was full of cardboard boxes. You doubtless assume that the word 'full' is an exaggeration; an expression of artistic licence.

It isn't.

The house was as full of cardboard boxes as a house can be without gluing them to the ceiling.

There were boxes in the hallway (that I had to clamber over) and as I passed along the hall I couldn't help noticing that the living room was packed with boxes. There were cardboard boxes on the floor, on the sofa and sitting on all the chairs. It was the same thing in the kitchen. There were boxes on the table and on the floor.

I walked up the stairs behind the mistress of the house; a forty something woman who, even though it was late morning, was still in her nightie and dressing gown. The dressing gown was pink and so were the fluffy mules she was wearing on her feet. What I could see of the nightie was also pink. When she stood she did so with a wide-legged, solid stance and when she walked she did so like a woman, who was no stranger to the obstetrics ward and the delivery room. Or, perhaps, someone on their first day of a sea cruise on a small boat without stabilisers. She seemed proud and naturally comfortable with her femininity, and rather stately – a tricky impression to pull off when you're dressed entirely in pink and wearing fluffy mules.

Climbing the stairs was a challenge because there was a cardboard box balanced on each tread. The boxes were wider than the treads so each box rested on the box below it and the box on the bottom tread rested on a box on the floor. The boxes were higher than the treads so this meant that all the boxes were balanced at an uncomfortable angle.

'Mind the boxes,' said Mrs Onions as we neared the top of the staircase, though it was a little late by then.

There were boxes on the landing, too. And there were boxes in the bedroom where Mr Onions was lying flat on his back in bed. I think I knew what was wrong with him before I even saw him.

'It's my back, doctor,' he said, not moving an inch.

'Let me guess,' I said. 'You've been moving boxes?'

He smiled but it was the hollow sort of smile that people produce when they don't feel like smiling but think they should.

Suddenly, I heard a commotion downstairs. It sounded as though someone had fallen over in the hallway. There was some swearing, which came from a male voice belonging to someone who was exceptionally adept at expressing anger through words.

'I'm sorry, doctor, I better go and see him,' said Mrs Onions. She turned to her husband. 'That'll be Paul,' she said. 'He said he'd come round and pick up half a dozen.'

'I take it the boxes are heavy,' I said, when Mrs Onions had gone.

'I thought I could store them all in the garage,' he said. 'But I filled the garage and the garden shed. I had to put the mower outside. You can't stack them because the boxes aren't strong enough.'

'What's in them?' I asked.

'Television sets,' he told me. '180 brand new television sets.'

I muttered something non-committal. I'm afraid I assumed that the televisions had probably been acquired illegally. Most people who buy 180 brand new television sets have a shop or a warehouse.

'The pain came on after all the lifting?' I asked him.

'During it,' he replied. 'It was bringing these upstairs that finally did me. The wife brought the last half dozen upstairs.'

His wife, she of the pink mules, was a muscular woman; taller, wider and stronger than most men. She was an artist. She painted men and always painted them in various stages of distress. Some of the men she painted had axes in their skulls. Some had knives stuck in their chests. And some had what looked like bullet wounds. Half were dead and half were alive and, judging by their facial expressions, the ones who were alive were in excruciating pain. It wasn't difficult to suspect that she harboured a dislike of men. A year or so later she complained that she had never sold a picture and regarded this failure as a sign that she was one of those artistic geniuses who, like van Gogh would not be discovered until a century or so after her death.

Her brother, I remember, was also a patient of mine. He was waiting for a living transplant. He and his wife never left their home in case the hospital rang with news that a suitable liver had been found. He kept a bag ready packed in case he needed to go to the hospital at a moment's notice. I confess I thought it was a terrible

171

way to have to live.

I examined Mr Onions, told him he'd simply strained some muscles and joints, prescribed some simple painkillers and advised him to keep warm. 'A hot bath will help,' I said. 'And a couple of hot water bottles.'

'Can I have a note for work?' he asked. 'I'll never be able to get in to work this week.'

'What's your job?' I asked, taking an official sick notepad out of my black bag.

'I'm a policeman,' he replied, rather to my surprise.

'Well, when you move your television sets I suggest you either get some help or borrow a sack truck. And remember to bend at the knees!'

'I won't have to move them all at once again,' he said. 'They'll be going out in ones and twos. A couple of blokes have bought half a dozen each. But you can't get more than four in an ordinary car.'

I nodded. I was still puzzled.

'They're not stolen by the way,' he said, obviously reading my mind. 'The police auction off lost property and stuff where the owner can't be identified. These were in an auction last week and I got the lot dirt cheap. They're supposed to be the latest thing in television technology – made by a big Japanese company.'

'I hope you manage to sell them all quickly!' I said.

'I can let you have one for half the retail price, doctor,' he said. 'And if you buy more than one you can have them even cheaper. You could make yourself a nice little bundle.'

I thanked him and told him that I already had a television set. Despite his explanation I had a feeling that, policeman or not, he probably had more skeletons rattling around than you could find in the catacombs of Paris.

Downstairs, Mrs Onions was helping a man in a policeman's uniform put a boxed television set onto the back seat of a police car. There was already one other set on the back seat and I could see that the boot lid was tied shut with a piece of string because there were two boxes almost packed into the boot. Mrs Onions was holding a small bundle of notes in her fist.

I couldn't move my car until the police car had gone so I stood and waited for a moment.

'Would you like a television set?' asked Mrs Onions as I waited

172

while the policeman did a five point turn in the driveway. 'We can let you have one at half price.'

I thanked her and explained that I didn't need another TV set.

A month later I heard that a policeman had been arrested for dealing in stolen goods. It was Mr Onions. It turned out that for two years or so he'd been acting as a fence for a couple of local thieves. He told them about shops and warehouses which had poor security and were worth their attention. The thieves lifted the goods and passed them to him. The stuff he'd told me about a police auction was all lies. He assumed that, as a policeman, he would be above suspicion. Sadly, for him, this turned out not to be the case. He sold the stolen goods on – mainly to other police officers. There was quite a scandal about it in the local press and I was rather grateful that I had resisted his offer of a cheap television set.

Constable Onions was eventually discharged from the force and sent to prison. His wife, who originally claimed not to have noticed the 120 television sets in their home, was found not guilty after her second attempt at a defence ('I thought he was just holding some evidence at home because the police station evidence room was full') was considered more acceptable. She stayed in the same house and spent most of her time painting.

It might not be a particularly solid reason for doing home visits, but I'd have missed all that excitement if I hadn't been prepared to visit patients at home.

The crash

When I was a medical student and a house officer working in hospital it was by no means unusual to work a 168 week. (Mind you, it was good money. As a junior doctor I was paid around £12 a week, though my board and lodging for living in the hospital was taken out of that.) I do not mean that I was up and rushing about for 168 hours a week but that when I wasn't actually working (e.g. seeing patients) I was on call. These days a doctor who is 'on call' is deemed to be working but in the 1970s a doctor who was asleep, or trying to sleep, with a bleeper or a telephone inches away from his head, or simply reading a book and waiting to be called, was officially resting and not working.

I was often so tired that even when both my bleeper and the phone by my head were ringing continually I occasionally didn't hear either of them and only woke when someone opened my bedroom door and physically woke me up and dragged me out of bed.

Being tired much of the time was dangerous – for me as well as my patients.

I remember having a weekend off and decided to drive home to see my parents for the first time in many weeks. I set off down the motorway. An hour into the journey I woke up to find the car bouncing around on the grass of the central reservation. There were no barriers at the time on that stretch of motorway. I was woken partly by the bouncing and partly by a good deal of horn blowing from other motorists. I swerved back into the appropriate fast lane just yards before I would have crashed into the central concrete pillar of a bridge across the motorway. Someone must have stopped and called the police because a mile or two down the road I was pulled over by a patrol car. They were sympathetic and drove behind me until I left the motorway (though I'm not sure what help this would have been if I'd fallen asleep again). I stopped at the first café I came to and drank two cups of black coffee. It didn't help. A few miles further on, at Stow on the Wold, I fell asleep again and drove into a ditch. The car was written off but I survived with nothing more than a stiff neck. My parents picked me up and drove me home. I was so tired I fell asleep in the back of their car.

The medical man

Back in the 1970s and 1980s, family doctors weren't paid bucket loads of gold, as GPs are today, and one of the ways most of us made a little extra money was to do insurance medicals. I have no idea whether GPs bother with them these days. Maybe the insurance companies can obtain all the information they require from the mass of information they have stored on their computers.

These medicals which doctors did in the 1970s and 1980s would take thirty to forty minutes each and were always done outside normal surgery hours. Patients who were taking out insurance (usually because they were buying a house and needed the policy to satisfy their mortgage company that they weren't likely to drop dead within days, or taking out life insurance or borrowing big chunk of money with which to buy a yacht) would make an appointment and then turn up carrying a huge form which had to be completed. The people I saw weren't actually patients of mine, of course, since, for ethical reasons long ago lost, it was considered improper for a doctor to perform an insurance examination on one of their own patients. I suppose the insurance companies were worried that doctors might be over generous if their own patients were involved.

If anything significant turned up (sugar in the urine or a raised blood pressure for example, it was considered normal practice to ask the patient for permission to write to their GP and let them know).

The insurance company paid the doctor a standard and fairly modest fee – it was, I think, a fee which had been agreed between the British Medical Association (the doctors' trade union) and the insurance companies. The fee wasn't huge – just about enough to pay for a tankful of petrol and a bagful of buns – but some retired doctors used to do two or three of them a week for a little pocket money. These days daft rules don't allow retired doctors to see patients at all – or to do anything vaguely medical.

The first part of the form consisted of questions about the customer's medical history, both personal and family, their habits (smoking and drinking) and their employment. That was the easy bit.

The second part of the form required a fairly full medical examination, including heart, nervous system, weight and so on. The examining doctor had to peer into every available orifice (though some insurance companies were more demanding and curious than others) and write down the findings. I sometimes wondered who on earth tried to read all those scribbled, indecipherable comments. And at the end of the whole exercise the examining doctor had to sign the form to say that in his or her opinion the patient was or was not in a satisfactory medical condition to take on a mortgage. Occasionally, the insurance would be taken out to accompany a job application. But usually there was a bank or a building society involved, or a life insurance policy.

I remember seeing a man who used to make an appointment every six months or so for a full insurance medical. He'd bring in his form, I'd ask him all the usual questions (to most of which I already knew the answers) and then I'd perform an examination.

'I hope you have better luck this time,' I said to him, after I'd completed the fourth or fifth insurance medical form for him.

He looked a little embarrassed. 'Oh, you mean with my loan application?'

'Exactly!' I said. 'I can't imagine why none of the other companies has gone ahead and lent you the money. I've never found anything wrong with you.'

'Oh, it's me that doesn't go ahead with the application,' replied the man.

I still didn't get it.

'I'm afraid it's just a way to get a regular check-up without it costing me anything,' said the man, completely without embarrassment. 'I used to worry a lot about my health but with the insurance companies paying for my health checks I don't worry anywhere near so much.'

I was slightly startled by this admission. It seemed as though he were cheating the insurance companies. But when I thought about it I couldn't get terribly upset about someone 'playing' the insurance companies. They cheat their customers all the time – by refusing to pay out or by pushing up their premiums massively if a claim is made.

'Aren't you running out of insurance companies?' I asked.

'Oh no, there are dozens of building societies and banks. I just go in and say I want to buy a house and will they give me a mortgage. They then write to me and ask me to have a medical examination to satisfy their insurance company. If I run out of banks and building societies I'll just start again at the beginning.'

The morality, or immorality of it didn't worry me too much and I happily accepted the fees I was paid by the various insurance companies involved.

Tilting at windmills

It is obviously true that all occupations change with time. The modern policeman has rather different responsibilities and attitudes to his forerunner in Victorian times. The modern shop assistant wouldn't put up with the sort of life endured by shop assistants just after World War II, when shop assistants worked ten hour days, had half an hour for lunch and may have had Saturday afternoons off if they had an exceptionally congenial employer. Train drivers no longer have to worry about the fire going out if their fireman doesn't work hard enough and fast enough.

But, although I am undoubtedly biased, I honestly don't think that any profession has changed as much as general practice.

Today, the average GP in Britain works a 26 hour week and spends much of that short week filling in forms, sitting staring at a computer and complaining that she or he cannot cope with the workload. Most of the practical day to day work is done by health assistants (who, you may be surprised or even shocked to hear, may or may not have any formal training in medicine) and the GP is available for consultations only between very limited hours. Indeed, in some parts of the United Kingdom GPs are now available only via the telephone or some sort of computer link involving software usually favoured by the sort of salesmen who insist on taking part in noisy meetings and conferences while sitting in restaurants and railway station waiting rooms.

When I was a GP, back in the 1970s and 1980s, things were very different and I truly believe that medicine was never better and never fairer than in the three decades after the end of the Second World War. The 50s, the 60s and the 70s saw the best of Britain's National Health Service. Since then the quality of care has gone downhill and medicine today is managed solely for the benefit of the practitioners. Patients are regarded as an irrelevant nuisance and treated as second class citizens with few if any rights. I strongly believe that one of the causes of this deterioration is the fact that doctors no longer control their own lives, or the way they work. This is not, of course, a problem unique to medicine. Farmers, small businessmen of all shapes and sizes and publicans are all controlled by regulations (some general and some specific to their particular trade) which give all control to anonymous bureaucrats who care for nothing other than the rules.

The average modern GP never visits patients in their homes and is never available outside consulting hours (which I have to say make banks look open and welcoming). Half a century ago patients could ask their doctor to visit them at home any time of day or night and expect not to be disappointed. There were no mobile phones, of course, so visiting patients at home was far more difficult than it would be today. It was surprisingly common for a doctor to visit a house on the far side of town, go back home or to the surgery and find that there was a call to a patient living two doors away from the one he'd just visited. All family doctors had to make sure that their staff knew exactly where they could be reached when they were on duty. There is some irony in the fact that although today's doctors would find home visiting much easier, because of mobile phones, they don't do any home visits. Back in the 1970s and 1980s, some of my patients didn't have landline telephones in their homes so if I needed an ambulance I had to find a phone box or a helpful neighbour.

Three things changed medicine dramatically.

The first was the decision, taken back in the 1960s, to give precedence to girls who wanted to be doctors. It was a strange decision to make because women doctors have often preferred to work part-time. Today, most doctors are female, and they insist on working part time and so it's not surprising that there appears to be a shortage. (Quite naturally, they also take time out to have babies, and that reduces the number of doctors available for work. It is customary for a female doctor to take a year off work every time she has a baby.)

The second change was, as I have already explained, the compulsory introduction of appointment systems.

The third significant difference between a GP in the 1970s and a GP today is the question of attitude. And that difference in attitude has played a large part in changing the sense of satisfaction enjoyed both by patients and by doctors.

Many things are responsible for the fundamental change in the relationship between doctors and patients but fundamentally it is, I suppose, the disappearance of the sense of vocation and personal responsibility that always used to be so important. So, for example, just a few decades ago, confidentiality was considered of primary importance to the doctor-patient relationship. The principle was that you couldn't be a bit confidential any more than you could be a tiny bit pregnant or a little bit dead. Today, confidentiality is regarded as an irrelevance, a luxury of little more than historical significance.

But by far the most important change has been in the availability of the doctor both in terms of time and of place. Back in the 1970s it was common for patients to be seen in their own homes. Visiting patients at home, either during the day or at night, enabled the doctor to develop a very more intimate relationship with their patients. When you've been into a patient's bedroom, bathroom and kitchen you know them much more closely than you know them when you and they sit on opposite sides of a desk. The relationship is quite different. You understand your patients much better and they are much more likely to tell you things about themselves.

Doctors need, above all else, to be observant. When you're talking to a patient in their living room or in their bedroom you see things, and learn things, that you never see when you're meeting them in the inevitably rather sterile surrounding of a surgery or clinic. You understand their lives, their stresses and so on much more easily in their own environment. With absolutely no disrespect, the difference is as great as watching a wild animal in its own habitat and watching it in a zoo. The majority of doctors today don't make any effort to know or understand their patients as people. But I honestly don't see any point in becoming a doctor if you aren't interested in people – and wanting to help them.

Sadly, for both patients and doctors, everything seems to have changed.

In health care today, patients are likely to be met with the sort of universally, dull, mindless, insolent, defiant, uncaring expression previously associated with the tax office and the Post Office. It is the standard face of communist bureaucracy as exemplified in East Germany in the 1970s. (I was in East Berlin in the 1970s, by the way, so this is not an empty comparison.) It is not a look of welcome or comfort. It is a look without caring or passion and it is a look which tells you that the owner of the look doesn't care about you.

They don't care if you live or die. Robots could (and doubtless will) be programmed to offer more compassion. General practice has adopted the awful old-fashioned hospital habit of treating patients as 'the liver in the end bed' and 'the kidney in the bed just after the door to the day room'.

GPs no longer do night calls or visit their patients at home over the weekend. They don't visit their patients at 3am or at lunchtime on Christmas Day. I really don't understand this. If there are five doctors in a practice and they share the out of hours responsibility, each doctor will have to be on call for one night a week, one weekend in five and one in five bank holidays. It's hardly onerous, is it?

Not doing calls means that doctors never actually save any lives. What I mean by this is that they never stick a needle into a patient and bring them back from the one way boat journey over the river Styx. For problems such as those, a GP can be far more use than an ambulance crew – and faster too. If I was called to a patient at the same time as an ambulance, I usually got there first – largely because I lived near to my patients. Mind you, modern GPs do so little practical medicine that they probably don't even know what a needle looks like.

It has been decided, by the medical establishment and the doctors' trade union, that visiting patients in their homes is a waste of valuable time for doctors. Today the surgery telephone is always engaged (often with the same regiment of desperate patients trying to get through to make an appointment) or else goes unanswered. The telephone will probably be fitted with an annoying message which warns callers that patients with urgent problems must find their way to the nearest Accident and Emergency Department (where they will be expected to wait 10, 12 or 16 hours before they are seen).

Many GPs in the UK now refuse to see patients 'live' at all; insisting that patients are treated over the telephone or by computer, apparently unconcerned about the fact that the evidence proves without a shadow of doubt that this is second-class medicine and very likely to lead to missed diagnoses and serious and deadly mistakes.

And, of course, for those doctors still prepared to see patients face to face (or, mask to mask) across a desk there is still the hurdle of the appointment system, which was designed and introduced to create a barrier between patient and doctor and which, to resurrect an old joke, should be renamed the disappointment system.

Visiting patients at home increases the chances that the patient will benefit in the long term, as well as in the short term, and dramatically increases the chances that the doctor will enjoy her or his work and obtain real satisfaction from her or his practice. It is the failure of this traditional relationship which has destroyed the essence of general practice and taken away much of the professional sense of satisfaction which used to be a vital part of the work of a family doctor.

I was only a GP for a decade or so. With great sadness, I resigned from the National Health Service when I felt that I was being asked to betray the fundamental rules of confidentiality which govern the relationship between doctor and patient. (The explanation appears in Memories 1.) The NHS bureaucrats insisted that I break the rule of confidentiality – even when it had no bearing on a patient's medical treatment but a massive bearing on their life – and I had no choice but to resign. I was fined for refusing to break the basic rule of confidentiality and it was made very clear to me that unless I was prepared to reveal details of my patients' conditions to their employers (and everyone else who wanted to know) then I would continue to be fined. Fortunately, bureaucrats and the medical establishment must have eventually realised that they were wrong because the rules were subsequently changed. By then, however, I'd resigned my position as a principal in general practice.

In my decade as a family doctor, I learned a tremendous amount about many different worlds. I learned about the life of a farmer, the life of a small business owner, the lives of men and women in the police force, the lives of people in professional show business, the lives of patients in the armed forces, the lives of people in horse racing and so on and so on. I even learned about the lives of criminals – and how having a criminal in a family can, and must, affect the lives of everyone else. I once knew a man who specialised in collecting seaweed. He kept bladder wrack, knobbed wrack, notched wrack and heaven knows how many other types of wrack in his bathtub and wrote learned works about them. I had a patient who was a pavement artist in London. He used to catch the train to the city every morning, just as if he worked in a bank.

Much of what I learned was gleaned because I visited patients in their own homes, in the daytime, during the night, at weekends and on bank holidays.

If a GP simply sits in his neat, sterile consulting room and doesn't go out into the real world then he or she has absolutely no chance of ever understanding his or her patients, or building any sort of relationship with them. The GP who does not visit his patients becomes a professional form-filler. He or she certainly cannot describe themselves as a family doctor. I suspect that the great sense of dissatisfaction which today runs through general practice is almost entirely a result of doctors refusing to practice medicine outside their consulting room. The chances are that many diagnoses will be missed and if a GP doesn't develop a relationship with, and an understanding of, his patients then no one else in health care ever will.

As an added extra, of course, being prepared to see patients at home offers other advantages. Some patients, the elderly and the chronically ill, often find it extremely difficult to make their way to the doctor's consulting rooms, surgery or clinic. It is a betrayal of the doctor's purpose to insist that such patients make the massive effort involved just to save the doctors a few minutes driving time. And by the time the elderly or disabled patient in the surgery has managed to undress (and dress again) the chances are that more time will have been taken than if the doctor had taken the trouble to visit the patient at home.

And as I've suggested, it is undeniable, too, that the best opportunity that general practitioners have to save lives occurs when they are available to see patients at home. When patients ring their GP today, they are likely to hear a recorded message telling them that if their call is urgent they should telephone for an ambulance or find some way to get themselves to the nearest hospital which has an open Accident and Emergency department. (Most small hospitals have closed and the ones which are left usually have no facilities for treating emergencies. And some Accident and Emergency departments have fixed opening hours, like public libraries and firms of accountants. It is hard luck if you are foolish enough to fall ill outside the official healing hours.)

I can remember a number of occasions when I know I definitely saved a patient's life. I remember, for example, a patient who was in status asthmaticus and an occasion when a patient had a severe

184

allergy reaction. On both occasions I was there fifteen minutes before the ambulance and on both occasions that fifteen minutes made the difference between life and death. Every GP who worked in the days when doctors were available 24 hours a day could give similar examples and will confirm that the joy of saving a patient's life was one of the blessings of general practice. Today, those patients would die.

A GP who visits patients at home in an emergency can deal with a diabetic crisis in minutes by giving the patient a sugary drink or a sweet; a patient with a wheeze can often be cured with a strong cup of coffee rather than a powerful drug (the caffeine breaks the spasm) and a child screaming with an ear ache can be temporarily soothed and calmed in just a few minutes by the application of a hot water bottle wrapped in a towel. A patient in severe pain who doesn't need to go hospital can be treated in moments with an injection of a powerful painkiller. And an elderly gentleman who can't pass urine can be cured (albeit temporarily) by getting into a warm bath. Even if he needs catheterising that can be done quickly (and with far less risk of infection) if it is done in his bedroom, rather than in a hospital bed some hours later.

A child with an ear infection might simply need an antibiotic. GPs always used to carry starter packs of suitable drugs so that patients could start treatment immediately. Today, a child with an ear infection might be ill for a day before they could be seen in an Accident and Emergency department.

The reluctance or downright refusal to visit a patient at home often means that the patient must make an entirely unnecessary visit to a hospital, helping to clog up the Accident and Emergency department, wasting ambulance time and spending long hours in a potentially dangerous (bug laden) hospital department when their problem could have been dealt with in minutes by a GP. I believe my father's death was triggered because his GP refused to visit him at his home and told him to ring for an ambulance to take him to hospital. My father then acquired a series of hospital infections and was much weakened.

(Why, incidentally, do all doctors, nurses, porters, cleaners and so on working in hospitals in the UK now all wear what look like pyjamas? It is impossible for patients or visitors to know if they are speaking to a consultant surgeon or a floor scrubbing specialist.

Everything within the NHS is designed to make things worse for patients – but do they have to be blatant about it?)

If a doctor doesn't understand his or her patients' lives, and how they live, he or she can't really hope to be able to help them when they are ill.

That sounds so obvious that it's almost embarrassing to put it down in black and white. But the way most doctors practice these days shows that they aren't aware of this simple truth. The vast majority of doctors are completely out of touch with the world in which their patients live. For example, doctors can learn a good deal about their patients by asking them what they do for a living, how they live and what their hobbies and interests are. Asking the relevant questions really doesn't take long and yet it provides vital information. I doubt if more than a few doctors bother to do this these days.

Watch how you walk

I once knew a psychiatrist who had consulting rooms in Harley Street. It was, he admitted, expensive to have rooms there but the advantage was that being in Harley Street meant that he could double his fees because of the address. He said that doctors with rooms in Wimpole Street and other nearby streets charged slightly smaller fees, unless they could let it be known that they looked after members of the royal family or film industry aristocracy.

I visited his rooms once to discuss a magazine article he was writing for a journal I was editing. (I was very young and editing soon gave me up). I'd met him a couple of times on social occasions when he'd been wearing an ordinary suit so I was slightly surprised to find him wearing a tail coat and grey trousers – the sort of outfit usually favoured by head waiters and people going to weddings. He saw me looking slightly startled and explained that he believed that people took him more seriously because he looked 'special'. (I think he meant that the formal clothing enabled him to add 25% to his fees.)

His consulting room was enormously long. You could have held a ball or a wedding reception in it. His desk was right up at the far end of the room and the only other furniture consisted of a couple of chairs in front of the desk, a small table upon which stood a vase of lilies and a glass-fronted bookcase full of what looked like first editions. There were no diplomas on the walls.

'It's a long walk from the door,' I pointed out needlessly, as I sat down on my side of the desk.

The psychiatrist, who had stood up when I'd entered the room, sat down and grinned. 'You'd be surprised how much you can learn from how people walk from the door to here,' he said. 'It's only the length of a cricket pitch but I've deliberately made the walk as long as possible.'

He explained that he always watched people carefully as they walked up towards his desk – and then listened carefully to the first words they uttered when they reached his end of the room. He said that even people who were usually very confident and full of themselves seemed to lose something of their veneer by the time they reached him.

The idea of assessing people before you actually managed to speak to them reminded me Cardinal Richelieu. In Cardinal Richelieu's ante room were two groups of pictures. On one side there were scenes of battles, assassination and torture and on the other there were peaceful pictures of green meadows, country scenes, lovers, old people sitting in the sunshine, cats sleeping, comfortable fireside pictures and so on.

Every man who applied for a job was shown into the room and the Cardinal watched him through a peephole. If the man looked at the brutal pictures he was classified as a timid, peaceful bloke who was fascinated by brutal stuff and Richelieu put him down as suitable for a job as a clerk. But if the arrival looked at the domestic, sentimental pictures then he was classified as adventurous and strong and more suitable for action, and a job requiring a risk taker.

And it reminded me of my interview when I went to Birmingham Medical School for the first time. There were, I suppose, around a dozen consultants and professors sitting in the room, waiting to quiz prospective students. Some of the questions were designed to find out whether the prospective student knew anything about medicine, some were designed to find out why the prospective student wanted to study medicine and some were designed to find out if the prospective student could think quickly under pressure.

But the thing I remember most was that a table had been positioned just inside the doorway. As I walked into the room I walked straight into the table which served no obvious practical purpose. There was nothing on it and no one sitting behind it.

Only afterwards did I suspect that the table had been put there to discomfort and to put the prospective student under even more stress.

I mentioned the incident with the table to my psychiatrist friend who told me that he'd attended one of the London medical schools and that at his interview he had hardly entered the room before a rugby ball was thrown at him – very hard and neck height.

'Did you catch it?' I asked him.

'Oh yes,' he replied. 'And I threw it back to the professor who'd thrown it at me.'

'What happened?'

'He fumbled the ball and dropped it. And they ended the interview there and then and offered me a place at the medical school without further ado.'

What I remembered, but my friend was too modest to remind me about, was that at the time he was a Rugby international. The dean of the medical school, a keen rugby follower and President of the medical school's rugby club, desperately wanted him for the team.

He leaves his bicycle in my back passage

'Do you have any trouble with your back passage?' I once asked an old lady. I was proud of my command of idiomatic English.

I was a medical student at the time. In those days, when a patient was admitted to the hospital, a junior doctor or senior medical student had to take an extensive medical and social history and perform a full medical examination.

'Why do you want to know that?' the old woman asked, clearly puzzled.

'It might help me make a diagnosis,' I explained.

'Oh, well, you know best I suppose,' said the old lady, still puzzled. She beckoned me closer and whispered. 'I have trouble with the boy next door,' she confided.

I looked at her, slightly startled by this admission. She was well into her 80s.

'I share the back passage with the neighbours and he leaves his bicycle in it when he comes home from school,' she said.

I stared at her.

'I've tripped over it once or twice in the dark,' she added. 'I've mentioned it to his mother but she doesn't take any notice of me.'

A box of chocolates

I once had a patient who was diabetic but whose diabetes was hardly ever under control. She had been seen at a specialist clinic and she'd been given a massive amount of help and advice. She had been given extensive advice about her diet and the treatment regime which had been recommended for her. But her blood sugar levels were, it seemed, almost impossible to control.

I got called one day by her husband who said his wife was almost unconscious again. I temporarily abandoned my morning surgery and rushed round to their home to find my patient drifting in and out of consciousness.

Now, the symptoms of excessively high blood sugar can be similar to the symptoms of very low blood sugar and so when known diabetics fell ill it was common to give them some sugar, either in the form of a sweet or in the form of a sugary drink. There weren't any machines around in those days to measure blood sugar levels easily in the home and giving a little sugar wouldn't do any additional harm to a patient with too much sugar in their blood but it would cure a patient with too little sugar. It was a standard diagnostic treatment and test which could cure those cases where the patient was having a 'hypoglycaemic' attack. These days most patients have their own blood sugar measuring machine and the patient, a relative or a visiting doctor can see straight away what is wrong.

I was about to get the husband to make up a drink with lots of sugar dissolved in it when I noticed a box of chocolates on the table. The box was open and half the chocolates had gone. They weren't the type of chocolates sold as suitable for diabetic patients. They were ordinary chocolates.

'Who has been eating those?' I asked the husband.

'Oh my wife ate them,' he replied. 'Her sister brought them last night as a birthday present. She loves chocolate and since she can't eat sweets she eats chocolates.'

I stared at him in disbelief.

'Your wife has eaten all those chocolates?'

'I think I ate one or two,' said the husband. 'No more than two. I'm not terribly keen on chocolate.'

'But she's diabetic!' I pointed out.

'Oh, she's very careful,' said the man. 'She never eats sweets of any kind though she used to love toffees.'

'But she shouldn't be eating chocolates!' I said. I think I actually put my head in my hands for a moment. It occurred to me that if the pair of them had decided to leave their brains to the nation, the curator of the lucky museum would have been able to save valuable shelf space by fitting both their brains into an unusually small jar – a mustard pot would be more than big enough, leaving plenty of room left over for a large quantity of pickling fluid and perhaps a dozen small onions to add a little je ne sais quoi to the arrangement.

Obviously, she wasn't going to be helped, after all, by a drink full of sugar so I gave her an extra dose of insulin and minutes later she was bright and full of beans again.

I then had to have a serious talk with her. And I explained that 'chocolates' come under the heading of 'sweets'.

If I hadn't visited her at home and seen that opened box of chocolates I doubt if her diabetes would have ever been brought under control.

That was another patient who proved the importance of GPs visiting their patients in their own homes.

Penny for a push

A patient of mine was a bit of a rogue. As far as I know he never had what might be called a proper job. Instead, he did a bit of anything and everything. These days, it's called having a portfolio of jobs. But he'd have said he was a jack of all trades or an odd job man. He'd cut your hedge, take away your unwanted old mattress, do your shopping, walk your dog or stand in a queue at the Post Office to get your Christmas parcels stamped and posted. He was meticulously honest and his clients trusted him completely. He did a lot of odd jobs for me.

'Were you ever tempted to find one job with hours and a wage?' I asked him once.

He looked quite shocked. 'Oh no, that wouldn't be for me,' he replied.

He told me that he'd always been the same.

'When I was a boy of eleven or twelve, we lived at the bottom of a steep hill,' he told me. 'I'd stand at the bottom of the hill, where the local shop was, and I'd carry people's shopping up the hill for a penny. Sometimes, if they didn't have any shopping I'd push them up the hill. That was a penny too. There was one woman who was over twenty stones. I was always exhausted when I'd pushed her up the hill. I'd have to sit down for five minutes and take a breather. But I charged her one penny too, the same as everyone else. It wouldn't have seemed right to have charged her more.'

Omphalomancy, gyromancy and gastromancy

Over the years I met a lot of quacks and charlatans. I once interviewed a man who claimed he could cure people with cancer by putting rubber bands onto their fingers. He treated different types of cancer by putting rubber bands on different fingers. A well-known publisher turned him into a best-selling author though I was proud when I managed to dent his reputation by exposing his ignorance and the danger of his advice on television. (It's curious isn't it, that a publisher would print, market and promote such a book but wouldn't dream of publishing a book which questioned the efficacy and safety of vaccination.)

Some quacks were incredibly successful, building up enviable reputations and making huge amounts of money. Some of the ones I met gave their trickeries impressive sounding names.

There were (and for all I know still are) people who offered medical advice who confidently asserted that they could makes diagnoses by studying a patient's navel.

Navel gazing is known as omphalomancy.

And then there was gyromancy in which patients were instructed to walk round in a circle until, dizzy, they fell down. Where and how they landed gave the quack the answers they sought.

And there were quacks who claimed that they could make diagnoses by listening to the gurgling of the patient's stomach and intestines. This too had a scientific sounding name: gastromancy.

Honestly.

And people believe in this stuff and trust these people.

Memorable ends

Occasionally, when invited, I went to funerals for my patients.

Like most people I never liked funerals but some of the ones I attended were memorable.

A former brewery manager told his widow (when she was his wife) that he wanted an old-fashioned funeral with a horse drawn hearse and with the mourners walking behind the hearse. With considerable difficulty, she managed to arrange this. She couldn't find a proper carriage so had to settle for a farm cart with a rather lively horse between the shafts. Unfortunately, no one had told the horse that it was supposed to be taking part in a solemn occasion. When the horse broke into a canter the mourners had to run to keep up with it. When the horse began to gallop, the mourners abandoned the chase and let the makeshift hearse, complete with coffin, race ahead on its own with the driver of the hearse yelling loudly at the horse to slow down. The hearse arrived at the cemetery a good fifteen minutes before the allotted time for the ceremony, and well ahead of breathless mourners. The former brewery manager was, I suspect, the only person ever to have been early for his own funeral.

A woman in her 40s went to her husband's funeral wearing the costume she had worn for their wedding. It was obviously a wedding outfit, though she had, so I was told, removed the spray of artificial orchids which had been attached to the lapel. She later explained that her wedding day was the only happy day she'd had in 17 years of marriage. She also said it was the only decent outfit she had since her husband had never given her any money for clothes.

A man in his 70s had been ill in bed for six months. He'd had open heart surgery and never properly recovered. But he insisted on getting out of bed to go to the funeral of a business rival. He said his only regret was that he wasn't strong enough to dance on the grave. Nevertheless, the exertion was too much for him. Weakened by the operation, the unaccustomed exertion and the excitement he picked up an infection and died a week and a half later.

A glass of port

We were in the operating theatre and, as we had scrubbed up a few minutes earlier, I had been painfully aware that his breath smelt of alcohol. I noticed with relief that the mask he had put on was now preventing anyone else from smelling the alcohol. The surgeon had been chewing sweets which I recognised as Palma Violets but the sweet aroma of the English delicacy had failed entirely to mask the smell of the alcohol. It had been a valiant attempt but an unsuccessful one. I had wondered if I should say anything. But he had seemed perfectly capable and although his face was a little flushed he did not seem to be in any way dangerously over-lubricated.

The truth is that I did not say anything for a very good reason. I'll explain.

Motorists often claim that their drinking makes them more confident and less hesitant. I've always found this argument to be rather specious and self-serving. It is, for example, well known that although motorists always think they drive better after a couple of drinks their skills and judgement are invariably worse than they would be if they were sober. Alcohol increases an individual's confidence but reduces their performance.

But an operating theatre is a strange, alien environment.

The only real way to judge a surgeon's skill is to measure his success rate when compared to colleagues performing similar operations on a similar group of patients.

I worked with two surgeons during one of my hospital jobs and they were completely different characters.

One of the two surgeons, the younger, was very slow, very methodical and very cautious. He had a very smart, powerful motor car but on motorways he was the driver settled in the slow lane, travelling at 50 mph with the lorries. He had a boat, grew dahlias and painted watercolours. He gave signed (but unframed) prints of his work to the staff every Christmas which was kind of him, though not terribly popular because the other consultants gave bottles containing alcohol. He was actually a terrible painter. Giotto, the 14th century Italian artist was, it was said, able to draw a perfect circle freehand but this surgeon, though nifty enough around a gall bladder and undoubtedly far more adept with a scalpel and a pair of Spencer Wells forceps than Giotto would have been, couldn't draw a straight line if you gave him a ruler. If he'd been a house painter he would have taken three weeks to paint a modest sized house but he would have done an acceptable job and there wouldn't have been a drop of paint spilt anywhere. He was very straight-laced and liked everyone to call him 'sir'. And he was vain too. He needed spectacles but wouldn't wear them because he thought they made him look old. That sort of vanity is not a good thing in a surgeon. One of my colleagues suggested that the real reason he wouldn't wear his spectacles was that he was worried that if he used them too much he'd wear out the lenses and have to buy another pair. I saw him once out on his boat. He wore one of those broad brimmed, all weather hats which have a chin strap to stop them blowing off. No one ever uses the chin strap because it's impossible not to look rather silly while wearing a soft hat with a strap tied under your chin. But even on still days he used the chin strap to stop his hat blowing away.

The other surgeon, the older of the two, was rather slapdash and if he had been a house painter there would have been paint on the windows and on the carpets. He would, however, have taken less than a week to complete the job. (Though someone else would have to spend two days cleaning up the mess he'd made.) He worked very quickly and took half the time his colleague took to complete an operation. He was great fun and liked everyone he worked with, even or perhaps especially, the junior nurses, to call him by his Christian name. He lived in a massive old country house with a pool, a miniature golf course and its own maze. (He did a good deal of private work and made a lot of money from work at a local private hospital.) I remember that one Christmas a group of us took his car apart and then reassembled it at the centre of his maze. He had to get a crane to lift it out of the maze but he thought it was hysterically funny.

You might have thought that the slow, methodical surgeon would have the better success rate but you would have been wrong.

The fast surgeon, the one who attacked his patients as though he were tackling the undergrowth in an overgrown garden, wielding his scalpel with gusto, had a far better success rate. His patients were more likely to live and more likely to get better quickly. The scar he left them with wasn't always neat but they lived. On the other hand, the patients who had been operated on by the slow surgeon had very neat scars, the sort that fade to a thin almost indiscernible white line, but too many of them did not live to parade upon the beach.

There is a simple reason for this.

When a patient is on the operating table they are, inevitably, under an anaesthetic and their bodies are subjected to a whole series of abnormal physical insults. The risk of a patient faring badly, and developing complications or dying, depends to a very considerable extent upon the length of time an operation takes. If one surgeon routinely completes his work in two hours and another surgeon takes four hours for the same operation then, all things being equal, the surgeon who completes his operations in the shorter time will have by far the better success rate. His patients will make a quicker recovery and they will be more likely to survive.

I was in the hospital mess when the slow and methodical surgeon, aware of the fact that too many of his patients were dying, asked his colleague what he thought he could do to improve his success rate. The careful surgeon was in a bad way; even talking of giving up surgery completely and retraining as a pathologist. He said that at least all the patients he dealt with would be dead when he started. Five of his last six patients had died on the operating table and the sixth was still seriously ill in the Intensive Care Unit. That is a heavy burden to carry with you when you next scrub up and approach an unconscious patient lying on your operating table.

'Ah that's easy,' said the fast surgeon with a laugh. 'You're a damned good surgeon but you're far too uptight. You fuss too much, you're too nervous and you take too long over your cutting and your stitching. Your patients are under the anaesthetic for too long. You need to speed things up a bit.'

'But what can I do about it?' asked the methodical surgeon. 'I'm a naturally cautious sort of fellow,' he added unnecessarily.

'Have a drink before you start work. Not enough to make you drunk of course. But enough to get rid of some of your inhibitions.'

And so the slow surgeon started having a modest sized glass of port before he put on his operating mask and gown. The nurses and other staff were scandalised for the surgeon made no secret of his new habit. He kept a bottle of good port and an appropriate crystal, drinking glass in his locker.

But the glass of port did its job. His operations didn't take quite as long and his patients started doing better almost immediately. As long as I was working for him the surgeon never exceeded his one glass of port. And everyone was delighted that his terrible run of failure came to an end.

So I never said anything when I smelt alcohol on the surgeon's breath.

Better than a punch in the nose

A good friend went to see his GP, a woman. She was uncaring, rude and inconsiderate.

'I felt like punching her in the nose,' he said.

'But you didn't,' I said.

'No,' he replied. 'I wouldn't punch a woman. Instead of hitting her I told her she had fat ankles. And that she'd always have fat ankles.'

'What did she say?'

'She didn't say anything. But when I got to the door I turned round and she was looking down under the desk.'

The tourist

I wrote my first book 'The Medicine Men' a year or so after I'd started work in general practice. The book dealt with the way the pharmaceutical industry had taken control of the medical profession, and I'd been researching and working on the book since I'd been a medical student. It had always seemed to me that the medical establishment had become far too closely integrated with the drug industry and that as a result, patients were often exposed to unnecessary risks. Research I did while writing the book showed that every doctor or administrator whom I could identify as being involved in the official analysis or assessment of new drugs had close financial links with the drug industry. Senior members of the medical establishment, including those advising the Government on the safety of the medicines, all seemed to have significant financial links to the drug industry. And the doctor's trade union received huge amounts of money from the drug industry as payment for advertising in its journal 'The British Medical Journal'. Every time doctors met for a lecture or a conference, or even a social meeting, the food and drink was supplied by one or more drug companies.

In 'The Medicine Men' I explained that the drug companies had literally bought doctors' leaders by paying them huge sums of money for consultancy and advisory work, had bought the establishment, by paying huge sums of money to sponsor meetings and conferences and had effectively bought many of the apparently reputable medical journals by paying absurdly high fees for advertisements published in those journals. (The medical journals, which mostly have quite modest circulations, still charge vastly higher fees for their advertising space than do almost any other publications.) At the grass roots level, the drug industry bought prescribing loyalty by sponsoring regularly luncheons and dinners and by giving doctors free television sets and video recorders (theoretically, so that they could watch promotional videos they'd been given) and by paying for them (and their partners, of course) to attend lectures in, for example, the South of France – reachable only, of course, via an expensive journey on the Orient Express.

After I had revealed all this wanton corruption, some changes were made to the way that the drug companies could operate, but I had made myself some very powerful enemies within the medical establishment.

'The Medicine Men' attracted a good deal of publicity. The BBC made a special ten to fifteen minute film about the book for its prime time evening news programme and a British newspaper called 'The Guardian' (which, at the time, had a significant circulation and a solid reputation) serialised the book. As a result I found myself making regular appearances on national and local radio and television programmes.

Back in the 1970s there weren't many doctors appearing on television or radio and I not infrequently found myself accosted in the street, in restaurants or on public transport by strangers who wanted medical advice. This sometimes led to bizarre situations.

I remember once appearing on a late night, live television show in Birmingham and, since it was a pleasant night and the television studio wasn't far from where I was staying, I told the producer of the programme that I'd walk to the hotel where they had booked me a room. I could actually see the hotel from the studio windows. It couldn't have been more than half a mile away.

(Although I was travelling I had very luggage with me. Whenever I was on a book promotion tour I took very little stuff with me because I spent so much of my time running between studios or to catch a train. While touring the country I jumped aboard so many trains that were moving that I almost forgot that most people boarded trains when they were standing still in the railway station. I always carried no more than a canvas shoulder bag. It was actually sold as a fishing bag and I've seen many television travellers using similar luggage. You can stuff a spare shirt and so on inside the main part of the bag and cram books into the smaller pockets. And, of course, jacket pockets can be filled with all sorts of useful things. Every jacket I own has pockets which bulge even when they are empty; their shape ruined eternally by overloading. The pockets of any jacket I wear will always contain a couple of notebooks, several pens, a number of pencils, a pencil sharpener, a large Swiss Army penknife , a Leatherman, a spare shoelace, a small torch, a pair of dice, a couple of conkers, a wallet, a credit card holder (which

carries my driving licence and other useful cards), a pair of
sunglasses, a pair of folding reading glasses in case I lose my
spectacles, a loupe and half a dozen small bulldog clips. I'll usually
also carry at least one paperback book in my jacket. I should explain
that I always buy jackets which are well equipped with pockets (the
pockets are the first thing I look for) and I often used to have one or
two extra, large pockets added, making sure that they fasten with
zips, to make life a little harder for pick pockets.)

'No, you mustn't do that!' screamed the producer when I told him
I intended to walk to the hotel. 'I forbid it. I absolutely forbid it!'
Television producers tend to be excitable people and their emotional
state reaches an apogee at the end of a programme.

He told me that a number of people had recently been attacked,
mugged and beaten up in the city centre and that the underpass I had
to use was a notoriously dangerous thoroughfare. He was so worried
that I would be attacked in the street that he insisted on calling me a
taxi to take me to the hotel.

'You're that doctor off the telly, aren't you?' said the taxi driver
as he drove me round the city's one way system.

I mumbled something appropriate, looked out at the city and
wondered, for the umpteenth time why I was sitting in the back of a
taxi when if I'd walked I'd have been tucked up in my hotel by now.
Because it was late at night, or early in the morning, the taxi had
taken nearly twenty minutes to arrive.

'Here you are, doctor!' said the taxi driver, pulling up outside the
hotel. I didn't have to pay him because the taxi had a contract with
the TV company, but I handed him a generous tip, grabbed my bag
and started to climb out of the taxi. The hotel was a large one with its
own drive-way. The reception area was still well lit and a night
porter was standing by the doorway, ready to open the door.

'Could I trouble you just a moment?' said the taxi driver.

I looked back into the vehicle.

'I'd like to ask you about something, if I may,' he said.

I waited.

He opened his door, climbed out of the taxi and came round to
where I was standing.

'I've got this lump,' he said. 'I don't know whether it's something
I ought to be worried about.'

I waited. He clearly didn't need any encouragement from me. I assumed he was going to tell me the location of the lump, and describe it to me. But instead he suddenly unzipped the leather jacket he was wearing, removed it and placed it carefully on the bonnet of his taxi, making sure that the zip didn't scratch the paintwork. And then, to my astonishment, he speedily unbuttoned his shirt. When he'd unbuttoned all the buttons he pulled the shirt out of his trousers and bared his chest. From where I was standing I could see the hotel's night porter staring in astonishment.

'It's here, doctor,' said the taxi driver, pointing to an area just above his right nipple. 'It feels like a lump.'

I could see the lump without any difficulty. And his nipple on that side of his chest was sunk into the little breast tissue that he had. There seemed to be an eczematous type of rash on and around the nipple.

Without much choice in the matter I rubbed my hands to try to warm them up a little and then examined the lump. It was hard and seemed fixed.

'Have you seen anyone about this?' I asked him, making sure I kept my voice calm so as not to alarm him at all.

'No,' he replied. 'Only you.'

Just then the night porter came out to see what we were doing. He was a very short fellow in a coat and peaked cap that seemed too large for him.

'It's OK,' I told him, before he could speak. 'I'm a doctor.'

'Oh, that's fine then, doctor,' replied the porter, rather surprisingly. He turned and went back into the hotel. I have often found that it is possible to get away with the strangest behaviour if you tell people that you're a doctor.

'What do you think it is?' asked the taxi driver. 'It can't be cancer, can it? Men don't get breast cancer, do they?'

Part of me didn't want to alarm him. But part of me also knew that it was imperative that he visited his doctor without any delay. I was pretty sure that he did have breast cancer and that it needed looking at sooner rather than later.

I reached round to his armpit but couldn't feel any swollen glands. The glands in his neck weren't swollen either.

'You must go and see your doctor tomorrow,' I told him.

'It's Saturday tomorrow,' the taxi driver pointed out.

'On Monday morning, then,' I told him.

'I made him promise that he would.

'Is it serious?' he asked.

'It needs looking at,' I told him. 'You may need an operation.'

'Is it cancer?' he asked.

'It could be,' I told him, wanting to be sure he did as I had advised. 'But you need to have some tests done. And there is no earthly point in delaying things.'

He buttoned up his shirt, picked up his jacket and put it back on.

'I'll ring up on Monday morning and get an appointment,' he promised.

'If you have any trouble with the receptionists,' I said, knowing that GPs' staff are sometimes rather defensive about handing out appointments, 'tell them that you saw a doctor who said you needed to be seen immediately.'

He thanked me, insisted that I take back the tip I'd given him, promised he would do as I had advised, climbed back into his cab and drove off. (Seven years later, I was in the same city, coming out of the railway station when a man rushed up to me with a big smile on his face. It was that taxi driver. He insisted on shaking my hand. He told me he'd had an operation for breast cancer and was doing well.)

As I walked into the hotel, the night porter approached me. 'Sorry, I didn't recognise you, doctor,' he said. He smiled and touched his cap. 'I've just been watching you on the television.'

I nodded, said good evening and headed for the reception desk to collect my room key. The porter followed me.

'I hope you don't mind, doctor,' he said. 'But could I just ask you something?'

Inwardly, I groaned but I turned back to face him and tried to look alert and interested. I looked around to see how many other people there were in the lobby. I really didn't feel like conducting an impromptu surgery in the lobby at 1.00am.

'Could I have your autograph, doctor?'

I signed the hotel card he offered me, collected my key and hurried up to my room.

First gold digger

Miss Oliver (not her real name or her stage name, of course) was an actress who had married and buried three four husbands and seen five lovers into their graves. ('I must be doing something right,' she laughed when she told me this. I confess I shivered a little.) If Shakespeare had known her he would have rewritten Hamlet to include a character known as the First Gold Digger.

She lived in a large cottage which had roses by the front door. There were antimacassars, aspidistra and china dogs everywhere and the walls were covered with pictures of her. In some of the pictures she was alone. And in some of the pictures she was posing with other famous actors and actresses.

Her main asset was that she was generously built, her god had definitely not skimped when putting her together, and even in her late eighties she always wore a v low cut dress. 'It's my shop window,' she explained, though I was never quite sure what sort of customers she was hoping to attract.

Miss Oliver had always lived her life beyond her emotional means – just as some people live beyond their financial means – and when I was her GP her main occupation seemed to be reading romantic novels. There were thousands of them in her home. Every bookcase was full of them and there were piles of them on the floor. 'I am a heroine addict, she told me with a throaty laugh.

She had two sons whom I met just after Christmas one year. They were the sons of her second husband. And the two sons had wives.

It was a Saturday, I was on call and I was at home in the garden desperately trying to unblock a blocked drain. I didn't usually try to do gardening or odd jobs when I was on call. Indeed, I didn't usually try to do anything very much other than wait for the telephone to ring. If I tried to work on an article or a book I was writing, the phone would go and ruin my concentration. But the drain was blocked and the chances of finding someone able and willing to come out and help me deal with it were somewhere between 'very slight' and 'you must be joking'. I did know of an odd job man, who usually did things like this, but he was a patient of mine and I knew that he was in hospital after a hernia operation.

So I'd changed into my oldest clothes and I was busy using some drain rods which I'd found in the garage in an attempt to budge the blockage.

And then the telephone went.

One of Miss Oliver's sons was at the other end of the line, demanding that I visit his mother immediately, if not sooner.

'What's the trouble?' I asked him. I'd seen Miss Oliver the week before and she'd been fine then.

'My brother and I are here and we need to see you immediately,' said the son. He refused to tell me why but he used the word 'immediately' and 'urgent' quite a lot and told me that he knew the Assistant Chief Constable (I wasn't sure of the relevance of that) and that he wouldn't hesitate to complain about me to the General Medical Council if I didn't turn up straight away.

So, with a sigh, I told him I was on my way. I thought about changing my clothes but I thought that I'd just throw an old rug over the driving seat in the car and go as I was. I stank of...well, I'd been trying to clear the drains so you can guess what sort of smell it was.

But when I got into the car it wouldn't start. I had no idea why it wouldn't start, but it wouldn't. (Three hours later it started perfectly well. I think maybe that it just didn't want to take me to see Miss Oliver's son. Or maybe the car felt that the stink was too much for it.) Our truck was in the garage having something incomprehensible but expensive doing to it.

I'd have gone on my bicycle but Miss Oliver's cottage was five miles away and I didn't fancy balancing my black medical bag on the handlebars for five miles. So I went next door and borrowed a truck belonging to the neighbour. The truck was 30-years-old, it was covered in rust, it emitted a good deal of ghastly smoke whenever it moved and most of the dents had dents in them.

'I'll start it for you,' said my neighbour. 'But don't let the engine stop. When you get where you're going leave it in neutral and put a brick on the accelerator to keep the engine running. There's a brick in the passenger foot-well.'

So off I went. The truck, though it seemed surprisingly powerful, was puffing and wheezing and I was stinking.

I knew I was in trouble when I got there and saw a BMW and a

Jaguar parked on the gravel driveway. Both cars were new and immaculate.

I put the brick on the accelerator and got out of the truck. I didn't have to ring the doorbell because one of the sons had come to the door to see what was making all the noise.

'What the hell do you want?' demanded a short, rotund fellow in a blue, three piece suit. He was bald and had a little moustache that would have made him look like Hitler if he'd had some hair and a uniform.

I explained that I was the doctor.

He looked disgusted and took some convincing but he eventually let me into the cottage where his brother and their two wives were sitting waiting. Miss Oliver was sat in her usual rocking chair.

'What's the problem?' I asked Miss Oliver. The sons and daughters stared at me, clearly horrified, but then ignored me and so it seemed polite to ignore them.

'There's no problem,' said Miss Oliver. 'I'm sorry you were brought out today,' she apologised. 'My sons want to put me into some sort of home. But I'm not budging from here so they're wasting their time and now they've wasted your time and I apologise for that.'

'Is that all?'

'That's all, doctor,' she said firmly. 'I told my son not to call you but they've spent the last fifteen minutes trying, unsuccessfully, to change my mind about going into a home. I'm so sorry you were bothered unnecessarily.' She looked over her half-moon spectacles at me, obviously inspecting my unexpectedly ragged jacket and filthy trousers. She sniffed a little. And then sniffed again. 'Is that a new aftershave you're wearing?'

I said it was something new and very special called 'eaux d'egout', promised to see her in a couple of weeks as usual, turned round and headed for the door.

'When you come again you must let me know where you get that aftershave,' she called. 'I'd like to buy some for my sons for Christmas.'

I turned back, grinned at her, winked to let her know I knew it wasn't her fault that I'd been called out unnecessarily, and left. I got back into my neighbour's truck, carefully replaced the brick on the accelerator with my foot so that the engine didn't stall, and, with a

209

roar, left in a spray of gravel and a cloud of blue smoke. As I disappeared out of the driveway, I could hear the comforting ping of a thousand pieces of gravel smacking into the well-polished bodies of the two smart saloons belonging to Miss Oliver's sons.

There's a child in us all and I have always felt that it is the little things, the unexpected delights, which make life worth living.

The great deceit

While I was writing my first book 'The Medicine Men', I realised that in addition to pretty well controlling the medical profession, the pharmaceutical industry also controlled medical research throughout the world, and so, for my second book, I chose to take on medical researchers in a book called 'Paper Doctors' which was subtitled 'A critical assessment of medical research'.

(For reasons which I never understood the publisher, Maurice Temple-Smith, who was a wonderful old school publisher with offices opposite the British Museum in the heart of Bloomsbury, chose to illustrate the cover with a slightly out of focus photograph of an empty glass bottle which had an ill-fitting cork stuffed in the top. On close examination, the bottle appeared to have contained spirits of some kind – probably whisky. I should have questioned the jacket but it was my second book and authors – particularly young and inexperienced ones – aren't encouraged to have opinions on how their books are presented or promoted.)

Having pretty well destroyed my chances of ever having any sort of medical career, I continued to destroy what small hope might have remained by writing a blistering attack on the very large, very powerful and very well connected medical research industry.

It is, incidentally, a common mistake to assume that medical researchers are quiet, serious academics who have stepped aside from commerce to devote themselves to making discoveries that will improve the world. Nothing, I'm afraid, could be further from the truth. Medical researchers are, almost exclusively, hired by, and work for, drug companies. They research what they are told to research (mostly into the usefulness of 'me-too' drugs – which are drugs which will be promoted as alternatives to existing drugs) and if their findings are commercially inconvenient (i.e. if the product being tested proves useless or dangerous or both) then their research will never be published.

The big myth about medical research (which is constantly restated by the drug industry and the medical establishment) is that it is discoveries made by researchers which have extended life expectancy and improved the quality as well as the quantity of life for most of us. This is, I'm afraid, a complete fabrication, made because it is commercially expedient. It is, possibly, the most profitable myth in existence and it has been promoted (without much opposition from anyone except me) by doctors, scientists, politicians and journalists for decades. I've spent much of my life trying hard to counter this myth (which has for over a century been the main promotional tool of the medical profession and the drug industry and the main excuse for all the risky endeavours promoted by doctors and drug companies). The truth is that most useful discoveries (the discovery of X-rays and the discovery of penicillin are good examples) were entirely serendipitous.

In 'Paper Doctors' I began by pointing out that doctors have traditionally believed that improvements in health will automatically follow if we acquire a greater under-standing of the structure and function of the human body. After all, it isn't difficult to show that modern medical practice developed hugely during the last two centuries and that, during that same time interval, life expectation apparently increased rapidly.

It is assumed that the two are linked but, I'm afraid, that this is an outrageous fallacy and a perfect and very useful example of the 'post hoc ergo propter hoc' fallacy – which is Latin for 'after this, therefore because of this' and which expresses the idea that because something happened after something else happened then the second happening must be a result of the first happening. In order words, the assumption here is that because lots of medical research has been done then any improvement in life expectancy must be a result of that research. Not so.

The reliable identification of individual diseases (and the accurate understanding of disease processes) really began in the 19th century.

The ancient physicians, such as Galen and Hippocrates, had always blamed the development of disease on the defective mixing of 'humours' in the body, but in 1761 an Italian called Giovanni Battista Morgagni published a book entitled 'On the Seats and Causes of Diseases', based on a great number of post mortems in which he showed convincingly that different diseases involve different organs. Forty years after that, a Frenchman, Marie Francois Xavier Bichat, took knowledge one step further and showed that organs are made up of many different kinds of tissue, and that different tissues are responsible for different disease processes.

It wasn't until 1833 that medicine really moved away from a philosophical approach and towards a genuinely scientific approach. The change was triggered when a German, Johannes Muller, published the first volume of his 'Handbook of Human Physiology'.

And it was another German, Rudolf Virchow, who, in 1855, used microscopes to study cells and who introduced the idea of 'cellular pathology'. It had taken nearly a century to move from organs, to tissues and to cells. Virchow's book 'Cellular Pathology as based upon Physiological and Pathological History' was published in 1858 and it marked the beginning of modern medicine as a science.

Also in the 19th century, the fight against infection started in earnest. Jan Ignaz Semmelweiss, an assistant in the Obstetrics Unit in Vienna, believed that puerperal fever, an infection which affects women who have just given birth, was caused by a 'poison' of some sort from dead bodies. He was scorned, his theories were rejected and he was ruined professionally but he was later proved right.

In 1882, Robert Koch discovered the tubercle bacillus and the following year he identified the organism which causes cholera. In the 1860s, Pasteur developed his theory of the cause of infectious diseases and in 1865, an English surgeon, developed the antisepsis principle which helped to save patients on the operating table. Before Lister came along, surgeons used to wear their oldest and filthiest clothes in the operating theatre and their instruments, which were rarely, if ever, washed, would be sharpened on the soles of their boots. The mortality rate among patients who had been on the operating table was horrendous.

In the 19th century, the basis of modern anaesthesia was developing and the compound microscope was created, enabling scientists to study cells and micro-organisms associated with different diseases. In 1895, at the end of a magnificent century, which saw an explosion in the amount of information available, Roentgen, who was involved in basic physics research, serendipitously discovered X-rays and made the greatest single contribution to diagnostic medicine. Like so many of the inventions which dramatically improved medical practice, the X-ray machine was developed by someone who had no medical qualifications and no interest in either medical practice or medical research.

By the end of the 19th century, life expectation had improved dramatically.

Two centuries earlier, a baby had a life expectation of just 25 years. By the end of the 19th century, those who survived infancy had a good chance of reaching their allotted biblical life-span of three score years and ten. The secret of a long life was to get past infancy. The average one-year-old could expect to live to the age of 55 and anyone who reached 45 years could expect to live to nearly 70. During no other century in history had life expectation improved so dramatically.

Not surprisingly, there were some in the medical profession who claimed that this improvement in life expectancy was due to the acquisition of information.

But it wasn't.

There was absolutely no evidence whatsoever to show that the increase in knowledge about the body had made any difference at all to life expectancy. It was, however, clear that there were several factors responsible for the fact that people were living longer.

First, the increase in the supply of good food (resulting from better farming methods, better transport and more wealth) helped keep people healthier and stronger.

Second the increase in the supply of clean drinking water dramatically reduced the impact of infectious diseases. (After Dr John Snow removed the handle from a pump delivering contaminated water the incidence of cholera in the area fell dramatically and the relationship between drinking water and the disease was noticed.) Cholera had been one of the biggest killers of the nineteenth century but it was brought under control by hygienic measures, before Koch discovered the existence of the cholera vibrio. Tuberculosis declined not after the discovery of the tubercle bacillus but as a result of improved nutritional standards.

Third, Victorian technology had led to the building of efficient systems for removing household waste and this inevitably helped make people healthier. The provision of clean water supplies helped massively.

Fourth, the improvement in the quality of available housing helped keep people healthier. And better education, progress in road building (and transport links in general) also played an important part.

But doctors and the medical profession played only a very small part in the improvement of life expectancy. The technically important, and undoubtedly fascinating, discoveries of the 19th century were important to academics but far less important to the health of the people than the fact that environmental and public health improvements had brought typhoid, scarlet fever, dysentery and infective diarrhoeas under control.

And it was the reduction in infant mortality (which came about entirely because of improved water supplies, improved sewage disposal techniques, better housing and better food) which led to the dramatic improvement in life expectancy which marked the end of the 19th century and the beginning of the 20th century.

The effect of this improvement in infant health is still often misunderstood. But it was vital. If one child dies in the first few months of life and another child lives a long life and dies at the age of 80 years, then the average life expectancy will be quoted as 40 years. But if both children live to be 80 years of age then the average life expectancy will be 80 years. Infant mortality in Victorian Britain was one of the main reasons for the popularity of large families. If two thirds of your children are going to die before they can walk then it makes more sense to have nine children (in the hope and expectation that three of them will live) than to have three children (in the expectation that just one of them will survive.) In 1900 about 150 children in every 1,000 born in England and Wales were still dying within their first year. By 1950 this had been reduced to 30 per 1,000.

The practical advances that came in medicine came after the start of the 20th century and these did play a part (but a surprisingly small part) in the improvement of health and life expectancy. The international pharmaceutical industry first appeared in 1899 when the first aspirin tablet was made, and during the first decades of the 20th century many great advances were made (a number of them being accidental). In 1901, it was found that blood transfusions between human beings were possible if the patient received blood from a donor with the same blood group. In 1914, the usefulness of quinidine in the treatment of heart arrhythmias was discovered. The discovery of the hormone insulin in 1922 brought about a revolution in the treatment of diabetes. And, of course, the discovery of drugs such as penicillin (another serendipitous accident) made it possible

215

to treat infective diseases. The sulphonamides were also introduced.

The twentieth century saw the introduction of ultrasound, artificial heart valves, artificial kidneys and so on. However, many of the advances introduced in the 20th century took a great deal of effort and money but did not make much difference to the general quality or quantity of life.

The small improvements in life expectation that occurred in the 20th century were largely a result of better knowledge about staying healthy (cutting down on cigarette smoking has saved far more lives than any medical discovery), better surgical techniques and so on.

I stress, however, that the importance of the discovery of drugs for the treatment of infectious diseases has been greatly exaggerated by doctors and drug companies. In 1901, a 45-year-old male could expect to live another 25 years or so, and by 1971 a 45-year-old male could still expect to live another 25 years. Medical research has had surprisingly little effect on life expectation. A few people who might otherwise have died have benefited enormously but the mass of people have benefited very little.

And the sad truth is that after around 1970, life expectancy and general health started to decline. About one third of all young Americans called up for the Vietnam draft were rejected for medical or psychiatric reasons.

In the last third of the 20th century, and the first years of the 21st century, there has been a steady but significant fall in life expectation (particularly among women – almost certainly as a result of increased smoking, increased alcohol consumption and the taking on of stress-heavy jobs) and an increase in illness. The number of people taking daily medication has risen to epidemic proportions as has the incidence of mental illness. Around four out of five modern cancers are thought to be caused by carcinogenic chemicals in foods, in household chemicals and in the air we breathe.

The bottom line is that the evidence shows that medical research has had little effect on morbidity or mortality rates or on the quality of life enjoyed by most people. Indeed, there is evidence that medical research and medical practice have detracted from the quality of life for millions and that money which could have been used more wisely (on educational programmes) has been wasted on programmes which have had little or no useful effect. Moreover, there is a considerable amount of evidence to prove that programmes of mass vaccination (enthusiastically promoted by the drug industry and by doctors who are very well paid to give the jabs) have done far more harm than good. Sadly, very little research has been done to assess the value of mass vaccination programmes. All around the world, infants and children are now subjected to a seemingly endless series of assaults on their immune systems. The vaccines used have never been adequately tested to see how they might interact or how they might affect other medications. Very few long-term trials have been done though the few trials available confirm my scepticism. For example, in 2017, the Danish Government and a Danish vaccine maker, funded a study of the DTP vaccine. The WHO and the medical establishment claim that the DTP vaccine saves millions of lives but, after looking at 30 years of data, the scientists concluded that the DTP vaccine was probably killing more children than had died from diphtheria, pertussis and tetanus prior to the vaccines introduction. The vaccine had ruined the immune systems of children rendering them susceptible to death from pneumonia, leukaemia, bilharzia, malaria and dysentery. Sadly, the results of that trial changed nothing. The vaccination continued unhindered. And if the pro-vaccine enthusiasts (paid for by the industry responsible) chance to see this paragraph they will pounce on this book and try to kill it with one star reviews.

It was when writing 'Paper Doctors' that I first offered the thought that if a patient has two medical conditions there is a very good chance that one of those diseases was caused by the treatment for the other. That observation would become 'Coleman's First Law of Medicine' and was the first sign of a book I would write 40 years later called 'Coleman's Laws', in which I would collect together twelve laws I'd formulated.

The evidence supporting my sceptical view about the value of modern medicine is widely available. Writing in the Journal of Human Resources, an American researcher Charles T. Stewart showed that life expectation is approximately the same in countries with between 4 and 16 doctors per 10,000 people. It is true that the number of patients being treated is increasing massively, and the quantities of pharmaceutical drugs consumed are rising dramatically (with huge costs, of course) but the number of people being saved is falling dramatically.

And there is no little irony in the fact that whenever doctors go on strike the number of people dying always falls.

I've written about my book 'Paper Doctors' because researching and writing it played a massively important part in how my views about medicine developed. And most of my 'straight' medical books have, in some way or other, been built upon those views and that knowledge.

The widow

When I first started work as a GP, one of the partners of the practice which was employing me as an assistant found me accommodation in the home of a widowed patient. The partner pointed out that, since I was single, I needed accommodation where there was someone available to answer the telephone at night when I was out on a call. I was, of course, thrown in at the deep end and although I had been qualified for little more than a year I was expected to deal with whatever emergencies came up.

It quickly became apparent that the arrangement wasn't quite as convenient as the partner might have hoped. I found that while I was out the widow, who was in her sixties, was giving advice to patients who telephoned out of hours. I'd go out on a call and if another call came through while I was out the widow would give the patient the benefit of her advice and leave things at that. I found this rather scary since she had absolutely no training or medical knowledge other than the sort of stuff that can be picked up from reading the Daily Mail and Readers' Digest on a regular basis.

There was worse to come.

While I'd been at medical school I'd started writing several columns and producing articles for a variety of papers. Now that I was medically qualified I was writing articles on health matters for a variety of national publications. When editors or journalists telephoned for advice or a quote or for an article to be dictated, my landlady would oblige by providing quotes and opinions – which she happily gave in my name. I found this out by accident when I saw that I'd been quoted in one of the national papers and had no recollection of ever being interviewed.

'Oh, I thought you wouldn't mind,' the widow would say, with a smile which happened to be both fawning and patronising. 'I thought I was being a help.' She was, I quickly discovered, a woman who knew her own mind and everyone else's too and she was never one to let ignorance get in the way of giving advice. Actually, she never gave advice: she gave orders. I began to suspect that in a previous life she'd been a high ranking officer in the German army.

After two weeks, I moved out of the widow's house and, still needing someone to answer the phone at night and at weekends when I was out on calls, I moved into a local four star hotel, which was the only hotel which had a night porter available to answer the phone. Since I was a resident in the hotel, they gave me a good deal on accommodation and meals. However, I found the whole business of living in a hotel rather oppressive since the maids insisted on putting away all the things I'd left out and tidying up papers and books which I'd been using and I quickly found a flat where I could sleep, eat and work when I wasn't on call and in need of the hall porter. Actually, it was more of a bed-sitting room than a flat and my accumulating books and files meant that I didn't stay there long. I moved into a massive top floor flat that had five bedrooms and, whenever it rained, cold water in every room.

It looks like privet

I've employed one or two house-keepers over the years but I've never felt comfortable having anyone working in the house.

When she worked full-time, my mum used to have a cleaner who came in two or three times a week, just for an hour or so, but my mum never felt comfortable with having anyone doing housework for her. She used to get up early and go through the house with a vacuum cleaner and duster before Mrs Pettifer arrived, so that the house would be as clean as a new pin when she arrived. There was, of course, then nothing for Mrs Pettifer to do but with commendable industriousness she hoovered and dusted again. I once bought a box full of old postcards at an auction and, by an amazing coincidence, somewhere near the bottom of the box, I found a postcard my mum had sent to Mrs Pettifer when she and my dad had been away on holiday. It was the sort of chatty card you'd send to a good friend, rather than an employee.

Having help in the garden is different, mainly because as long as you have an outdoor (or gardener's loo) the gardener doesn't have to come into the house at all and can be left outside like a flowering shrub or a wisteria plant.

Over the years I have usually tried to do all my own gardening. Indeed, I've always found grass-cutting to be an immensely peaceful activity. You have to concentrate a little but not too much. (Though our home now is on the edge of a cliff and the edge of our lawn is a 100 foot drop to the sea and the rocks below and I do try to concentrate more when I'm cutting that stretch of the grass.)

Nevertheless, I have, from time to time, employed a variety of gardeners (usually because I was so busy rushing around the country that I didn't have time to mow, cut, prune and trim) and I have been constantly surprised by the variety of those who choose this way of earning a living, although I suppose some may not choose to be gardeners but may drift into it in much the same sort of way that people drift into becoming traffic wardens, car park attendants or Chancellors of the Exchequer.

221

One gardener whom I employed knew absolutely nothing about plants. When I first hired him I took him around the garden to show him what needed doing. He attempted to display his knowledge by pointing things out to me but this was a mistake for he described every bush as privet and every tree as an oak tree. He didn't bother naming flowers at all and had absolutely no knowledge enabling him to distinguish between flowers that were supposed to be where they were and flowers which were not. He insisted on being paid in cash after every session and refused to use the outside loo (which we laughingly called the gardeners' loo) because he said it smelt a little musty and probably contained spiders. He arrived in an old van which leaked oil and always left a large stain on our driveway. I noticed that he always managed to park in a slightly different spot, but just outside the front door, so that the driveway there was eventually pretty well covered with oil stains. I often wondered if he did this knowingly, as some sort of protest. Or maybe he was, like a cat, simply marking what he thought of as his territory.

Another gardener seemed slightly less knowledgeable than one might have expected. For years we've fed nuts to the squirrels and when this gardener first arrived (complete with a van load of very impressive looking and doubtless expensive equipment) he saw some walnut shells on the ground. He then looked up and proceeded to identify three walnut trees in our garden. We didn't have any walnut trees and if he looked more closely he'd have seen the words 'Produce of California' stamped in red on the nut shells.

A third gardener, who was marvellous and the most knowledgeable plants-man, worked in all weathers and always did so wearing only a potato sack over his upper body. He had made holes for his head and arms and looked wonderfully primitive. He would never shelter, nor even on the hottest or coldest days, would he accept a drink of any kind. He used to bring wonderful little cakes which his wife made and he wept when I told him I had sold the house and was leaving.

A fourth gardener sent his teenage daughter to cut the grass while he sat on a bench in the garden and did more arduous work (smoking cigarettes while reading the paper was a speciality and a fine example of male multi-tasking). Unfortunately, she couldn't manage the weight of the mower and when cutting the croquet lawn she used to crash into a ditch quite regularly. Since she couldn't lift the

222

mower out of the ditch, and her father, was always too busy multi-tasking to take notice of her screams for help, I used to have to abandon whatever I was doing and rush to help her.

A fifth gardener charged us by the hour and insisted on being paid by a monthly direct debit 'for our convenience'. He did very little work. He preferred to gossip with our neighbours. I would hear him arrive (in a van which rattled and did not seem to have an exhaust pipe) and then I would hear him try to start his mower. After half an hour of silence I would look out of the window and see him chatting to a neighbour. Eventually, he would cut the grass (leaving it looking as if it had been cut by a blind man with a blunt scythe) and disappear, leaving grass cuttings widely distributed.

A sixth gardener came and trimmed and pruned but never picked up his trimmings and prunings. He said that was work for a labourer. So after he had gone I had to go out and clean up after him. He always brought his two Alsatian dogs with him. They tore around the garden, scaring all the birds and squirrels, digging up non-existent bones and doing what dogs do best when they are well fed and well watered. The dogs were very noisy and rather frightening and neither Antoinette nor I would leave the house for any reason while they were in the garden.

The seventh gardener was an economist who told me he had given up a well-paid job at an investment bank 'to find himself, rework his work-life balance, and get closer to nature'. He had no gardening equipment, refused to use the ancient power driven lawnmower I had (which worked perfectly well) and insisted that I buy something new and powerful, preferably made by Honda, with which he could cut the grass. He also insisted that I purchase a leaf blower, a hedge trimmer, a strimmer and various other pieces of equipment which, he declared, were essential. Desperate to find someone prepared to look after the garden, and thinking the fellow sounded promising, I agreed to his demands and spent half a day and a medium sized fortune at the garden equipment centre. After two weeks, the gardener decided that he could only get in touch with his real self, and properly re-balance his work-life ratio, by going back into banking and took a job at an investment bank in Frankfurt.

Antoinette and I now deal with our garden ourselves, though we are becoming increasingly enthusiastic about the Government's proposed re-wilding programme which seems to offer us an excellent excuse to sit in comfy chairs, with a pair of long cool drinks while watching the squirrels run around burying nuts and then digging them up again. People who haven't watched squirrels at work assume that the nut burying process is a simple one. It isn't. The squirrel will dig a hole, drop in the nut, and then cover the nut with earth. He (or she) will then place a number of fallen leaves over the fresh earth, to disguise the hiding place. Two minutes later he (or she) will return, dig up the nut and repeat the process.

Zoladex

It is sad but true that most doctors know very little about side effects of the drugs they prescribe. And they know next to nothing about the interactions that can take place when a patient takes more than one drug at the same time. Little or no research has been done to find out how all the different drugs and vaccines which are available might interact with one another in the human body.

Six months after Antoinette had her surgery for breast cancer, the oncologist suggested that she take Zoladex for a few months. She had been taking tamoxifen since the operation.

Zoladex is given by injection and our first worry was that the injections would be given at the GP's surgery, rather than the hospital. And they would almost certainly be given by a care assistant – rather than a doctor or a nurse. The injections, into the abdomen, involve a large needle and are fairly sophisticated as injections go. I didn't want the care assistant giving these.

But when we looked at the possible advantage of adding Zoladex to the tamoxifen and the potential side effects with Zoladex we were appalled.

Our first shock was finding a scientific paper which compared the advantage of adding Zoladex to the tamoxifen. The paper dealt with around 2,700 patients who were followed for ten years and showed, convincingly, that there was absolutely no advantage to adding the Zoladex to the other drug. Importantly, I found much other scientific evidence showing that there was absolutely no advantage to having Zoladex as well as tamoxifen. A meta-analysis which assessed four controlled trials comprising 6,279 patients (the paper we found was entitled 'Tamoxifen with ovarian function suppression versus tamoxifen alone as an adjuvant treatment for premenopausal breast cancer: a meta-analysis of published randomized controlled trials') concluded: 'Based on the available studies, concurrent administration of OFS (Ovarian function suppression with a drug such as Zoladex) and adjuvant tamoxifen treatment for premenopausal women with breast cancer has no effect on prolonging disease-free survival and over-all survival...'

It was clear that the drug would have to be very safe – and complete free of side effects – for us even to consider using it.

The first and most obvious danger was that of having regular injections into body fat. There was the risk of infection and the risk of an anaphylactic shock. There was the mental trauma of having to have regular, tricky and painful injections – possibly given by someone with little training.

And, of course, there were the specific side effects.

I have been writing about drug side effects for half a century and have written a number of books on the subject. I had never in my life seen a drug with such horrid side effects occurring commonly. And, remember, most side effects are never reported to the authorities because doctors don't recognise them for what they are, or don't bother to report them. In the past I have seen estimates that less than 10% of side effects are reported by doctors. In America it is believed that only 1% of side effects are reported.

One of the common problems listed was an increase in blood sugar.

This is vitally important because cancer cells thrive on sugar so if you take something which pushes up the blood sugar levels then the cancer will thrive.

The British National Formulary (published by Britain's NICE, the National Institute for Health and Care Excellence) lists the indications and side effects for all drugs.

Here is the list of the common or very common side effects which it lists for Zoladex: alopecia; arthralgia; bone pain; breast abnormalities; depression; glucose tolerance impaired; gynaecomastia; headache; heart failure; hot flushes; hyperhidrosis; mood alteration; myocardial infarction (heart attack); diabetes; neoplasm complications; paraesthesia; sexual dysfunction; skin reactions; spinal cord compression; tiredness; vulvo-vaginal disorders; weight increase.

Those are the common or very common side effects. The potential bone problems are so bad that it is recommended that all patients have a bone scan before their treatment starts.

I have studied side effects for decades and usually the common side effects are things like skin rashes, intestinal upsets such as nausea and diarrhoea and headaches.

Why would anyone prescribe a drug which can commonly cause heart attacks, heart failure, spinal cord compression, neoplasm complications and depression and which can affect blood sugar levels?

In my considered opinion, Zoladex is one of the most evil and mis-appropriately prescribed drugs. It is no exaggeration to say that I would be reluctant to use Zoladex as drain cleaner. The idea of asking a patient to swallow the stuff makes me nauseous.

I am reminded yet again how important it is for cancer patients to take some control of their own destiny.

When I had looked at all the evidence, Antoinette and I decided that mainlining bleach would make more sense than adding Zoladex.

Compared to Zoladex, the tamoxifen which Antoinette takes is as safe as jam.

Trains, planes and travelling pains

I used to love travelling and, in particular, I loved travelling by train. Back in the 1970s and 1980s, when I did a good deal of travelling in the UK, the railways in the UK were nationalised and, looking back, they were cleaner, better organised, better run and more likely to arrive on time than the trains of today. The staff were, on the whole, friendlier and more enthusiastic and more likely to treat passengers as welcome guests rather than as an irritating annoyance. Ticket office staff were capable and knowledgeable, and most trains used to have dining cars in which white coated waiters served simple but hot and edible food and drinks at very reasonable prices. There were trains with sleeping compartments too. I used to travel hundreds of miles to TV and radio studios and I can't remember ever missing a programme because a train was very late or missing. It is true that the trains then weren't as fast as today's trains, but they were stable and steady (so travellers could read or write quite easily) and they were nearly always on time or within five minutes of being on time.

Travelling by road was quicker and more fun, too. I reckon that today (in 2022) it takes at least twice as long to get anywhere by car as it took back in the 1970s and 1980s. Moreover, the traffic jams caused by absurdly misnamed smart motorways, and by all the 40 mph limits which spring up for no apparent reason, mean that only the foolhardy travel by road if they have an appointment to keep.

Antoinette and I used to travel regularly to France by Eurostar and by the time we'd given up, sold our apartment in Paris and abandoned the struggle with a local council which hated foreigners, we were allowing three times as long as should have been necessary to drive to Ashford or Ebbsfleet (the two Eurostar railway stations outside London). And even then we would find ourselves worrying that we were going to miss the train because of road works and utterly pointless speed limits. Travel had become a nightmare. Once we arrived at the station we were met with inefficiency and aggression and the process became increasingly combative. In order to cut a few minutes off the journey to Paris, old, comfortable trains

228

were replaced with over-bright trains which bumped and lurched and leapt about and made almost everyone (including the train crew) feel nauseous. As far as I know no customers had asked for the change – the company seemed to have decided to spend a huge amount of money just to annoy its passengers. The carriages and the service were infinitely better at the end of the 20th century.

Travel by aeroplane was easier too, back in the 20th century. I used to fly to European destinations, or to Scotland where I made several TV series, and the whole process was almost always pain free. I'd arrive at the airport with half an hour to spare before take-off, park within walking distance of the lounge, and be in the air without any fuss at all. Customs officers were usually polite and the whole process of checking in and passing through passport control could be done in five or ten minutes.

It had always been my ambition to evolve slowly, but with a quiet dignity, into a pleasantly irascible old man. I'd hoped to travel a little with Antoinette, but to travel quietly and without haste; to see the castles of Scotland; to visit the fading piers of England; to take Antoinette on the train to Venice or Amsterdam. I imagined long, slow journeys in quiet compartments with a well-filled picnic hamper and a bag of books.

I fear that all that has now been abandoned. The world has changed too fast for me. Circumstances prevailed and we have become anchorites. I don't even go to Worcester to watch the cricket any more. These days we hardly leave home, and when we do we rarely travel more than 20 miles. We both had places we wanted to visit, and trips we wanted to make, but the pain of travel has simply become too much.

Bad publicity

In commercial (rather than personal) terms there is no such thing as bad publicity.

In the 1990s, a newspaper (now deservedly dead and pretty much forgotten) called 'The Independent on Sunday', published a lengthy profile of me in its colour magazine. The article was accompanied by an absolutely awful full page photograph. I don't usually care what photos of me look like but this one, taken after hours of effort by a fussy photographer, was worse than the sort of pictures I used to take with my Brownie camera when I was twelve. It was awful, and to be honest I think that was the intention.

The article was what is known in the trade as a 'hatchet' piece (an article in which the writer takes every opportunity to be snide about the subject) and I am convinced that the piece was commissioned by an editor responding to pressure from the drug industry. In the same week that the Independent on Sunday interviewed me, I was interviewed at length by the Sunday Telegraph magazine.

The article in 'The Independent on Sunday' was so biased, inaccurate and patently unfair that the newspaper ended up publishing a lengthy letter from me. The editor 'left' a few weeks later. And the writer of the piece, whose name I have honestly forgotten (and who, indeed, seemed to disappear) was later discredited when it appeared that she had been, to say the least, very naughty.

The point of dredging up this nonsense is that the same issue of the 'Independent on Sunday' which published the demonising profile also carried an advertisement for a book of mine. You might imagine that, under the circumstances, the advertisement would be a failure. But it wasn't. One of the beauties of mail order advertising is that it is possible to tell immediately whether or not a particular advert was a success or a failure. And this advert, appearing in an issue which contained an article attacking me (and my work) resulted in a dramatic rise in sales. So, here was a small piece of proof that in commercial terms there is no such thing as bad publicity.

Of course, in personal terms things are very different.

And the post-covid demonization has been far more effective. When you have been lied about on the most of the mainstream media and the big internet sites, and are completely banned from all the former and the latter, things are rather more difficult.

Nearing the end

I saw myself visiting all the glorious English cricket grounds I remembered with pleasure.

I saw myself, on a warm summer day, sitting wrapped in a woollen jumper, the jumper fitting snugly under an old sports jacket (for we older folk like to keep warm), watching a quiet match between two counties at the Lord's cricket ground or the grounds at Edgbaston or Worcester, perhaps.

Yes, Worcester would be good: a beautiful, county ground next to the river Severn. Antoinette would be nearby, sitting painting the view across the river, with the cathedral resplendent on the other bank.

At the end of my final day a steward would notice me still sitting there, staring at a field with no players. He would touch me lightly on the shoulder and I would topple sideways.

That's the way to go.

Appendix 1

Thirty Nine things I've learned (and which I wish I'd known at 20)

Some years ago I wrote a book called '101 Things I have Learned'. Readers have been kind enough to say that they found it useful as well as entertaining. Since I wrote that book I've remembered more valuable stuff and expanded a little on old thoughts.

So, here's a selection of things I wish I had known when I was 20:

Everyone should endeavour to find out what they are good at. Once you've found what you're good at, try to do it for a living.

Don't allow the young think they own wisdom, just as they believe they have exclusive ownership of grief, compassion and every other human emotion. It is this arrogant misconception which explains why young people join left wing organisations and believe they have a monopoly of concern for the planet and the environment. The only thing the young can do better than the old is to climb trees. And that particular talent starts to fade at the age of eight.

Children are intrinsically cruel. It is only as they age that they learn to behave in a civilised way. Of course, some children never age, and remain cruel all their lives even when they have apparently reached adulthood.

Never drink wine served in a carafe – it was probably made in a bucket in the proprietor's shed or garage and is unlikely to have been within a mile of a grape.

Some people know more than they tell, others tell more than they know. It helps a great deal if you can put the people you meet into the correct category.

A gentleman always behaves with honour, dignity, kindness, respect, loyalty and integrity. And he sticks to his word. However, just because someone wears an expensive suit, an Eton tie and well-polished shoes, he is not necessarily a gentleman. Ditto a lady, with the obvious sartorial variations.

Quiet confidence should come not with breeding (that tends to produce a confidence which too often drifts over across the border into the hinterlands of self-satisfaction and arrogance) but with a good helping of a genuine sense of compassion and a generosity of spirit.

I'm sure I've mentioned this before, somewhere, but it is worth repeating. If, when you are away from home, you buy water in a plastic bottle, always remove the top yourself and make sure that the top clicks when you turn it. In Paris, on hot days, the tourist buses are often invaded by men selling bottles of water. When giving the bottle to the purchaser, the salesman will often pretend to twist the top to open the bottle – as a small gesture of goodwill to the customer. These bottles of water are pricey items but the true cost will not usually be met for some hours. I have seen those salesmen filling empty Evian bottles with water taken from the River Seine. I wonder how many holidays and honeymoons have been ruined by these cheats – who could have easily made a very decent 200-300% profit by buying new bottles of water from a supermarket.

If someone asks you to do something for a charity, you should do it free of charge rather than for a cut price rate. I have, over the years, found that whenever I provide a piece of writing or a drawing for a charity (or even make an appearance somewhere) they will sometimes offer to pay a fee or, at least, to pay my expenses. I think it is more acceptable for everyone concerned to do things without any charge rather than to make a special price. If I am going to do something for a cause I regard as worthy then it seems to me to be unwholesome to charge any fee or expenses at all.

Networking is a vital part of life these days. You will never get on, or achieve anything, if you do not network. Sadly, I have never, ever been able to network.

I have spent much of my life campaigning on issues which I regard as important and I have found that the worst abuse will invariably come not from the opposition but from those who claim to be on the same side. My back is heavily scarred from the thrusting of knives – most of it done by egotistical empire builders and control freaks. I first found this many decades ago when fighting against animal abuses (such as vivisection and hunting) but it has come to the fore in recent years, though of course some of the knife wielding has doubtless been done by those best identified as controlled

234

opposition.

Without purpose there is very little point to life. I once asked a patient about his hobbies and his interests outside his work. He sat and thought for a while and then admitted that he didn't have any and couldn't think of any. I then asked him what he did at weekends. He said he washed the car and, in the summer, cut the lawn, though I may have mis-remembered and he may have said he cut the car and washed the lawn. Somehow, it doesn't really seem enough.

I have always found that it pays to be prepared. In 2019, for example, realising that the 'group think' that was driving the global warming conspiracy was going to cause serious problems and shortages of heat and power, Antoinette and I bought a medium sized, fairly new caravan. We had no intention of using it for holidays and we asked the seller to park the caravan on a stretch of spare tarmacadam in the grounds of our home. Before the caravan was delivered we had solar panels fitted to the roof – as many as could be put in place. We bought the caravan simply because our home was built in the 19th century and is rather draughty. It also has high ceilings. We realised that at some time in the future there would be problems with obtaining heating for the house (because of energy shortages) and so we wanted somewhere small and safe to which we could retreat when necessary. The caravan has a cooker connected to a bottled gas supply – giving us an alternative way to heat food. We also made sure that we had a camping stove (together with a good many bottles of gas), a large supply of logs (for the open fires in the house) and a stored supply of bottled water. We also had a greenhouse built so that we could grow some of our own food. (I discovered to my astonishment that kale and spinach plants can be harvested endlessly and will produce food for many months. I've never had a green thumb but I found kale incredibly easy to grow.). And we had five large water butts fitted to the greenhouse to collect rainwater to use for washing, loo flushing and watering the plants. We also bought filters and purifying tablets so that we could, if necessary, drink the rainwater we collected.

At an auction, it is vital to identify the professional dealers. If you find yourself bidding against a dealer (who will need to buy the lot for a price that allows him room to make a profit) you will almost always buy something for a fair price. It isn't difficult to spot dealers. They only show interest in a few lots. They seem to know a good many of the other buyers and, indeed, will probably be known to the auctioneer by name. If they don't arrive in a van they will usually arrive in an estate car, often with a large, strong looking roof rack fitted. The estate cars always used to be elderly, slightly battered Volvos but this is no longer inevitable. These days the dealers sometimes drive fancy 4x4s or small trucks. They often wear sheepskin coats.

Always take a percentage and never a fee. In the 1980s I was invited to record a series of tapes for a telephone advisory service. I was given a choice of a generous fee or a percentage of the profits. I chose the percentage, became The Telephone Doctor, and eventually, within a year or two, I had earned several hundred times what I would have earned if I had accepted the flat fee. Here's another example: in the 1860s, Dr Joseph Lawrence created a formula for cleaning wounds. A chemist wanted to buy the formula but instead of accepting a lump sum fee, Dr Lawrence asked for, and received, a royalty. His original contract stated that for every 144 bottles of Listerine which were sold, the pharmacist would pay Dr Lawrence (or his heirs) $20. The right to manufacture and sell Listerine is now owned by a company called Johnson&Johnson which still pays royalties. The ownership of the licence has been split and the owner of a 0.5% share in the royalty income still earns around $120,000 a year. Similarly, fortunes have been made by many other inventors who retained control (in whole or in part) of their invention. The men who invented the paperclip, had the idea of putting a rubber onto the end of a pencil and invented the cats' eyes in the centre of the road all did very well, thank you.

Purchase an extendable brass toasting fork. Toast tastes much better when made over an open log fire. And the smell is much more satisfying. But to avoid burning your hand you really do need an extendable fork. The toasting fork can be sterilised before being used by holding it in the flames.

Learn how to layer a hedge. It's easier than you think and magnificently satisfying. Think of the kudos to be obtained by saying you spent Saturday afternoon layering a hedge. Of course, you do need a hedge to start with though if you haven't got one you could, I suppose, always borrow one.

Never accept financial advice from anyone poorer than you are (even if they are professional financial advisors).

Unless you are under 12-years-old, don't ever be tempted to use an emoji hieroglyphic in an email.

Using fire lighters to start a fire or a bonfire is cheating and un-gentlemanly, as is wearing an elasticated bow tie or a clip on tie of any kind. The trick with lighting a bonfire (and I have lit bonfires in rainstorms and in heavy snow) is to remember that a fire needs plenty of air. My favourite trick is to use an upturned cardboard box as the basis for a fire. Put newspaper underneath the box and light it. You can then pile the material to be burned on top of the box. I don't wish to sound like a pyromaniac but I also recommend owning a house with a fireplace. Again, judicious use of the dogs or andirons will make lighting a fire relatively easy. The secret is to use the supports to prepare your kindling in such a way that the fire has access to plenty of oxygen. (Collecting your own kindling and cutting your own logs are extraordinarily satisfying activities.)

An English gentleman never wears an overcoat over his shoulders, without his arms through the sleeves, and never wears a jumper with the sleeves tied or draped over his shoulders. The French do these things, and also spend hours tying their scarves, but no Frenchman would ever claim to be a gentleman. A gentleman never wears a tie lighter than his shirt, never has anything visible (pens, handkerchief) in his jacket breast pocket and always has working buttons on the sleeve of his jacket just in case he needs to deliver a baby.

No one (whatever the weather, and whether male or female) should leave home without a hat.

A gentleman should never button the bottom button of waistcoat or jacket (the buttons are there so gentlemen can be identified at a distance).

No one respectable should ever use metric measurements; own, drive or sit in an electric car; read The Guardian newspaper (or even pick one up on the train); pay the BBC licence fee (find a legal way to avoid paying it); bank online or put ice into whisky.

Decent, good people are never cruel to animals, never hunt or shoot, never clean a car, never wear driving gloves and never park with the wheels of their vehicle on or over the defining lines of a parking bay.

No one (male or female) should ever wear shorts after the age of 20 unless they are playing tennis, either professionally or on a private court.

Respectable folk never buy brand new furniture. Heirlooms make the best furniture but although it is tacky to inherit them it is decent to buy someone else's – preferably at an auction. Old brown Victorian furniture is of a better quality and cheaper than the new stuff, which is largely made out of compressed cardboard. No home should contain furniture which has been put together like something made out of Lego or Meccano.

Understand that the English language is full of subtleties. The English never say precisely what they mean. So the phrases: 'I really don't mind'; 'Don't worry about it' and 'That's alright' all mean: 'That's terrible, but I suppose I'll have to put up with it if I want to avoid a scene'. And the phrase 'There's no hurry, take your time' really means 'I've been waiting for an hour and it's hardly worth going now'.' The phrase 'I don't mind if I do…' is polite English for 'Yes please'.

Accept that it's never a good time to change a light bulb (you switched on the light because it was too dark to see) and it's never a good time to change a flat tyre (you were going somewhere).

Whatever it is that you're buying, buy the best you can find and afford. It will probably do the job better and last longer. Avoid cluttering up your home with chattels which will need to be replaced in six months. If you do, you'll have the extra problem of getting rid of them.

Remember that the weight you should give to criticism should depend upon who is doing the criticising. I have learned, at last, that the internet is well-populated with trolls whose views are of no value.

The single most important question to ask is: 'Why?' The second most important question is: 'So what?'

Everyone should own, and know how to use sealing wax. Now that the guinea has gone, it is, quite possibly, our last link with civilised life.

Whether male or female you should wear a hat when out of doors. And you should carry a mugger's wallet or purse. (The wallet or purse should contain a few bank notes and coins, an old phone that doesn't work and maybe a few expired club cards. Nothing should contain your address.) After the age of 40, men and women who need help with their vision should consider using a monocle, a pince nez or a lorgnette.

When giving a speech, remember that hardly anyone ever complains that a speech was too short.

No one who is not starving ever eats tripe, heart or brains.

It is indecent to see the sun rising. Respectable folk wait until it has risen, washed its face and dressed before they arise. No one other than a farm labourer ever sets the alarm clock for 5 a.m. so that they can get a good start on the day.

If you complain (even politely and justifiably) about a large organisation then you must be prepared for anonymous members of staff to make your life miserable. They will block your phone (to stop you calling) and they will ignore your letters and lose your paperwork. I am never rude or aggressive to people working for utilities, insurance companies and so on (partly because I feel too sorry for them) but I find that if I ever try to stick up for myself when I am the victim of corporate bullying I will, in turn, be victimised in some petty and vindictive way.

Never stop watching and learning and always be prepared to learn from others. Every time you meet someone successful – whose work or life you admire – observe them and learn from what they do. Find out their philosophies. Find out what drives them. When Antoinette became a professional artist I learned from her to properly enjoy skies, clouds, seas and landscapes. Every day our landscape, whether rural or urban, is constantly renewed and recreated by sunshine or moonlight. Without light there is no shadow and no landscape.

At the end of the day most of these things don't matter very much. The two truly important things I have learned are that the biggest sin is cruelty and the greatest virtue is kindness. And I know that the people who are kind to animals are invariably kind to people whereas, conversely, the people who are cruel to animals will also be cruel to humans. Fight for justice and freedom and root for the underdog. Distrust your government, avoid mass media and fight the lies.

Appendix 2
Author biography

Sunday Times bestselling author Vernon Coleman qualified as a doctor in 1970 and has worked both in hospitals and as a principal in general practice. Vernon Coleman is a multi-million selling author and since 1975, he has written over 100 books which have sold over three million copies in the UK, been in bestseller lists around the world and been translated into 26 languages. Several of his books have been on the bestseller lists and in the UK paperback editions of his books have been published by Pan, Penguin, Corgi, Arrow, Century, RKP, Mandarin and Star among many others. His novel 'Mrs Caldicot's Cabbage War' was turned into a successful, award winning movie. He has appeared on Top Gear (the motoring programme), written for a DIY magazine and contributed to a cookery video. He has presented numerous programmes on television and radio, including several series based on his best-selling book Bodypower which was voted one of the 100 most popular books.

Vernon Coleman has written columns for the Daily Star, Sun, Sunday Express, Planet on Sunday and The People (resigning from the latter when the editor refused to publish a column questioning the morality and legality of invading Iraq) and many other publications and has contributed over 5,000 articles, columns and reviews to 100 leading British publications including Daily Telegraph, Sunday Telegraph, Guardian, Observer, Sunday Times, Daily Mail, Mail on Sunday, Daily Express, Woman, Woman's Own, Punch and Spectator. His columns and articles have also appeared in hundreds of leading magazines and newspapers throughout the rest of the world. He edited the British Clinical Journal and for twenty years he wrote a column which was syndicated to over 40 leading regional newspapers in the UK and to papers all around the world. Local health officials were often so irritated by the column that they paid doctors to write competing columns without charge. Fortunately, with a few exceptions, this made little difference to the success of the column.

In the UK, Vernon Coleman was the TV AM doctor on breakfast TV and when he commented that fatty food had killed more people than Hitler he wasn't fired until several weeks after a large food lobbyist had threatened to pull all its advertising. He was the first networked television Agony Aunt, working on the BBC. Many millions consulted his Telephone Doctor advice lines and for six years he wrote a monthly newsletter which had subscribers in 17 countries.

In recent years Vernon has been banned from all mainstream media because his views are often at variance with those of the medical establishment. Since March 2020 the ban has been extended to include most of the internet and he is currently banned using or even accessing YouTube because the videos he made contained uncomfortable truths. He made over 300 videos which have all been censored or banned. He was refused admittance to Facebook, being told that he would be 'a threat to the Facebook community', expelled from LinkedIn (with no reason given) and banned from all social media. For over 30 years he has had a website (www.vernoncoleman.com) and right from the start the site has been visited regularly by representatives of the CIA, the FBI and by members of armed forces around the world.

Vernon Coleman has a medical degree, and an honorary science doctorate. He has worked for the Open University in the UK and was an honorary Professor of Holistic Medical Sciences at the Open International University based in Sri Lanka. He worked as a general practitioner for ten years (resigning from the NHS after being fined for refusing to divulge confidential information about his patients to State bureaucrats) and has organised numerous campaigns both for people and for animals. He can ride a bicycle and swim, though not at the same time. He likes animals, cricket (before they started painting slogans on the grass), cycling, cafés and collecting cigarette cards. Vernon Coleman is a bibliophile and has a library larger than most towns. He used to enjoy cricket when it was played as a sport by gentlemen and loves log fires and making bonfires.

Since 1999 he has been very happily married to the professional artist and author, Donna Antoinette Coleman to whom he is devoted and with whom he has co-written five books. They live in the delightful if isolated village of Bilbury in Devon where they have designed for themselves a unique world to sustain and nourish them in these dark and difficult times. They rarely leave home.

Note
If you enjoyed this book (and it is the author's sincere hope that you did) it would be an enormous help if you would write a review for Amazon or any other internet site.

Printed in Great Britain
by Amazon